The Author

James Moffett, who died in 1996, was a national consultant, workshop leader, lecturer, and author in language education and total learning environments. During his long and distinguished career he taught at Philips Exeter Academy and served on the faculties of Harvard, the University of California, Berkeley, San Diego State, and Middlebury College's Bread Loaf School of English. He wrote numerous influential books including *Active Voice* (1981, 1992), *Coming on Center* (1981, 1988), *Teaching the Universe of Discourse* (1983), *Storm in the Mountains* (1988) and *Harmonic Learning* (1992). *The Universal Schoolhouse* was his last book.

A fuller note about the author can be found on pages xxi–xxii.

THE UNIVERSAL SCHOOLHOUSE

▲

THE
UNIVERSAL
SCHOOLHOUSE

▲

Spiritual Awakening
Through Education

▼

JAMES MOFFETT

Area 3 Writing Project

Calendar Islands Publishers
Portland, Maine

Calendar Islands Publishers LLC
477 Congress Street, Portland, Maine 04101

First published in hardcover by Jossey-Bass Inc., Publishers 1994

First published in paperback by Calendar Islands Publishers LLC 1998

ISBN (Calendar Islands Paperback) 0-9663233-2-7

Library of Congress Cataloging-in-Publication Data
Moffett, James.
    The universal schoolhouse: spiritual awakening through education / James Moffett.
    p. cm.
    Originally published: 1st ed. San Francisco: Jossey-Bass, c1994.
    Includes bibliographical references (p. 361–367).
    ISBN 0-9663233-2-7 (pbk.)
    1. Moral education—United States. 2. Education—Social aspects-United States. 3. Critical pedagogy—United States. 4. Education, Humanistic—United States. 5. Educational change—United States.
I. Title.
LC268.M64   1998
370.11'4'0973—dc21   98–15939
                                                                      CIP

Cover design by Darci Mehall, Aureo Design

Printed in the United States of America on recycled paper

03 02 01 00 99 98   10 9 8 7 6 5 4 3 2 1

CONTENTS

▲

PREFACE

▲

The Universal Schoolhouse addresses itself both to professional educators and to the public. An increasing number of thoughtful citizens are alarmed not merely about the plight of schools but about the fate of society—and the pilgrimage of individuals. This book proposes profound change argued on common knowledge and the experience of an independent educator who has devoted a long career almost entirely to renovating public education. For me, school reform has been a full-time, lifelong effort—through teaching teachers, consulting with schools and universities, speaking to professional organizations, publishing, and just plain stumping the country. Through these efforts I have tried to center learning on personal growth, which ultimately means spiritual development.

While acknowledging current school reform efforts, this book takes off from a different beginning and aims toward a different end. It takes issue, in fact, with most of the usual premises of school reform—that curriculum, for example, should be set by the state, that the chief goals of schooling are economic and nationalistic, and that testing and competition should be major tools of change. Other common school reform ideas like site management and parental choice are submerged here in far more radical suggestions. A major purpose of this book is to try to head off the well-meaning but wrongheaded approach of current "reform" before it worsens the situation of public education and delays societal transformation beyond the term of possibility.

The many interlocking problems of this nation and this world are escalating so rapidly that only swift changes in thought and action can save either. The generation about to enter schools may be the last who can still reverse the negative megatrends converging today. In order for these children to learn the needed new ways of thinking, the present generation in charge of society must begin to set up for them a kind of education it never had and arrange to educate itself further at the same time.

This isn't done by plastering on a new course or program to counter each affliction—AIDS, addiction, gangs, selfish ethics, and so on—in the ludicrous way we now try to use schools as band-aid cure-all. Public education will have to be totally reconceived—what it's for and how it's to work. The very idea that it might *transform* society would be a reversal, since schools have always been regarded as a transmitter of tradition. And it would have to go far beyond teaching people how to get a job and get ahead. We have to think now not just about personal success and class mobility but about planetary survival and human co-evolution. This means that we will have to elevate schooling to a spiritual level heretofore unknown in public education.

In trying to take a bigger view of schooling, reformers have resorted, with numbing reiteration, to the use of the word "systemic," which has become a synonym for "holistic." They are certainly right that we need to look at learning as a whole. A longer school day or year, magnet schools, parental involvement, or curricular integration mean little in themselves. Everything depends on the total learning environment of which they might partake. But systemic reform refers so far only to reorganization of a bureaucracy or of a curriculum. Increasingly, as policy makers have dominated educators, a systemic approach has come to mean enlisting, or drafting, local and state governments into a national system of curriculum and assessment coordinated by the federal government in close consultation with business leadership. Systemic thinking has been extraordinarily political, featuring originally the local school district and then successively more inclusive governmental jurisdictions. The time has come to situate education in a perspective that comprises far more than management of schooling and that thus redirects thinking to intrinsic issues of human development.

Some wholes are larger than others. I worked my way up organically through ever broader systemic views, starting as a secondary English teacher in a private school in the 1950s who became by the 1960s and 1970s a developer at large of K-12 language arts curriculum for public schools in North America. In the process I discovered that not only did reading, writing, listening, and speaking have to be integrated with each other but that the language arts had in turn to be learned through the other academic subjects, the other media, and the other arts. Since for me the "whole" became the learner, I called this integrated curriculum *student-centered*. At the same time, I was realizing that students, schools, and subjects all have to be considered in their cultural contexts. I was myself growing by integrating my awareness across more inclusive fields of thought and value. Through both professional and personal development, I have come to regard not only school but school reform as suffering from systemic thinking that is too limited because the system on which it is based is partial.

The only solution consists of making the most inclusive system of all the framework for education. If you think of successively more comprehensive contexts for the learner, spanning from personal to transpersonal, they range from the system of an individual mind to that of the society and on through that of all of nature—that is, from consciousness through culture to cosmos, the biggest whole of all. The ultimate systemic thinking is cosmological, metaphysical. Human development deserves no less. After all, an educational system would most sensibly sponsor the quest for the nature, meaning, and purpose of life that underlies not only science, art, and philosophy but also the personal acts of everyday life. This book suggests how education might be so envisioned and realized.

Within this cosmic framework, not politics and economics but culture and consciousness should provide the dual focus for a new sort of education. This is the argument introduced in Part One, "Reform for the Right Reasons." Schools should not be political and commercial instruments. Officials in government and business are not the right people to lead school reform, though they must be deeply involved. Politicians would sacrifice their careers were they to analyze honestly what makes schools the way they now are, as is done in Part Two, "Reform by the Right Means," or were they to propose the radical solutions that are required, as outlined in Part Three, "The Universal Schoolhouse."

Officeholders and their appointees have to cater to the partialities of both special-interest lobbies and a public that has not had the benefit of a cosmopolitan education for personal maturation. Most official forums inhibit discussion of personal and social realities as being over the heads of, or too strong for the stomachs of, the public. But a democracy must assume an electorate with some capacity to face truth and deal with it maturely. The interests of most businesspeople are too narrow and even self-serving. Neither government nor industry seems likely at present to consider the total aims of education that serve the deepest needs of the society and of its individual members.

Nationalistic economics must not remain the chief determiner of educational policy-making. People are people before they are employees or employers. Placing money first makes the whole society so materialistic that people fail each other and the society breaks down. This is exactly what is happening in America. When everybody is squeezing everybody else and thinking solely of their own ambitions, families, or companies, the whole cycle of development, production, and delivery degenerates, and *no* systems or programs or policies work well. Yes, public education should help people get jobs, get along, and get ahead, but that had better happen as part of benefiting human culture and consciousness. The quality of society and of individuals is really all one, so intimately do they influence each other. Both are evolving, co-evolving. How may public education best affect culture and the individual consciousness it interacts with? We will never answer this question as public officials and blue-ribbon commissions have gone about reform so far.

Setting and meeting national standards through a system of universal assessment has long been a de facto reality of public schooling. This sort of systemic thinking is not only old hat but is clearly part of the problem, not any sort of solution. We have had a test-driven education for generations that has been tried and found calamitously ineffectual. As for accountability, test scores mean little. Ask the disgruntled employers, colleges, and families. Most students pass, but most citizens regard public education as a failure. Rightly, they do not judge schools by scores but by the results demonstrated out of school, which they measure by values no standardized assessment system designed to rank schools or sort students can accommodate. Only individuals can make this ultimate assessment, and only their collective judgment, which no technocratic numbers game should displace, can make for a truly democratic educational system.

I argue that personal development must be central, because

all solutions to public problems, no matter how collective the action, depend on mature, enlightened individuals to call for and indeed insist on these solutions. Democracy simply cannot work otherwise, and we will lose it if political leaders continue to have to pander to the selfish, childish, bigoted, and short-sighted elements of the electorate. So it is not only for the sake of self-fulfillment that individuals should set and assess their own educational programs but for the sake of the common-weal, which needs members who, in learning to think and do for themselves, can think about and take care of each other. All learners would participate in community service, and social agencies would be built into the educational system as major arenas of learning. Expanding personal awareness must occur socially, as part of transforming the culture. Only individual maturation will make either capitalism or democracy work, because freedom in both the market and individual behavior presupposes a consciousness and identity that go beyond mere egoism.

Each community should organize a totally individualized, far-flung learning network giving all people of all ages access to any learning resource at any time. Nothing is required, but everything is made available. Users make the decisions but avail themselves of constant counseling by a variety of parties. The very concept of schools, classes, courses, exams, and curriculum is superseded. Subjects and methods are reorganized around individual learners forging their personal curricula in interaction with others doing the same across a whole spectrum of learning sites, situations, and technologies. This is what I am calling the universal schoolhouse.

Since school buildings would no longer be the educational units, school reform loses meaning except as an interim stage toward a total transformation of public education. I have al-lotted, however, a considerable part of the book, Part Three, to bridging from schooling as we know it to such a universal learning network, because those people who are to effect this difficult transition need not merely a vision but considerable practical help. I have sketched stages that build from the best we now know and do toward implementation of that vision. These include all good learning activities, wherever and however they occur. The means to a splendid education are not mysteries but lie at hand all around us all the time. Certain elements in our psyche and society have blocked us, however, from gathering these together and putting them to use in public schools.

I have associated educational reform with societal transformation to the point of proposing that most social services be merged with public education (Part Four, "Social and Personal Rebirth"). Consolidate the problems, consolidate the resources. Problems can then be shifted from damage control to prevention, from numerous costly and ineffectual agencies in all levels of government to one local learning system that, through this merger with other social services, makes communal problems part of its subject matter and learning methods. In one stroke, personal learning becomes realistic and public problem solving efficient.

Part of this radical proposal is that the functions and funds of government be redeployed so that each level of government from municipal to federal does only what it can do better than the others. This means decentralizing education and most other social services from state capitols and Washington to local communities, where most tax monies would remain but with provisions for overcoming funding inequities and for certain other checks and balances. The current decentralization of some school districts is being nullified by state legislatures and national examinations, which more than ever control curriculum over the heads of districts, defeat reform of it by standardizing it, and misuse tax money to maintain it as a "core" to which everyone must submit—all in violation of American ideals of democracy and liberty.

In this proposal, control of education would pass to private citizens, because no party determines in an individualized learning network what another learns—not even on-site or neighborhood committees, which can be as misguided or tyrannical as the state. The people must take education into their own hands—but for their individual selves only, not for others. Majority rule does not apply to something so personal as learning. That is a political concept based on voting. Book censorship, for example, becomes impossible, because no one is subject to some other party's decision. By the same token, users who want to include study of a certain religion needn't attend private schools to do so. If the state isn't setting curriculum, there can be no issue of separating church and state. Using common resources to customize one's own education most nearly accommodates both the ideals and the pluralism of America. Paradoxically, the way to bring everyone together is to let them go their own ways—together, in the same communal learning network.

Finally, this fusion of idealism and realism embodies the perception that the truly practical way is the spiritual way. Just as only more fully developed individuals can avoid becoming part of problems like corruption, crime, addiction, pollution, unemployment, unwanted pregnancy, or unnecessary poor health, only the most holistic perspectives on learning will save education in time for it to save the society. People have to construe these problems as at bottom educational and deal with all of them *simultaneously*, through integrative ways of relating to each other and to nature. By pushing holistic thinking all the way, to its basis in holiness, this proposal ultimately grounds educational and social transformation in spiritual evolution, as developed most fully in the first and last chapters of the book.

Building a bridge from today's herd-mind, nationalistic school system to a thoroughly individualized and cosmopolitan learning network will take place by the coalescing of desirable practices already implemented or envisioned but not brought together as a whole. This and the further coalescence of this new educational system with other social services require a thoroughgoing holistic approach, which tends to be a spiritual approach, whether one thinks of it that way or not, because identifying with other people and creatures, and ultimately with the All, really defines spirituality in a nonsectarian way. The more inclusive the wholes that individuals dwell in, the holier the society they create together.

In this book *spiritual* does not mean polyanna, puritanical, or pietistic. Nor does it refer to a sect or even to religion in general, inasmuch as all religions are embodied in cultural institutions that are partial. Spirituality is totally cosmopolitan, because only the cosmic framework is all-inclusive. To be spiritual is to perceive our oneness with everybody and everything and to act on this perception. It is to be whole within oneself and with the world. Morality ensues. From this feeling of unity proceed all positive things, just as from *whole* proceed all the words for these things—*wholesome, hale, healthy,* and *holy.*

A society can become sacred through secular means. Spiritualizing education does not require any religious indoctrination or moralistic preaching. All it takes is the setting of certain relationships among people and between people and the rest of nature. Children who grow up sharing resources and knowledge, collaborating to realize common goals, helping and being helped, serving a community that gives them access to everything it has, and identifying across social boundaries will become empathic, compassionate adults. Also growing up empowered with choice and self-direction, convinced by this of their innate worth and capacity, they will feel their inner divinity, the highest form of self-esteem. Such people create a sacred society, which can prosper materially as a side effect of making holistic knowing—spiritual understanding—the framework for every act within it.[1]

January 1994   James Moffett
Mariposa, California

THE
AUTHOR

▲

James Moffett taught English and French at Phillips Exeter Academy from 1955 to 1965 after receiving his A.B. degree (1952) in English and A.M. degree (1953) in French from Harvard University. He graduated Phi Beta Kappa, magna cum laude with highest honors in English, and won the Bowdoin Essay Prize. Awarded a Carnegie Corporation grant in 1965 to write up theory and practice for an innovative English curriculum, he was a research associate at the Harvard Graduate School of Education from 1965 to 1968. This resulted in *Teaching the Universe of Discourse* (1968) and *Student-Centered Language Arts, K-12* (1968). Since then he has worked freelance as a national consultant, workshop leader, lecturer, and author in language education and total learning environments.

In 1970 he was a visiting lecturer at the School of Education, University of California, Berkeley; in 1984, Distinguished Visiting Professor in the English Department of San Diego State University in California. Occasionally he has also taught at the Bread Loaf School of English of Middlebury College, Vermont. He is a former member of the National Humanities Faculty of the National Endowment for the Humanities. From 1973 to 1978 he studied yoga and spiritual discipline under Swami Sivalingam.

In 1982 he received the Distinguished Author Award from the California Association of Teachers of English for *Active Voice: A Writing Program Across the Curriculum* (1981) and *Coming on Center: Essays in English Education* (1981) and in 1992 received from the National Council of Teachers of English the David H. Russell Award for Distinguished Research in the Teaching of English for *Storm in the Mountains: A Case Study of Censorship, Conflict, and Consciousness* (1988). He is coeditor of *Points of View: An Anthology of Short Stories* (1966), senior editor of *Interaction: A K-12 Language Arts and Reading Program* (1973), and editor of *Points of Departure: An Anthology of Nonfiction* (1985). Other works include *Detecting Growth in Language* (1992) and *Harmonic Learning: Keynoting School Reform* (1992).

James Moffett died in December 1996.

THE UNIVERSAL SCHOOLHOUSE

▲

PART ONE

▲

Reform for the
Right Reasons

The urgency of school reform is recognized but most often for the wrong reasons. Envisioning future education must include sorting out the various reasons for reform to determine which are right for today. Efforts to do that in this first part of the book will refer to successively more inclusive frameworks of personal, social, and natural life—to consciousness, culture, and cosmos. We may regard these expanding contexts as concentric or nested one within another. The present educational framework of politics and economics falls somewhere in the mid-range, well short of the most comprehensive perspective. This is why school reform geared to government and business will continue to fail both the practical goals it aims at and the spiritual ones it does not.

Just as context holds the key to text, any "whole" taken as a framework governs the thought and action that can take place in the arena it stakes out. Every whole becomes only a part when viewed from the meta-perspective of the next larger whole. While it is sometimes necessary to study plants and animals as participants in a relatively self-contained ecosystem like a swamp or savannah, for the fullest understanding and wisest decision making we have to look at that local ecosystem within the region of coast, plains, or river drainage of which it forms only a part. Or within the whole continent. The more importance we give to long-range, widespread effects like climatic origins, migrations, or evolutionary variations in species, the more comprehensive the ecosystem we need to work within. The more tightly national ecologies, economies, and cultures interact, the more we have to think and act internationally even within our own bailiwick. Hence the slogan, "Act locally, think globally."

But we also have to consider our actions in relation to extraterrestrial factors like the heat of the sun, as in global warming, or the sun's cyclic magnetic storms, which affect our electrical transmissions and perhaps ourselves, much as the moon causes tides and influences behavior. Now that scientists consider how asteroids may have determined part of earth's history and how planets may partially trigger earthquakes by shifting gravitational pull, and now that they monitor radio signals from distant galaxies and acknowledge our constant irradiation from outer space, perhaps we can see part of the point of the ancients' belief that our environment includes the stars—that ultimate ecosystem, the cosmos.

What is a cosmic or spiritual perspective? Before contrasting politics and economics with culture and consciousness, as educational settings, let's take a big step back and work our way into a metaphysical framework. This framework will be introduced in Chapter One through an emphasis on evolution and then developed in the final chapter through an emphasis on incarnation. Between these bookends we will examine education across the range of the various subsystems of which it is a part.

1

▲

Spirituality and
Education

A few decades from now people will regard the schooling of today with revulsion, as astonishingly primitive, in the same way we deplore the eighteenth-century treatment of the mentally ill. Our successors will not be able to understand how citizens dedicated to personal liberty and democracy could have placed learning on a *compulsory* basis, such that citizens had to report to certain buildings every working day of their youth in order to be bossed about by agents of the state. All the requirements that we take for granted—subjects and courses, textbooks and examinations, credits and certificates—will be properly seen as crude efforts to gear education with society in ways that throw back to the Chinese bureaucracy of 1000 B.C., which dictated the kind of schooling needed to staff its huge organization of clerks, scribes, and savants.

The very idea of a state compelling people to attend schools contradicts the foundations of modern democracy, however much practical reason there may have been for it when America's population was predominantly rural and illiterate. Far from creating an enlightened electorate, compulsory state-set education has resulted in a populace that is currently throwing democracy away. By refusing to face problems and by voting for leaders who just make them feel good, Americans have supported political practices that erode their civil rights and the powers of Congress and that defer the solution of problems until only some sort of fascism will prevent total collapse.

Making people learn, and making them learn certain things in certain ways, teaches them to abide by decisions from above instead of learning to think for themselves. Homogenizing a populace through a cookie-cutter curriculum at once nullifies the diversity that ensures collective survival and thwarts the individualization on which self-realization depends. Thus it works equally against the social and the personal, the practical and the spiritual.

I think that education will out of sheer necessity move in the direction described in this book. As public schooling continues to fail, and as unresolved societal problems threaten catastrophe, the realization will take hold that only personal development will save the situation. Governments themselves will have to undertake this redirection, because they have charge of resources, and through them the people must take action. The state has to sponsor personal development for the sake of the social body, because there is no public problem one can name—unwanted children, unemployment, corruption in government—that would not be dramatically improved if the people involved were more mature, capable, and moral. Selfishness, ignorance, and immaturity can spoil any political and economic system, as indeed they have both communism and capitalism.

Of the three common aims of education—social responsibility, productive employment, and personal development—governments inevitably slight the last, which policy makers and business leaders fear will subvert the other two. Personal development interests legislators less than law and business, which are their meat and potatoes, but without personal development you cannot hope for the enlightened electorate that democracy requires, nor the maturity and self-fulfillment that make people responsible, nor the development of talent, intellect, and social skills that the workplace is crying for. If there is a priority among these three main aims, surely it goes to personal development, because learning takes places only in individuals, and because social responsibility and productive employment depend on the maturation and self-realization of individuals.

Total personal development naturally includes, after all, relating well to other people and creatures. Individualization is needed not just to cultivate talent and intellect but to foster the full human being, which best safeguards any society. As mathematician Alfred North Whitehead said in 1922, "The claim for freedom in education carries with it the corollary that the development of the whole personality must be attended to."[1] This calls for learning conditions that facilitate self-education, compared to which the concept of choice bandied about in school reform discussion is paltry. So long as learning is organized around *schools* of any sort, and not around personal learning programs benefiting from maximum resources, we will not have the self-education that freedom and democracy require.

This was, I suspect, the main reason that Ivan Illich proposed "deschooling society" in favor of a community learning network. There are four principal knowledge sources, he said—objects, models, elders, and peers. An educational system should aim to give learners access to these four sources by means of referral and exchange services that put learners in contact with learning objects and facilities, match them with peer partners, and find for them those experts and educators who can serve as models and tutors. Illich assumed three essential sorts of people to make the system work—educational administrators to build access roads, pedagogues to counsel individuals, and "leaders" who are not professional teachers but who know or do something so well that they act as mentors or gurus.[2]

Although my own thinking does not particularly derive from Illich's, my experience leads me to very similar conclusions. I think he was right that we should reconstruct the fundamental ways that people learn by providing everyone access to these ways all the time. Educators did not respond much to his proposals, because societal problems had not gotten bad enough yet and because few people saw then how closely these problems interrelated with each other and with education.

Since then, the holistic mode of perceiving has become more established in our consciousness by the globalization of economy and ecology, communication and transportation. This holistic experience has combined with the urgency of extremity to induce a preventive rather than remedial approach to solving problems. Early and continuous education seems the most effective way to head off the negative factors that cause the problems. Proposals such as Illich's that seemed too radical and risky in the 1970s appear far more feasible now that we feel we have nothing to lose—and now that we feel any change had *better* be radical in the sense of getting to the roots of the problems. Even in the 1970s Illich's society might have taken more seriously his deschooling of itself had he or others tried to envision more ways to bridge to it from conventional schooling.

Evolution and Education

Personalized, holistic, experiential learning has been advocated, experimented with, and sometimes implemented since at least the eighteenth century, starting with Jean-Jacques

Rousseau, Johann Heinrich Pestalozzi, and Friedrich Froebel, and continuing with the American Transcendentalists, all of whom worked frankly within a spiritual framework. It was reintroduced later in their different ways by Maria Montessori, Rudolf Steiner, and John Dewey. Across these differences runs a strong continuity that detractors always want to call "romantic" but which amounts to an insistence on the total growth of each person—physical, emotional, social, intellectual, and spiritual.

The fear that personal development will turn narcissistic and destroy the political and social fabric has always overwhelmed or marginalized these movements. This fear stems from a chronic misunderstanding of history, which seems to tell us that personal development disrupts and eventually destroys a culture, as exemplified by Athens and Rome. According to these cautionary tales, when Athenian education shifted from preparation for political and military leadership to self-cultivation, the society decayed and fell victim to Sparta, which focused entirely on citizenship training, even perhaps to the exclusion of literacy. Similarly, Roman civilization supposedly declined once a middle-class, individualistic way of life developed.

But lessons of history concern not just what has happened but what is happening, the long-range drifts that include our own time. Seen in this largest perspective, history becomes evolution. The relation between the individual and his or her culture is precisely one of the things that is evolving. In antiquity, self-cultivation could take place only by enslaving others. Thus history gives individualization a bad odor for modern people. The famous liberal arts education of which we still speak today was called such because it was designed for those who would never have to earn a living. It was "liberal" because its beneficiaries were free, supported by the labor of others, to whom alone the trades and crafts were taught. The elite studied only the "arts." Today anyone may pursue a liberal arts education, which means something different, because it has evolved so as to merge with education for making a living.

It is precisely such enormous societal changes that have invalidated the simple old equation between personal development and selfishness or narcissism. We boast of our personal liberty, but it is clear we still fear and distrust it, because historical experience seems to tell us that as individuals strengthen, society disintegrates. What once may have been true is what is evolving. How can that old truth not have changed when self-cultivation has become possible without slavery?

Starting as a sort of occasional mutation in extraordinary personages who became kings and spiritual leaders, individualization has grown in both quantity and kind. It has democratized, so that over the centuries more people have been gaining independence from the group, including more people of different socioeconomic classes, aided by the development of technology and communication media.

But the *nature* of individualization has also been evolving, some stages of which are selfish and narcissistic, attained by the majority now, and further stages of which, attained by a leading minority, are empathic and compassionate. The latter seem to return to the original group solidarity, but there is a world of difference between the primal herd feeling, which is unconscious and incapable of personal thought or action, and the expanded consciousness of the individual who has parlayed self-cultivation into self-transcendence. The American Transcendentalists well represent a highly evolved minority who experimented with social reforms, including educational. Highly individualistic, they nevertheless sought better community, sometimes through utopian social experiments. This is what happens if personal development is pursued with some consciousness of the drift of evolution; it gets beyond selfishness and narcissism, which are best viewed as temporary stages that lead to better ones if properly understood.

In his classic of 1901, *Cosmic Consciousness: A Study in the Evolution of the Human Mind*, Richard Bucke distinguished three stages of consciousness.[3] Upper animals are aware of things around them and of their own bodies and hence have *simple consciousness*. In addition to this, humans enjoy a second stage, *self-consciousness*, whereby each distinguishes itself from the rest of the world, treats its own mentation as an object, and becomes capable of language. A few people, increasingly more numerous, attain the third stage, which is characterized by cosmic illumination and exaltation. According to Bucke, more and more people will gradually shift from self-consciousness to *cosmic consciousness*, that is, into a spiritual state of direct revelation that will render religions obsolete. For evidence he examines the lives of several dozen historical figures like Buddha, Jesus, Mohammed, Socrates, Dante, Blake, and Whitman that he judges to have entered cosmic consciousness.[4]

Put a somewhat different way, consciousness seems to be evolving from collective to individual, from dependence on a group mind to independence of thought. Conformity may have been necessary in order for individuals to survive before they had developed enough self-consciousness to think for themselves and function in autonomy from their group. This is the thesis in psychologist Julian Jaynes's *The Origins of Consciousness in the Breakdown of the Bicameral Mind*.[5] Modern theosophists and rosicrucians always assume as part of esoteric spiritual traditions that the individual soul evolves from the group soul of the race, and we can see evidence of a parallel secular evolution in the history of Western government, economics, religion, and art.

As political and commercial liberty for individuals evolved, so did spiritual and aesthetic expression. Protestantism, capitalism, and democracy all arose as aspects of this evolution in the relationship between individuals and their society. Whether we compare the same civilization at different times or compare older and newer civilizations alive today, we see individual consciousness gradually emerging from its cultural background, pathos from ethos, like a statue emerging from stone. This can be traced in the shifts of literary mode from myths and epics through folk tales and romances to bourgeois novels and stories of the antihero. As the divine comedy yields to the human comedy, anonymous communal storytelling splinters into a multiplicity of character viewpoints. At first stories are still told only in the third person, but increasingly they are told in the first person by the characters themselves through purported diaries, letters, memoirs, autobiographies, and subjective monologues.[6]

It is no accident, as Jaynes points out, that individualism develops as races travel and mix. Where blood is purest, as in oriental and Middle Eastern countries, conformity still reigns. Amerindians bonded very tightly within a tribe, identifying and sharing with one another to the point of virtually eschewing self-assertion and personal possessions. In extant aboriginal cultures we are struck by the relative lack of self-consciousness, of feeling distinct from the group or environment. The individual counts on the collective power and knowledge of what I will call the race spirit and tends to pine and wither if the culture is diluted or destroyed. In insular or pocket cultures, group solidarity comes before all, leading often to intolerance, chauvinism, and xenophobia. At its extreme, outsiders are not recognized as similar to oneself, as people, and so the group's laws and morals, rigidly enforced within the group, may not apply beyond it.

As hunter-gatherers become herder-farmers and the nomadic egalitarian society becomes settled, populous, and complex, the lives of individuals differentiate into a variety of social and vocational roles. One way or another, through mixing of cultures or through diversifying within each culture, pluralism causes people to identify more selectively and fractionates the group consciousness. As individual consciousness increases, tolerance becomes more and more important for social cohesion. Large modern democracies comprise explosively diverse populations not only ethnically mixed and vocationally specialized but finely splintered into an infinity of interests and preferences. The evolution of consciousness seems to work by constantly refining this breakdown into subgroups of subgroups and hence down to individual members. Or perhaps it's rather that as individuals find themselves different, they seek some nearest of kind and form cells or clubs of similarity, often activist.

Confronting this evolution, liberals and conservatives typically fight over whether to change or stay the same. Radicals and reactionaries feel even more strongly about this issue. Rightists emphasize patriotism and the dangers of weakening tradition; leftists emphasize internationalism and the dangers of not reforming. We note that the issue of change is linked to ethnocentricity, to in-group loyalties based on the dependence of the individual on the group. Both partisans have a point, we can say, and their conflicts are needed to maintain equilibrium. But if technology, demography, and other factors are changing, then old ways may jeopardize survival more than adjusting to the changes. If the changes are within the control of the group, then a reactionary policy may be in order, like efforts to reverse the use of toxic substances. But suppose a group unleashes forces it cannot reverse, that get out of hand? Or suppose a change occurs that can be humanly controlled only by a collaboration that the groups cannot achieve because their other interests conflict?

In other words, conservatism serves a group only when the

world does not change or when the group can reestablish the status quo if the change is deemed undesirable. If change is constant and irreversible, a group will most likely have to keep adjusting to it.

Evolution is precisely such constant and irreversible change. If human evolution exists, as seems evident, it tips the scales toward the left. For if the human species is evolving from collective to individual behavior, or if an individual consciousness is evolving out of a collective, or if both culture and consciousness are evolving somehow in tandem, then groups will have to keep changing whether they like it or not, assuming that this evolution originates from beyond humanity itself. In this case, pluralization and hybridization make for a creative, flexible, self-correcting culture that has a better chance of surviving than a monolithic culture that tries to perpetuate itself by homogenizing its members and invoking the past.

If these considerations seem too philosophical for a pragmatic matter like learning, reflect that we are always saying education must prepare for the future. Does that mean we are really just trying to prophesy political, economic, and technological changes? These are, after all, of human origin, and with collaboration people could undo such changes or simply control them in the first place so as to *make* the future. However—and this is where we can't avoid some cosmological or metaphysical questions—what if there is an evolution beyond human control that inheres in nature or the universe? Suppose evolution might become a collaboration between humanity and nature or some other force behind nature?

So far, human evolution has worked willy-nilly, without much human collaboration. Change has occurred through extremity—wars, revolutions, plagues, mass migrations, and other social cataclysms—because the changes that comprise evolution had to be effected, so to speak, from the outside, as though through some deus ex machina. Evolution seems to press forward with a will of its own that gives history a direction no government ever planned. We must now become conscious of this direction and try to interpret its import for future society. Any reform has to reckon with it in one way or another. The more we take evolution into our own hands, the less destructive it needs to be.

Public education has ignored human evolution, whereas it must play into it—fit the present stage of culture and consciousness, not a prior stage. By basing education on the past we fight evolution and force it to force us, through extremity. That is, people who don't work with evolution will change only when cataclysm leaves them little choice. This is how change is still happening for the most part today, although a more evolved minority understands that much agony becomes unnecessary if you try to discern the direction of evolution and make the changes yourself instead of being clouted into them.

We are midway with individualism, contradictory about it, abusing it, as if a foreign force had thrust it upon us and we did not know what to do with it. Freedom can be proclaimed by legislating it, but it can be realized only by educating for it. Conformist education worked perhaps so long as society changed little and personal liberty was not an ideal. But if a state-set curriculum teaching everybody the same things were right for the present stage of human consciousness and culture, surely we would know so by now and would not be agonizing over the state of the world. Creating social coherence while fostering personal self-realization—the trick of our era—requires an education tuned to human evolution, which is shifting, however bloodily at present, from ethnocentricity and exclusion to a cosmopolitan inclusion.

The connection between this shift and the shift from collective to individual consciousness is this: as people solo out from the herd mind—the race spirit, the group soul—they not only start to think for themselves and take responsibility for themselves, they enter on a personal spiritual path unique to each that nevertheless entails joining increasingly expansive memberships of humanity and nature. This is the root reason why self-development leads not to egoism but to empathy. As the ancient esoteric adage expresses it, "Everything that rises must converge." Or as the slogan on U.S. coins puts it (borrowed by the Freemasonic founding fathers from the same tradition), *e pluribus unum*—out of many, one. As opposed to the exoteric meaning—about fusing the original colonies into one nation or the millions of immigrants into one people—the esoteric meaning is that fully developed individuals become one again because in essence they are consubstantial with each other and the All.

This evolution is far from merely Darwinian. It is cosmological, subsuming the physical. I believe even Darwin recognized it as a more general, even spiritual, framework for his work. The same may be true for Illich and Dewey. But scientists and reformers feel obliged to take a secular stance, on pain of being ignored or derided. Reformers of a secular society have to speak in the terms current in that society, and of course they are aware of the huge harm done in the name of religion.

On the other hand, the lack of a bridge from schooling to deschooling may have hindered acceptance of Illich's ideas, which seem to have needed an evolutionary framework to provide the understanding necessary to bridge from past to future. Such a framework involves the reformer in what are usually regarded as spiritual or cosmological matters—forces beyond the human world, which the Catholic Illich probably withheld and the secular Dewey simply eschewed. Whereas their proposals suffered, I think, from the omission of such a framework, it is equally true that Maria Montessori and Rudolf Steiner limited the number of their adherents by frankly relating education to a spiritual dimension.

The time has surely come for the pragmatic realization that

our colossal problems are forcing us beyond the customary materialism of our mainstream culture into another dimension, that we will never solve our problems except in the most comprehensive framework conceivable. Perhaps our culture has reached a stage of both aspiration and desperation such that it can now think about practical concerns within metaphysical or cosmological perspectives.

After all, treating problems holistically is now considered effective even in management circles. The question is—*how* holistic. Any area may be staked out as an arena beyond which the game is off the field, action doesn't count, and therefore the mind doesn't play. For educational reform and cultural transformation nothing should be considered off the map. In fact, our problems are colossal precisely because our maps are too small. We can't afford any longer, in a postmodern era, to let merely modern prejudices about the "supernatural" limit our thoughts and our problem-solving capacity. If physicists have for decades been acknowledging that they can't avoid metaphysics and cosmology in trying to account for what they observe and infer, it makes little sense for the rest of us to remain too embarrassed to entertain matters going beyond what we can palp and heft.

Defining Spirituality

If possible, I would avoid the word *spirituality*, because it makes red flags pop up in many minds—unctuous sermons by preachers no better than oneself, millionaire TV evangelists preying on the frail, superstition blocking the progress of science, religion as the opiate of the masses, not to mention religion as a no-no in public schools. I honor all these negative associations to the extent that they represent aspects of reality and in the measure that I share them. But the very unavoidability of the word is something I have to honor even more. Others writing on educational change today, like Clive Beck and David Purpel, have chosen to speak of the spiritual element of life despite their wish, like mine, not to alienate the very audience of thoughtful people that will have to initiate or support any reform.[7]

First, there are secular meanings of *spiritual* and *spirituality* that don't necessarily entail belief in God, immortality, the soul, and other metaphysical realities. Atheists or agnostics may understand, for example, that people or acts may be referred to as spiritual only in the sense of moral or benevolent. In common parlance, spirited people are simply full of life and of themselves. There's even team spirit and the spirit of '76 or the spirit of the law, that is, some characteristic energy or essence. In French *esprit* means 'spirit' or 'ghost', as well as 'mind', its English equivalent. *Spirituel* means 'witty' or 'lively' as well as 'sacred'. Typically, as society has secularized over the centuries, the sense of *spirit* and its cognates has also become more material and metaphorical. Consider the use of *spirits* to mean alcoholic beverages, something that volatilizes to nothing and that alters our own spirits when we drink it. In the same way, *soul* may now refer to food or music that is spirited or to characterize African-American sensibility, all the while sometimes retaining its original meaning of incarnated Spirit.

As a way of passing on now to the sacred or religious meaning of spirituality that many people today would object to, it is helpful to consider what the common denominator might be of morality and mind, energy and essence. Even these material meanings converge on the immaterial. Morality comes from mores or customs and therefore does not depend on religion. Nor do vitality and energy, mind and wit. The essence of something is abstract and may perfectly well be understood as purely a mental or psychological category. Morality contrasts with materialism in the sense of selfishness and meanness. Mind commonly contrasts with matter, as does energy in the scientific sense. Philosophers contrast essence with existence. So a concept of immateriality underlies even the secular, material meanings.

Even were we not to accept *any* metaphysical meanings of spirituality, this convergence of secular meanings alone warrants *spiritualizing education*, I believe, as a rallying call for reform. It is intended to include everyone, however they feel about other worlds or otherworldliness. It brings to our daily efforts to improve our life in this world a sorely needed focus on being good for one another because we're not just thinking of ourselves. It energizes these efforts with a life force common to everything but working through each of us in a particular way characteristic of our individuality. It validates the inner life of thought and feeling and the sense of personal being in the face of depersonalization and a preoccupation with physical things. It calls us back from surfaces to essences, to whatever may be at the bottom of things or beyond our immediate kin and ken. It invites us to seek commonalities beneath commonplaces, for the sake of mind as well as morality. It's a toast to wits with spirits.

We could stop here and never bother with those "impractical" imponderables, the religious meanings of spirituality. But education can be informed by *all* definitions of spirituality, for even the nonsecular meanings can help us understand what we are about, given that in America we should never impose religion on students. In this context, let's consider the chief metaphors for spirituality, any literal use of language being of course wholly inadequate for the job.[8]

Spirit compares to breath, unseen but felt, experienced from moment to moment with every respiration, representing the life force that animates us and the rest of creation, uniting all things within it. Inspiration is breathing in, aspiration is breathing toward, and conspiring is breathing together. When the yogis say, "I am in your breath," they mean they are in your mind and tuned to what you are experiencing. They see profound connections between breath and thought: change one, change the other. Vocalizing is a key to all spiritual traditions, which employ chanting and singing for altering consciousness but which also emphasize speech as incarnation, the acoustical embodiment of mind through language. One of the energy centers in the body of which yoga and some Western traditions speak is the throat chakra, associated with the thyroid gland. Halfway between the heart and the brain (the organs of knowledge), at the point where breath voices thought, this energy center aptly represents the intersection of matter and spirit.

The other most common metaphor for Spirit is the sun, the handiest way of symbolizing energy, radiance, and light. But in this comparison the point is often made that Spirit is to the sun as the sun is to darkness. This not only distinguishes mere sun worshipping from symbolism but uses the traits of the sun to help us imagine a reality beyond our conscious experience, some energy and radiance of another order or dimension. The main criterion Richard Bucke used in determining which individuals have entered cosmic consciousness was their experience (which he once had himself) of being immersed in a flame or a rose-colored cloud, accompanied by joyous exaltation and an illumination of the world as a whole. Such was the "light" that filled and surrounded Paul on the road to Damascus and that blinded Peter, James, and John during the Transfiguration, which was a glimpse of the Christ in its true nature as Spirit. When Spirit no longer appeared in its familiar form of incarnation as Jesus, they could not bear it. A remarkably similar moment occurs in the *Bhagavad-Gita* when Krishna grants Arjuna his wish to see Krishna in his pure, unincarnated form, which is also a "light" so powerul that Arjuna has to beg off.

This understanding of Spirit as a super-energy or radiance of inconceivable subtlety and power is not hard to square with the emphasis in modern physics on radiation of various frequency ranges and of the reordering of reality occurring beyond the speed of light. Even notions deriving from Spirit, like the soul, immortality, resurrection, the fall, and redemption, can easily seem compatible with scientific theories that, as they continually evolve, are becoming equally hard to believe on the basis of familiar, material experience. Just as energy becomes matter at a low enough frequency, Spirit incarnates into what we know as the physical universe. This may occur through a process of serial step-downs comparable to what power transformers do. The esoteric literature describes this as successive emanations, each of which precipitates another denser than itself, until there materializes the densest of all, the one of lowest frequency, our physical world. The seven "days" of Creation, the Christian Trinity, other series of "engenderings" like the pagan geneologies of gods, Jacob's Ladder, and the Pythagorean numerical cosmology all symbolize this series of transductions, which in effect creates multiple worlds or alternative realities, another concept of today's theoretical physics.[9]

Soul is Spirit as it incarnates in an individual human being. The individual spirit is immortal precisely because it partakes in origin of Spirit itself, taking on and dropping a body as it incarnates and disincarnates. More literal-minded Christians inveigh against immortality of the soul, insisting that resurrection refers only to the body levering itself up out of the sod, but most other religions assume the immortality of the spirit along with its logical corollary, reincarnation, and so did Christianity before the Romanizing of doctrine that culminated in the anathematizing of the early church's leading theologian, Origen.

The "fall" refers to the incarnation of an individual spirit, which loses consciousness, on the material plane, of its "divine" origin and nature and therefore has to be "redeemed" by a "savior" who reveals through his or her own identity the true identity of the lost soul. The basic story here is of a bewildered exile, "a stranger in a strange land." Sin and evil refer not to earthly misbehavior, at least not directly, but to the Fall as involution of the spirit into matter, from which ensue the ignorance and egoism, the fear and anger, that cause the abuse of others commonly known as sin and evil.

The chief issue in all this is education, a factor of evolution. Human being is evolving back out of the darkness and density of matter. You recover who you really are, and in the course of this, discover the multiple realities and how you comprise multiple selves corresponding to this spectrum. This is the ultimate mystery story.

Spirit can be thought of as the subtlest frequency, the one that propagates the spectrum of increasingly slower vibrations. To be spiritual is to identify with Spirit across these vibrations. By extending one's frequency range, one attunes to the whole gradient of reality, whatever that may prove to be. Although morals can be formulated and enforced as group rules and as part of a religion, people who extend the range of their identity and sympathy naturally do what is good for others as well as for themselves, because they dissolve the boundaries of the ego and feel always the connectedness. If evolution reverses involution, then its direction is spiritual in that, as Bucke believed, more and more people will see life whole and act accordingly.

Even in its most sacred sense, spirituality does not depend on religion. Spirituality may be what all religions share, but religions are human-made and partake of particular cultures, so much so that their adherents may confuse Spirit with race spirit and continually slaughter each other over cultural differences construed as conflicts between the holy and unholy. Along with church bureaucratization and corruption, ethnocentricity is a major reason why some of the most spiritual people avoid religions. But this institutionalization of the in-group herd mind is precisely what attracts many others to them. In this respect, a cross or crescent is like a flag. Whether in Christendom, Islam, or Judaism, religion seems about to succumb to takeover by fundamentalists, who interpret scripture literally, reality materially, and humanity narrowly.[10] Many people in the church do not represent spirituality, while many outside do. Unless one is dedicated to a particular religious order, in which case the special discipline may indeed develop spirituality in someone who is ready, church affiliation may have little to do with spirituality, which is a way of perceiving reality and a way of being in the world.

A Metaphysical Framework for Education

Americans associate moral or spiritual education so closely with religion that it's difficult for them to conceive of it as independent enough to avoid violating the First Amendment injunction against a state religion. But it's also difficult to imagine that the founding fathers envisioned a school system as materialistic as ours, devoid of any effective spiritual permeation, devoted rather to plugging students into a dispiriting, self-destructive social apparatus driven by commerce. Though devout Christians, the founding fathers wisely refrained from basing this nation on their own religion. From European history since the Reformation, they had learned that a theocracy would lead to religious persecution, civil war, or, at best, enforced devotion.

On the other hand, the majority of the signers of the Declaration of Independence, the drafters of the Constitution, the members of the Continental Congress, and the officers of the Continental Army belonged to an international spiritual fraternity drawing on ancient esoteric teachings—the Freemasons, who probably deserve major credit for establishing the first democracies.[11] This means that they recognized a universal spirituality such as I have been trying to describe, independent of particular religions or cultures. It seems fair to assume that the founding fathers had no intention of banning this spirituality from public education when they separated church from state.

On the contrary, they had to have understood that personal liberty and free enterprise would work *only* in the spiritualized culture they envisioned. Otherwise a society is vulnerable to the very selfishness and materialism that have brought our own to the brink of catastrophe. Every economic and political system depends on some degree of trust, good faith, goodwill, and fellow feeling, without which everything from auto traffic and public foodserving to banking procedures and judicial proceedings simply breaks down. The more intricate and far-flung the interdependence, the greater the vulnerability to egoism. Far from contradicting the Constitution or the intent of the founding fathers, an education that spiritualizes the society will alone fulfill their ideals.

Nothing is more practical than spirituality, understood at whatever level. This is not to say, as so many TV evangelists do, that God will make you wealthy (although it's often true in *their* case), nor even that things go better with God, although there is some truth in that if we understand God as Spirit or spirituality. Becoming centered and integrated, mature and perceptive, has numerous practical advantages in daily life. For about five years I underwent close discipleship with a spiritual master, a South Indian yogi who had no religious affiliation but honored and valued all the world's spiritual traditions. He emphasized mindfulness, attention, total awareness at all times of what is going on around you and within you. Because this sort of attunement can be focused on any being or object, it naturally develops empathy and illumination. Along with these goes an objectivity based not on alienation, on denying the subjective or passionate parts of oneself, but on impartiality, on giving full play to the totality of oneself at all levels of being so that one forms no controlling attachments. Like Arjuna in the *Bhagavad-Gita*, we do what has to be done in this world but without becoming attached to the fruits of our efforts.

All this bestows great knowledge and power that may be used for earthly accomplishments, and my teacher the yogi felt that *being able* to do what one wills on this material plane is critical. He did not approve of incompetence and fuzzy-headedness posing as otherworldliness. Not knowing the state of your finances or the hidden motives of someone you are dealing with are spiritual flaws because they show failures of attention and perception. Spirituality is gnostic in the sense that it is fully knowing. God marks the fall of every sparrow. A spiritual discipline trains for the omniscience and omnipotence of divinity itself. The pilgrim "worships" divinity only to identify with it and "follows" it only to emulate and become it. Christ expressed this intent in John 14:20 when he said, "I am in the Father, and ye in me, and I in you." Consider also "Be perfect even as your Father is perfect" (Matthew 5:48) and "He that believeth on me, the works that I do shall he do also" (John 14:12). As we identify, so we know.

Now, the practical advantages of this order of knowledge and power are so great that only spiritually evolved people have been entrusted to acquire it. The reason that the highest spiritual teaching has usually been secret and exclusive ("esoteric") and never mainstreamed in the churches of any religion is that it is potentially very dangerous. The more one understands, the more one can manipulate other people and the rest of nature for one's personal purposes. It is essential that the moral and spiritual nature of a person be awakened to a degree commensurate with the development of the person's intellect and will. Thus the mystery religions of antiquity had in common with other initiatory teaching that extraordinary revelations were permitted only to those who had demonstrated goodness and self-control in their ordinary behavior. If one's intents derive from the egoistic self and not from the God-being or transpersonal self, that Self of which all else partakes, then knowledge and intelligence become instruments of calamity.

This situation indeed characterizes the world today and its history so far. We blame ignorance and stupidity for evil, but knowledge and intelligence can wreak far more destruction precisely because they are more powerful. Most history is the story of brighter people exploiting the simpler. Fostering knowledge and power without commensurate development of morality and spirituality, as our society tends to do, is a formula for disaster. Bright, well-educated people sit around conference tables in government and business talking smartly about solving problems that to a great extent they create themselves. If bright, well-educated people quit taking advantage, through their professions of law, medicine, business, education, and so on, of the less intellectually developed, many of the problems we set out to solve in our strategy sessions would dissolve at the roots. Most social problems stem in some way from inequalities, which can be solved by sharing.

One of the laws of spiritual disciplines is that when you evolve, you must take others with you. Service is not merely pious; it is an essential part of your own growth. My teacher asked me to start teaching yoga when, flustered at the thought, I felt I was still a beginner myself. Navel-gazing may capture the imagination of Westerners because it's exotic to them, but it's not the whole story. You meditate in order to break through to new knowledge that will help others as well as yourself. As the Zen masters put it, at some time you come down out of the cave and go back into the marketplace. So spiritual education is practical not only in generating more knowledge and power but in keeping them within a safe, holistic context where consciousness and culture nourish each other.

Spirituality is practical not only in what it can enable you to do in the world but in how it can free you from the world. To be able to release things, to not need or want them, amounts to a tremendous advantage. Much suffering comes from feeling you *must* have this or *have* to do that. When you fail, you go through cycles of feeling defeated and impotent, thwarted and deprived, angry, envious, and resentful. The economic and societal losses are correspondingly devastating. I'm not talking hair-shirt renunciation here. It's a matter of being able to feel good or at least sound, whatever happens. People who don't expect much enjoy life more than those whose anticipations inflict constant disappointment on them. Most of us long for serenity, which is really some release from our own passions, some autonomy of the self from circumstances, peace *before* death. Happiness may come less from getting what you think you want—which limits your chances, after all, to a few conditions (which you may very well be wrong about)—than from finding pleasure or satisfaction in many things.

We talk of freedom politically, as if it depended merely on someone else to grant it, or as if legislatures and courts could guarantee it. "How small of all that human hearts endure/That part which laws or kings can cause or cure" (Oliver Goldsmith). Of course what governments do can sometimes make an enormous difference to us, especially given the interdependence of life today, but our own compulsions and other inner constraints limit us at least as much as external conditions. Actually, we tend to internalize these conditions, so that many of the things we feel we must have or do or avoid originate in the culture. This is true because we still participate in a collective consciousness.

Perodically suspending habits, dependencies, and attachments both wakes us up and frees us. It represents a major element of the spiritualizing process, what I will call deconditioning, undoing the myriad ways our lives are determined by the inner and outer circumstances of consciousness and culture. All spiritual leaders regard ordinary life as a kind of sleep. This is why their goal is awakening. We are automatons living out the posthypnotic suggestions of our conditioning, which we take for free will and choice, just as we take the theater sets we have constructed around us as the real world.

Today's concept of "deconstructing" culture catches rather well the efforts of spiritual disciplines to find the hidden "subtexts" of the manifest world and to recognize how it seems real or true because we constructed it in the first place. The Hindu notion of the manifest world as *maya* or illusion has always assumed the "constructionist" view of knowledge that reigns today in cognitive psychology circles, that is, that humans *make* knowledge or meaning, collectively and individually, by putting together their perceptions of the world according to their needs, bents, lights, fears, desires, and circumstances of time and place. Any human version of reality is thus always situational and relative. The antidote is to undo or deconstruct one's personal and cultural conditioning. This awakening of mind and liberating of behavior would be an education indeed.

The very definition of spirituality as all-inclusion is the one that most applies to education. Advocates of holistic education, for example, insist on the total development of all levels of human being, just as advocates of minorities insist on total equity and access. This holism corresponds to the pure spiritual discipline perhaps most usefully typified by yoga, whose very name means 'union'. Yoga has managed to keep unusually intact and explicit some spiritual practices common to all cultures but mostly lost, blurred, or hidden in today's industrial civilization. These means specialize yoga into physical (hatha), emotional and devotional (bhakti), intellectual (jnani), action or service (karma), and meditational (raja or royal, which may bring all these together).

These multiple pathways develop body, heart, mind, and spirit for the realization of the individual at all levels of being. Were they offered as means to an ideal secular education, one might never suspect that they issued from a spiritual discipline aimed at enlightenment or awakening. As a program, these paths would fulfill the traditional American goals of citizenship, employment, and personal development. This is why I have drawn on so-called esoteric teachings as well as on exoteric or church teachings, which have been popularizations for the majority of what only a minority had evolved enough to perceive.

In an age of democracy, and in the spirit of total inclusion itself, the time has come to declassify mysteries, to erase the boundaries between esoteric and exoteric. Knowledge without spirituality remains as dangerous as ever, but the worst has already been largely realized, and we now have more to lose than gain by this sort of censoring. Suppose that the hierophants of the mystery religions were right to carefully screen the initiates whom they entombed in a three-day trance while they guided their spirit on an out-of-body tour of other realms. Suppose that the Christian church fathers were right to suppress reincarnation and the existence of the soul before birth on grounds that this knowledge would tempt the majority to live immorally. Better to tell the masses that they have only one life, at the end of which they will be held strictly accountable for their behavior by being sent off to dwell perpetually in bliss or agony.

In blandly posting "the pursuit of happiness" as the American dream, even the founding fathers seem to have withheld from their general constituency the deeper spiritual understanding they expressed only symbolically in Freemasonic em-

blems like the radiant eye and unfinished pyramid on the reverse (esoteric) side of the U.S. Seal (which, as thirty-third-
degree Masons themselves, Franklin Roosevelt and his vice
president Henry Wallace were later to place on the dollar bill).
Suppose the founding fathers were right in judging that the
first Americans were not yet ready to conceive personal liberty
as more than self-gratification, as an upturn in the spiritual
evolution of consciousness (the "new order of the ages," also
on the dollar bill) that would in fact make freedom hell if you
did not grow beyond yourself. As Emerson, Thoreau, Haw-
thorne, Melville, Dickinson, and Whitman were soon to say in
the Transcendentalist vein, both society and individuals suffer
greatly if they construe personal freedom as merely material
pursuit of happiness instead of as spiritual quest.

Even if the secrecy of an elite did succeed in curbing the
materialism of the masses in its day, now that our society has
committed itself to individual liberty and free enterprise, pater-
nalism has to go, along with theocracy and monarchy. Materialism is now doing its worst anyway, brought on precisely by
the unsolved challenge of freedom, so that at this point the
risks of the majority abusing spiritual truth, as we have freedom, seem far less than the risks of withholding from people
the very understanding that this freedom entails. Individual
consciousness has, after all, evolved over the course of the same
period as have political liberation and materialism. This has
made common people more equal to the new spiritual assignment than when they were patronized. What the founding fathers probably assumed but did not dare assert—the esoteric
meaning of "the pursuit of happiness"—ought now to be declassified in the sense of discovered for ourselves as we contemplate the failure of freedom to bring happiness in the exoteric
sense and look to education to set a new course for it. This
would be a course in learning to choose wisely when given
total access to both material and spiritual resources.

As for metaphysics being imponderable or problematical, isn't that true of life generally, whether you seek or shun metaphysics? Questions about how the universe is made, what it is for, and why you're in it can dog your days either way. Besides, there are advantages to accepting the *possibility*, as many scientists are doing, that other worlds, planes, or dimensions exist. The old polarity between spirit and matter may turn out, like the one between matter and energy, to be a costly habit of mind more than a representation of reality. Likewise, instead of contrasting the natural and the supernatural, we may simply expand the definition of nature to include experiences that seemed beyond it, just as scientists adjust a hypothesis to accommodate *all* the observations.

In any case, questions about the nature of the world and the purpose of life should undergird education just as they underlie our routine activities. Whether avoided or confronted, these are not only issues but *the* issues. Our lives are profoundly affected by these questions, whether we feel we have laid them to rest forever or whether we cannot rest for lack of answers. Humankind's greatest mental efforts have been exerted in science, philosophy, and literature to try to illuminate them. The ultimate ground of our being interests everybody. Consciously or not, the man in the street cries for meaning and purpose and will seek it in trivial or destructive ways if no framework exists through which to give significance to daily life. Education should make it possible to so continually and richly tie together experiences that making out in the world becomes the same as making out the world.

Finally, in keeping with a long American tradition of pragmatism and with the strategy of the seventeenth-century mathematician Blaise Pascal, why not *assume* that the spiritual view is true? Give it the benefit of the doubt? People who do so tend to feel better, treat others better, and fare better in their endeavors. If both the secular and sacred understandings of spirituality would bring to educational reform just what has been missing, what is there to lose? Even if you understand spirituality only as metaphor or myth, it can help you to think big and see deep when contemplating educational and societal transformation. You don't have to convert to benefit. Since an education that accommodates all possibilities for everybody is desirable anyway, it does not depend on your believing in Spirit. But if a metaphysical framework helps us learn to save either our hides or our souls, regenerate society and nature, why not bet on life being more rather than less?

2

▲

A Farewell to
Flag-and-Dollar
Schooling

Government and business are calling for educational change in order to compete better with foreign commerce. They complain that American students don't know enough science and math and that they lack skills in communicating, collaborating, analyzing, and creative problem solving. During the 1960s the federal government instigated curricular innovation for a similar reason. In launching *Sputnik* into orbit in 1957, the Soviet Union incited the United States to compete in a space race that was inseparable from military confrontation and rivalry for hegemony over other countries. Both then and now what spurred school reform was fear of a decline in technology as measured by nationalistic competition. This leads to wrongheaded thinking about public education.

The Waning of Nationhood

Nationalism already creates or feeds many of the problems education is supposed to relieve. It hardly needs encouraging and in any case is not the reason for which schools exist. Nationalistic commercial competition will soon obsolesce anyway as corporations continue to internationalize and as global trade becomes more collaborative in the manner of the European Community and the Confederation of Independent States.

Both corporations and governments are beginning to learn that they fare better in the long run by working with instead of against their foreign counterparts. American and Japanese automobile companies are marketing each other's products, building factories in each other's countries, and jointly producing some cars. No company or country is self-sufficient. Some countries have the capital, some the labor, some the natural resources, some the markets, and some the technology. In order to avail themselves of one or more of these, corporations are dispensing with the old national allegiance, which infuriates those workers and consumers who cling yet to a national economic identity. "Made in the USA" or "made in Taiwan" does not tell you the nationality of the company, of the capital, or of the components. Making this point in a *New Yorker* article, Richard J. Barnet echoed the question of policy expert Robert B. Reich—"Who is us?"—and quoted Thomas Jefferson: "Merchants have no country. The mere spot they stand on does not constitute so strong an attachment as that from which they draw their gain."[1] In this ironic sense, business is leading the way to global thinking.

Nations cannot help depending on each other economically, not only because they all need the five essentials listed above but also because no country alone can control its own economy now that trade, currency value, interest rates, stock markets, employment, and prices all fluctuate within any single nation on an international basis, according to what is going on in and between other countries. And now that both capitalist and communist empires have been dismantled and war virtually repudiated as a way of forcing economic advantage, countries have no choice but to collaborate. Besides, since rival countries are also potential markets, winning out over them means reducing their capacity to buy along with their capacity to sell.

Agreements will be made for certain countries to manufacture such-and-such items and other countries something else or to produce certain goods jointly. For their own advantage, the multinational corporations will have to sort out conflicts among themselves. This will enable them to share technology, to capitalize each other, and to otherwise collaborate. In today's global interdependence, competition no longer pays off, though for the moment multinational corporations still have not found all the necessary ways to replace it, just as nations still limit collaboration largely to regional alliances. The fact is that large national and multinational corporations have always found ways, despite laws against restraint of trade and despite the mystique of free-market competition, to work together to their mutual advantage within a given industry.

So long as the governments of other countries like Germany and Japan continue to work closely with their industries, American business will cry for similar subsidies and protection, but this mercantile capitalism of these other nations represents an earlier stage of free enterprise that will have to yield to the realities of global economics, which demand nationalistic concessions and eventually a coordinated world market. As perhaps the most committed practitioner of a free-market economy, the United States is being hardest hit at a time when it neither belongs to an economic bloc (though it has formed a weak one with Canada and Mexico) nor protects and subsidizes its own industries to the extent competing nations do.

Without war, all nations will have to negotiate the economic inequities among them, and this will result in a globally planned economy. War may remain fashionable for a while to express ethnic and religious differences, but warring over markets seems finished, for the fundamental reason that wars no longer pay off for a national economy (perhaps because they are fought less today with people than with high-tech equipment, which is far more expensive).

In other words, by the time we will have further ruined public education to remedy our current problems of competing with mercantile capitalism, these problems will have been absorbed into a different constellation of international relations. To base school reform on the old nationalistic economic competition would lock education into a past that is dying for good reasons. Indeed, the dominance of economics and nationalism has always been self-defeating and the curse of schooling.

Right now, moreover, the United States is caught in the grip of a virtual hysteria about losing its integrity and identity. While some factions cry that foreigners are buying up American companies and real estate, others, as in California and Florida, lobby for laws to declare English the official language, and still others propose restricting immigration or requiring the teaching of "our" heritage and "cultural literacy." We see all over the world the same frantic scrambling to reassert cultural identities following the breakup of empires, at the same time that the globalization of economics increases interdependence among countries. Thus at the very moment of breaking apart into Russians, Lithuanians, Ukrainians, Armenians, Moldovans, Azerbaijanis, and so on, the former members of the old Soviet Union formed new voluntary coalitions for economic, military, and ecological advantages.

Perhaps the most significant world trend, in fact, is this double movement toward economic integration on the one hand and ethnic fragmentation on the other. Out of all this is arising a new concept of governance comprising different levels for different purposes—the smallest ethnic, the largest economic and ecological, with others in the middle that may serve other purposes. The all-purpose, self-contained national government is on the way out.

The United States has always had several levels of governance within itself but will eventually have to join some international government for those matters it cannot control alone. It is not likely to break into separate ethnic states, because ethnicity in the United States never settled out geographically into the large and distinct regional cultures that are typical of older empires, which often forced separate countries to combine. The sole exception is the Hispanic Southwest, which might conceivably try to secede, as Quebec has repeatedly threatened to do from Canada. Generally, however, the United States already consists of a multicultural federation of states tolerating differences and committed (in principle at least) to protection of minorities. It is farther along in integrating ethnic groups within itself than it is in integrating itself economically into the rest of the world.

With this new understanding of a nation as only one of many concentric social organizations, the United States should sort out afresh which functions each level of government should fulfill. Some social programs should probably be shifted from federal and even state governments to local governments, with a corresponding shift in tax revenues. Some programs, like education itself, might be sponsored in different ways at different levels of government, but not in the same ways as now. Since the Depression and World War II, the federal government has increased considerably its powers and taxes, many of which should no doubt revert to lower levels of jurisdiction, where the programs actually have to be implemented. State governments have especially expanded in education during recent decades. *All* allocations of revenues and responsibilities need to be reexamined nationally if educational reform is to succeed, because the failures of schooling and other social programs owe partly to the fact that some levels of governance do too much or too little.

It would be a terrible mistake to found a new U.S. educational initiative on old blood-and-soil preoccupations, on old

▲

notions of economic nationalism, and on old allocations of governance. Nationhood is evolving into something better, based on relegating different sorts of governance to different levels of affiliation within and beyond itself, according to where different concerns can best be handled. People today belong in fact to several supercultures and subcultures at once and to several concentric economies and ecologies. We should adapt schooling to these plural identities and place it on the side of international cooperation and planetary consciousness.

The real danger comes, in fact, not from relaxing nationalism, which has to wane and is waning as part of the evolution of human consciousness, nor from decentralizing governance, which has to happen to halt the squandering of resources, but from another quarter entirely. It is in this direction that we should be looking.

Private Sector over Public

Corporations are becoming stronger than governments and therefore beyond the control of the citizenry of any country. At the same time that the interdependence of nations compels each to yield some sovereignty to advantageous transnational coalitions, all nations are moving toward democracy, individual liberty, and free enterprise. This means that just when corporations are conglomerating into formidable multinational forces, nations are yielding up some of their powers to both supranational confederations and to the private sector. Already too strong for federal and state regulation, how will commercial corporations be controlled in the future? Government should be addressing this critical problem, not pressing schools further into the service of business, which already outmatches government and is in fact pressing government into the service of its own ends.

When Bill Clinton took office as president, everyone focused on the long-neglected problem of the national deficit, the reduction of which appeared the ultimate in problem solving, but little thought was given to how to keep from incurring such a ridiculous debt all over again in the future. Clinton rightly understood that uncontrolled medical costs constituted nearly half of the debt. Without oversimplifying an intricate situation, it's fair to say that the bulk of the rest owed to unnecessary defense spending and to the failure of savings-and-loan companies, the biggest financial scandal in history. Not only did major defense contractors cheat and defraud the government out of enormous sums, but the defense budget itself was inflated by false reports of Soviet military menace right up to the moment Gorbachev himself officially let the cat out of the bag by admitting that the Soviet Union was far too close to economic disintegration to bother with war—something that U.S. intelligence and other experts on Russia had to have known years before. The common denominator of medical, military, and savings-and-loan costs is the domination of government by commercial interests, especially corporations. The deficit grew out of hand because the private sector is out of hand.

Significantly, two of the three outrageous excesses occurred in life-preserving industries—health care and national defense—where the people and their representatives fear most to challenge the professionals or to risk cutting costs. This setup invites greed to flourish, as it did among pharmaceutical and medical hardware companies, hospitals, doctors, and insurance companies. The situation was exacerbated by President Reagan's policy of getting government off our backs, which really applied only to corporations, since they were deregulated while an unprecedented federal debt was laid on the people.

Reagan and Bush refused to corral all those medical freebooters into any sort of coordinated national health plan and removed the controls over savings-and-loan companies that had

protected the Federal Insurance Deposit Corporation from precisely the unbridled pillaging that—quite foreseeably—took
place. We are told that through poor judgment these companies
loaned to risky ventures and overinvested in real estate, construction, and agriculture, but it's strange that a usually pru-
dent industry suddenly, after deregulation, began to dispense
money so debonairly. The savings-and-loan companies knew
they would not have to make good on losses; the public would.
Consequently, many officers in these companies made loans to
friends who kicked the money back or to other companies from
which they stood to gain through ingenious paper trails. Government officials in the pockets of the lending industry shielded
these operations and stalled investigations for years, during
which time government costs to reimburse citizen depositors
soared along with the interest on that debt. Money became
short for investors, and this in turn helped bring on the recession of the early 1990s. Similar but more longstanding collusion between defense contractors and the federal government
caused overspending and undersurveillance of military
spending.

Clinton's call for patriotic sacrifice attacked the immediate
problem of debt reduction but left Americans paying more not
to get new benefits but to rid themselves of a burden they
should never have had and could just as well fall victim to
again because nothing has happened to bring commercial corporations under the control of the people. We are constantly
warned of the dangerous state of banking. In fact, other fiascos,
as in the airlines industry, continue to happen because of inadequate government regulation. Antitrust laws have become a
farce since the breakup of AT&T, which actually increased
costs for the consumers, who are now paying larger phone
bills that include subsidizing a permanent and very expensive
advertising war among AT&T, MCI, and Sprint. Mergers and

takeovers abound, restricting or eliminating competition and frequently weakening the companies themselves. In fact, laxity in this area permitted the leveraged junk-bond buyouts and other paper games of the 1980s that played a large part in creating the 1990s recession.

To point out how the incorporated dominate the unincorporated is not to take an antibusiness position but to argue for the subordination of for-profit corporations to the general welfare, that is to say, for an equitable society. Unrestrained, corporations bully consumers and workers, endanger the environment, imperil the economy, and suborn the government. Leading companies with household names in virtually every major industry—chemicals, construction, pharmaceuticals, stock brokerage, publishing, automobile manufacture, and many others—have been indicted for or convicted of criminal behavior. Economically, corporate crime poses a far more serious problem than street crime. Governments spend huge sums up front apprehending and incarcerating burglars and robbers, but the hidden costs to the public of corporate crime and immorality permeate the whole economy so insidiously that we can only guess at them from the few examples that make the news. Organized crime syndicates have so deeply infiltrated the corporate world in order to launder and invest money that distinguishing legitimate from illegitimate business becomes increasingly difficult. Like any economic system, capitalism can work only if its participants are moral.

The decline of American sales and productivity, typified by the much bemoaned loss of auto markets to foreign competitors, need not have happened had U.S. corporate life taken a moral attitude and a long-range, holistic view. Both of these are attributes of spirituality, and this case in point may serve to demonstrate its practicality.

U.S. manufacturers lost both domestic and foreign sales by

one and the same immoral, shortsighted policy. They had all
the advantages after World War II of being part of the only
nation not just still standing but enjoying a fully mobilized
industrial capacity. Looking for new consumers after most
American families already had a car or two, Detroit decided
to simply resell to that same market by making shoddy products that had to be replaced far sooner than necessary. That
was the immoral part. The shortsighted part was that the auto
companies could have gone abroad instead and developed foreign markets. That would have required long-term vision and
investments. Rather than take advantage of their favored situation, they took advantage of the American consumers—who
have yet to forgive them. Foreign manufacturers did not make
products designed to obsolesce, and they did go abroad—to
America. The U.S. auto industry has whined ever since that
American consumers will not buy from them even though it
has started to make products to last.

Short-term thinking characterizes this managerial syndrome,
because it works in favor of the individual executive trying to
look good right away, whereas long-term thinking works in
favor of the enterprise, which needs a bigger view, as Japanese
companies know so well. American managers stint on research
and development because it may not pay off in time for them
to look good for their next big career move but may, instead,
reduce profits during their watch and thus make them look
ineffectual. More than any other single factor, this self-serving,
short-term style of American executives may account for the
decline of U.S. industry, which forsook real productivity during
the 1980s for paper deals like junk-bond buyouts that artifi-
cially and temporarily drove up market values or other credits.
School superintendents also opt for projects that pay off soon,
because they shift jobs a lot in order to keep moving into positions in larger districts, their only way of getting promoted.

Spiritual Thinking

Spirituality pays. So educate for it. No society can survive if it does not function holistically. No element of it can thrive at the expense of other elements. If the first law of parasitism is "Don't kill the host!" surely a people committed to equality and reciprocity cannot *afford* selfishness. When corporate business kills the goose that lays the golden egg, it commits suicide. The exploitative mind thinks that by walking over others, you can get to the top—but without the others, there may be nothing left at the top when you get there. Just as impoverished workers make poor consumers, a wasted landscape provides no resources, and beyond a certain stage of degeneration in society and nature, all the money and power in the world will not procure for you a safe home and pure food, air, and water. The sacred framework of Native Americans not only respected other forms of life as part of Spirit but included the wisdom of protecting even what you prey upon.

One reason that the unspiritual framework turns out to be impractical is that it impairs intellect and judgment. To assume that my destiny is distinct from those around me, that I and my lineage can long thrive despite the destitution of others, or by means of the destitution of others, is sloppy thinking, especially today. Before the equalizing effect of the two world wars, some families, it is true, lived well without having to work for a living, on the backs of the poor. Now that a sexually transmitted disease from Africa can in a few years untenant the mansions of Beverly Hills, it is time to think again.

Thought that is not spiritual is intellectually inferior because it is too partial. What connects the amoral attitude of the corporate world to short-term thinking is the lack of a holistic perspective. Both managers of corporations and elected government officials work within short time frames, the one imposed by quarterly and annual financial reports and the other by terms of office. Like school superintendents, they have to show a quick payoff in time to be reappointed or offered a bigger job somewhere else. This puts blinders on those people wielding the most power in the society. The dangerous limitations of this mentality have not been acknowledged nearly enough. Lawyers also contribute to the short-range, small-compass thinking that determines policy. Indispensable to business and government, they are trained and paid to divorce their arguments and counsel from any considerations larger than the aims of their clients. Based on such exclusion, amorality cripples thinking, which is richer and deeper the more it includes. The most brilliant logic and strategy suffer the limits of the cause they serve.

Evolution is pushing individuals at once to think more for themselves and more on behalf of others. Not long ago, morality was not left to personal discretion as it is today except when one breaks the law. Morality was codified and enforced by the group through religion and public disapproval. Navajos are split today between an old ethos requiring everyone to share goods and the European ethic of acquiring personal property. The acute question of today's individual freedom concerns how people can behave morally toward each other when neither social sanctions nor governmental authority force them to. After all, most of the behavior that holds society together goes far beyond criminal and civil law.

Furthermore, when criminal behavior itself becomes epidemic, as now, what avails the law? Police cannot arrest enough, courts convict enough, nor prisons hold enough to enforce compliance. At the rate crime is increasing, some futurists say, one out of every five to ten people will have to work for law enforcement to contain the problem. We think of a police state as instituted by a tyrannical government depriving citizens of freedom, but it could come about from a democratic government granting citizens a freedom to which they are not inwardly equal. At this stage of evolution, group authority will not make people moral, whether implemented through church, state, or public opinion. Only personal development will do this.

We can see the need for this sort of self-sufficiency even in the practical facts of the American workplace, which is changing from an authoritarian factory or office run hierarchically like an army, each worker doing one task for years on end, to a shifting complex of activities requiring flexible, self-directing workers commanding more mental than physical skills and capable of collaborating in teams. Employers say they want people who can rotate jobs, acquire new skills, take responsibility for themselves, and see how their work fits into the whole operation. These traits especially fit small businesses, which are creating most new jobs today and which can respond more rapidly to changes in technology, markets, and the many other fluctuating factors of business and the global economy. Finally, self-employment is increasing rapidly, and the home has become a significant workplace. Individuals have the fastest response time of all in adapting to changing economic conditions, and computer technology facilitates cottage industry, communication replacing transportation. Working on your own requires the utmost in self-reliance, self-responsibility, and self-teaching. All kinds of employment, then, are evolving toward more fully developed individuals. A state-set, state-assessed curriculum cannot prepare as well for this as a self-programmed, self-assessed education.

To focus for a moment on another great concern of industry, America must indeed drastically overhaul its math and science education. But one does not have to look to business or patriotism for compelling reasons. All people, no matter what job they aim for, should be fluent in math and science—for any number of important reasons ranging from utilitarian to political to philosophical. Democracy will not work if the lay electorate remains as ignorant of technology as it is today. Math and science must no longer seem preserves for students with special penchants. Everybody needs to incorporate them into their lives as part of normal human functioning. Math and science, after all, are only formalizations of logic and inquiry respectively and therefore of everyone's capacity to make sense of the world. Educators in math and science already look upon their subjects in just this way and are striving to realize this view in practice, which would greatly further personal development.

Emphasize math and science indeed, but don't just beef up the couple of high school courses that most students might ever take. Math and science should be subjects for everyone all the time, learned and used from all angles, not a miserly self-contained course in biology or algebra taken once, mostly forgotten, and rarely applied. Let's integrate math and science into all the other sorts of learning so that they are constantly used, reviewed, and related to other things. If the total curriculum and the very process of education are not renovated along with the teaching of math and science, a new emphasis on them will do no good but will instead continue to edge out the arts and humanities, which are vital not only to personal development but to the learning of math and science, best learned themselves as arts and humanities.

As for improving students' abilities to analyze, communicate, collaborate, and creatively solve problems, these are old goals that serve business no more than they do other human endeavors. The fact that schools have not fulfilled such fundamental goals owes principally to the subordination of personal development to nationalism and economics. The failure of students to acquire the abilities that business leaders and policy makers want costs us all socially and personally as well as economically and is precisely part of what we have to examine in this book—but in a much larger perspective than that of the governmental-industrial complex, which in insisting on state-set education defeats both its particular aims and general human growth.

3

▲

Education to Transform Culture

If nationalism and economics should no longer constitute the framework of public education, what should supplant them? Holistic thinking best accommodates all learning goals and best facilitates efficient problem solving. But we all live within any number of "wholes" ranging from a nuclear family and concentric social families of varying compasses on to all of nature. Each whole serves as context for the next smaller. The best framework for education is the most inclusive whole or context, because it illuminates the most and spiritualizes the most.

Imagine a set of nested contexts centered on the individual's personal consciousness and expanding outward through social contexts, nature, and our universe to the cosmos. As the concept of collective consciousness suggests, before individualism was born, consciousness and culture were essentially one. As the concept of cosmic consciousness suggests, consciousness and cosmos may become one. So through shifts in consciousness the individual, the society, and the universe interplay so as to dissolve their boundaries. Since it is within familiar human realms that we have to transform education, however, let's designate consciousness and culture as the new framework replacing nationalism and economics but understand that the transformation itself aims to make consciousness and culture cosmic.

Sociality for Individualization

Public education will have to do what the culture has so far failed to do—develop the individual's inner resources to match the freedom we have been granted. Freedom is not enough; one has to learn how to use it. This means *practicing* it all while growing up by making decisions about how to spend one's time. It will be said that many young people don't know what they want and don't know how to make decisions, that they really want elders to tell them what to do. This is far truer than it should be, because we infantalize children. But developing good judgment and learning how to make decisions is precisely what a good education ought to feature for the sake of both self-fulfillment and effective employment. Public education needs to be more personal in order to connect with individual will and intelligence. Exercise of will and mind go together. The school system cannot reserve will to itself and leave mind to the learner. When students become empowered to make choices, they take charge of their own education, and the main problem of schooling—alienation—rapidly diminishes.

But people have to be allowed to take charge of their own education in a situation affording maximum support. While granting liberty, a public education system must at the same time supply the individual with generous human resources—other people of all ages and abilities, from peers to seniors, in a variety of relationships, from partnering to apprenticing. Students will belong in effect to a number of families of various sizes, within which people of mixed ages work together.

School will not be a plant and site but a rich human and material network extending throughout the community and open to everybody all the time. It will comprise all public facilities such as libraries and museums, nurseries and senior centers, and it will arrange traffic between them and private facilities such as offices and factories, laboratories and farms. Crisscrossing and collaborating in this network, individuals make personal choices while influencing each other. This interaction grounds individualization in a social field and helps personal development become spiritual, because at the same time that self-direction is inducing self-knowledge, reciprocity is generating empathy.

Sociality is probably the best learning device of all time—and the one least used in public schools. A single authoritarian adult per isolated classroom gives it little chance to work. Commercial materials have been substitutes for human relations. Twenty to forty people is a lot in one room, but in the interest of control and standardization this tremendous human resource is wasted. Students have been forbidden to interact, and the teacher's role has been mostly limited to giving directions and monologuing or at best questioning and prompting a group according to a lesson plan. Outside of school, people are learning enormous amounts, both good and bad, from social experience, whether they're trying to learn or not. Interaction is the key, and here it is difficult to separate social experience from interaction with the material world in general, most of nature being socially mediated to us through an artifactual environment.

Culture is the big teacher, because it's the medium we live in. Schools segregate age groups off alone with a single adult committed to a preordained paper curriculum. This is hopelessly unrealistic. Were children simply turned loose for the twelve years of schooling they could learn a huge amount more. But this isn't necessary and would leave them at the mercy of

▲

neighborhoods or other local cultures, which are often cruel and restricted. People can capitalize on their great need for social relating to learn things not current in the local culture. Not only may students interact in activities composed of mixed ages and backgrounds but they may range afield to learn from others at work and interact with the broader environment. The point is not merely for them to learn to get along or get around but to learn about many subjects, including so-called academic ones, *by means of* getting along and getting around. Most skills and knowledge that really take and count are learned in the long run through other people, few of whom are professional teachers.

Learning is joining a certain culture. In learning to talk we join the human race. In learning to read and write we join the community of literate people and the time-space-spanning world of texts. Social groups are knowledge groups, whose members know certain things by virtue of belonging to and participating in that group. As we identify, so we know. Most learning is by acculturation, whether the group is a family, a neighborhood gang, an ethnic or religious body, a nation, an international youth culture, or a whole civilization. Through this sort of saturation learning, the new educational culture will pass down both higher mathematics and higher consciousness.

If a culture is a knowledge system that both imparts and limits knowledge within its membership, then a learning culture should constitute the richest possible knowledge pool and arrange total access among all its members. Instead of trying to teach everybody the same things, it is far more sensible to encourage individuals to learn different things. Then they can cross-fertilize each other, and all learn more, including many of the same things. Rippling across a whole community ensures, in fact, the maximum sharing of knowledge. In other words, we should create a learning culture so diversified by individualization that people immersed in it absorb far more than when curriculum aims at a common body of knowledge. We want to get the best of both the personal and social worlds.

Furthermore, if a certain body of knowledge were required for all, how would it be determined? Such decisions amount to mind control, because they can't avoid being partisan, nor can they avoid being exasperatingly arbitrary to students, who can see for themselves that schools sample in very biased fashion all that there is to know. Young people will have to know much more than formerly, but no one can predict exactly what they will need to know. Knowledge is proliferating and obsolescing so rapidly that schools haven't a prayer of covering it all or keeping up to date. Students have to learn how to survey, sift, and select knowledge. More, they also have to learn the very nature of knowledge—how it is made and used and what the various forms of it may be worth. They need to learn how to learn, how to investigate independently, how to truly think for themselves.

Letting different students do different things at the same time will entail radically restructuring the procedures of education. It means, for example, mixing ages, learning modalities, and subjects—in other words, abandoning standardization of both the subject matter and the learners. It is the *ensemble* of such changes we should consider and how they interact to make each other more feasible. Making education more personal, for example, actually becomes easier to do if it is made more social at the same time, for both will make learning more *relational*.

The strategy is to individualize and pluralize at the same time, that is, coach personal decision making but orchestrate the plurality of personal choices so that everybody is teaching everybody else and all learn enormously more than they would if herded through a common course set at a common denominator. We would then trade the pseudo-order of "scope-and-sequence" for the reality of how people actually learn, which is from inner agendas acted on through communal means.

Politically, the community-as-school aims to distribute power around the community so that no single faction or structure controls it. Decentralization should not mean merely handing over education to a staff at one plant site or merely letting parents choose a school. So obvious an obstacle to reform is bureaucracy that some communities have reassigned control of funds and hiring from the board or district level to the individual school or to a parent-teacher governing board of a school. This can change a school or make it more efficient, but it can also subject children to the sometimes severe limitations of a local culture, which may be racist or ignorant and narrow in other ways. Much more has to occur than merely handing down control from the top of the hierarchy to the bottom.

The whole purpose of public education is to introduce children to a broader world than the home alone can offer. A neighborhood needs outsiders, and a school needs a learning network in which to participate. The history of "common schools" in America, like the history of institutional learning anywhere, shows how some religious, ideological, ethnic, nationalistic, and socioeconomic groups use schools to control other groups. No effort to establish a single curriculum for all or a single set of standards for all can avoid subjecting some people to the will of others. Up to now American schools have been "common" only in the sense of being open to everyone and paid for by everyone, both attendance and taxation being legally enforced, but they have not been "common" in the sense of accommodating what everyone needs and wants. Democracy and freedom will never be realized until individuals take control of education not only away from governments but from local citizen groups as well.

It's frequently asked what a "liberal" approach like that of a free-choice system has to offer people "at-risk," as if self-determination and self-realization are luxuries only for the well-off. Inhabitants of a culture of poverty and crime need individualized learning even more than those whose favored environment naturally offers them more choice. Brutalized people need a personalized education most of all. Instead, we often hear that children of poverty need more "structure" and "authority" than others, on grounds that their lives have lacked order and they can respond only to force. The whole point of customizing learning is to do justice to *all* needs and backgrounds, not just by giving choices but by arraying everything there is to choose from, to ensure that old limits are offset. This personal attention does more for "at-risk" youth than anything else, because such people may have low self-esteem, negative identifications, and little sense of personal power, especially the power to make decisions and to realize intentions. Always they have to adjust to the environment—at home, in the streets, in school—and can assert themselves only by crime and other rebellion, by taunting the law and making their own rules in gangs. Many good inner-city projects like big-brother pairings, sports teams, choirs and orchestras, neighborhood improvement campaigns, and other organized activities for youth have shown how responsive young people are to caring adult sponsorship. But such projects are piecemeal, temporary, and specialized; they help a lucky few who happen to live in the right place at the right time or are ready for a certain activity. A community learning system *builds in* a plurality of venues, activities, partners, and mentors for just such purposes, so that no at-risk boys or girls fail to find plentiful alternatives to destitution and despair. Getting what you need through a customized curriculum serves most those who have least.

Likewise, it is unnecessary to muster special efforts to ensure equality of educational opportunity when at the outset every learner is given unlimited access to all resources and personal control over how to utilize them. Because of the inequities inherent in schools as educational units, in testing and tracking, classes and courses, grades and certification, school reform has understandably featured minority rights, social justice, and enforcement of democracy. But no faction should have to expend itself in lobbying for its rights. Build equality, justice, and democracy so firmly into the community learning network that no one can jeopardize these for anyone else. The "critical pedagogy" that Paolo Freire and others have urged, to make students aware of societal biases and injustices, need no longer occur as special guerrilla teaching but will shift into learner-initiated community projects, which will naturally derive from or raise these issues. None of this is possible so long as a government of whatever level sets learning aims and means, for then factions fight over control of the institution, and some dominate. The problem ends only when the power of choice is decentralized right down to the individual.

In a democracy, one may retort, governments and locally chosen groups represent the people, who after all must trust their representatives. But even representative democracy should not legislate the content and means of education, because group decision making at whatever level cannot do justice to the pluralism of individual learning aims and needs. In a matter so personal as learning, which takes place always within individuals, the principle of majority rule does not obtain. Parental disputes over what is read in schools raise this issue at the family level. Either to force or to withhold a certain kind of learning violates American traditions and ideals of personal liberty. Any predetermined program is bound to subvert the Constitutional guarantees of freedom of thought. So decentralization has to bypass groups of any sort and refine down to individuals, so that many parties are making decisions affecting themselves without interfering with other parties doing the same. How to set up such a mix-and-match learning network constitutes the central practical problem of educational reform.

In the new educational culture individuals will have every opportunity to find out what they can do and want to do, what they do and do not know. The community learning network will help people find themselves as early as possible, to play so fully as children as to prepare for their own particular adulthood. Traditional school has been so concerned to give students a general education, almost entirely bookish, that it has prevented them from developing talents. This is why so many gifted people have dropped out or put in only a token attendance at school. Magnet schools have revealed that many youngsters, even from very deprived environments, develop substantial talents if allowed to specialize somewhat in an activity or area they are drawn to.

A person with a musical or a graphic or a scientific bent should not have to drop out of school to find time to practice or tinker. Nor should he or she have to go to a specialized school, magnet or other. The new educational culture will be so committed to individual development and maximum accessibility to resources that everybody can be placed in relationships and circumstances where penchants can disclose themselves and develop. Specialization risks one-sidedness, it is true, but nothing safeguards against this better than the diverse social learning network within which individuals will be finding themselves. The secret is the multiple influences of this human web, which not only awaken one's particular propensities but show how these connect with others' specialties. In other words, the question is not just "What can I do in this world?" but "How does what I can do take part in the rest of the world?"

In a web everything connects with everything else. Learners who work for twelve years or so in this web can hardly avoid moving around over a considerable part of it. In particular, however, teacher-counselors will focus on how individuals may pursue an interest across these many connections—keep a direction but also keep moving. If one tracks an interest far enough, it comes out other places. Music, for example, often results in one-sidedness because of the practice time required to get good at playing an instrument, but music reaches out into many realms, any one of which might not only tie in with an individual's original motive but more fully realize it. As acoustics, music is scientific. As measure, it is mathematical. As an evolving art or rite, it is historical. As an influence on people, it is psychological. Music is structural, emotional, political, and so on. Teacher-counselors or others in the network, often by example, help the individual see and pursue these connections. Often music can be practiced in groups like bands or choirs that show the individual further possibilities.

Individuals contribute best when helped to discover what there is to do and what they in particular can do. The educational culture has to enable and empower people to do real things, now, that may lead to other real things later. Institutions exist for individuals, not the other way around. Youngsters have to feel positive about themselves and about finding a good place in the world. Even if their self-esteem has suffered in a negative environment, school can turn this around for them by giving them the gift of themselves. This is a gift they will return to the society.

Curative Education

Making the culture of education both far more personal and more social will at once improve academic learning and foster a spiritual and emotional life eventually capable of healing both individual and societal ills. This curative culture will be warm and personal and allow the individual a lot of choice and control over his or her own learning, confident that its powerful emphasis on human relating will balance the emphasis on personal development. To cure the parent culture, education will have to spiritualize it.

Future education should not merely mirror the society but should fashion selectively a special culture that will correct and complement the society. Now, however, schools contract all the diseases of the larger world. The more learning merely reflects the society, the less it can help improve it. This critical need for public education to have some independence from the body it serves has not been recognized in all the emphasis on transmitting the culture and on fitting students into the world as their elders know it. This approach has prolonged the selfish materialism, the herd mind, and the adult immaturity that characterize our society's ills, which schools have worsened by preparing youngsters for all too well.

Years of not being allowed to relate humanly in class have taught apathy and alienation. Years of being herded, prodded, goaded, ordered, and otherwise manipulated have taught passivity and fatalism. This makes for a zombie on the outside and a terrorist inside. Whenever I tell teachers, "This is not education, this is child molestation," they are not offended; they know what I mean. And when I joke, "If we did with their bodies what we do with their minds, we'd all be in jail," they laugh ruefully in recognition of a truth that we both understand goes with a world we never made but are now guilty accomplices to.

It is commonplace to remark today that American children constitute the new victim class of the poor and disadvantaged. It's also commonplace for Americans to chastize other countries for their poor civil rights records. The truth is, our school system violates children's civil rights so seriously that it plays a major role in their negative plight. No government or public institution has the right to compel its citizens—children or adults—to spend most of their waking life for years on end in conditions over which they have very little control and where their behavior is programmed by bureaucratic forces for reasons of state. The fact that we take for granted this appalling subjection of individuals to institutions shows how little our understanding matches our declarations of freedom and democracy. Human beings are not here to be molded by the state. Schooling as we know it breeds rigidity and neurosis in the lucky and despair and fury in the unlucky. This is not how a democratic state keeps hale and whole.

Years of forced competition for scores and grades have taught students that you set yourself up by putting others down, that selfishness and secrecy hold the key to success. Conflict and war will seem natural. Years of arbitrary programming and fragmented lessons have taught that life is essentially a meaningless thing that is done to you. Years of being treated as an object of testing, of being measured and monitored by external standards, of having one's worth constantly questioned have taught low self-esteem and anxiety. Most of the adult populace retains this feeling of being perpetually on probation.

School, moreover, is so stupefying and ungratifying that it sets up addiction to drugs and television, so dehumanizing and infuriating that it helps engender crime and violence. The natural reaction to all this is enormous resentment, which individuals act out toward each other and the society. The dysfunctional family can generate more resentment and usually does far more damage to children than school does, because its closer relationships intensify feeling, but wouldn't it be good if public education could, instead of reinforcing other traumas, offset them?

Schools, we hear, can't be expected to solve all the ills of the society. That's certainly true as schools are now conceived and constituted. Still, how else but by education are we to head off or offset our now uncontrollable problems? Where else foster the states of mind and feeling that redirecting the world will require? *Some* element of the society must create the setting for fundamental improvement. Public education may seem an unlikely candidate to do the job, but what other institution has even a prayer of getting to the roots of problems?

Some activist churches work courageously for needed change, but most remain too conventional and parochial to help much. Many single parents are trying to raise children alone. But even when not separated, most parents are too distraught by their own problems to give much to their children's upbringing. Often they both work because salaries are so low that two are required to support a family or because their status-seeking consumption of goods has blinded them to their children's welfare. For a while the New Age movement toward self-realization held out some hope of transforming consciousness, but it has been so assimilated into the corporate and commercial world that it is hard to trust and in any case is available only out of school and mostly just to affluent people with some leisure.

If I come back to public education, it's not—God knows—because I idealize schools. Not certainly after spending a discouraging twenty-five years trying to reform just their teaching of literacy and language. Not certainly that schools haven't fallen victim to every ill afflicting the society that spawns them, from a vast educational-industrial complex to drug peddlers dealing in the halls. Not certainly that schools are anywhere near teaching what is needed for even physical survival, much less psychological or spiritual. I come back to them for one reason. That's where the children are—by legal compulsion.

Virtually the whole populace grows up in school and grows into what it is to become while there. Public education reaches everybody and for a long time during the later formative years. Whatever it does or does not do is extremely important. Its influence is second only to that of the home, and in the most important cases—where home hardly exists—some schools already provide a safer, warmer, and more stable environment, the prerequisite for learning. These havens point the way to broader curative education. But the very fact that schools are necessarily part of the problem, by virtue of reflecting the society so faithfully, despite some valiant efforts by school personnel, is another reason to try for change there first. Then as young people go into society they can change it in turn. Let's take advantage of the fact that public education is built into our life, for better or for worse. That's where huge public resources are already committed, and that's where a citizenry can best exert its will to make profound societal change.

Going by the past, it might seem reasonable to say that school is neither church nor home and shouldn't try to usurp their functions by undertaking spiritual, moral, and therapeutic education. But schools can do whatever a society thinks it best for them to do. During the years of heavy immigration, just before and after the turn of the century, schools focused on teaching English as a second language and hence emphasized formal grammar, rightly or wrongly. Textbooks were very moralistic. The popular *McGuffey Readers* are said to be what really won the West because of their ambitious get-ahead ethic. And in the first years of American public schooling, religion itself was taught—Christianity only, of course—without anyone worrying, unfortunately, about the separation of church and state. Throughout history, societies have employed schooling for the whole gamut of purposes, from religious and intellectual to institutional and industrial, from patriotic to personal, from brainwashing to mind-expanding. When survival is at stake, it makes no sense to quibble over which part of the society should be doing this and which that.

The new educational culture will not so much supplant the home as strengthen it. Parents are former students, after all, and some become parents while in school, before they mean to, for lack of such a curative environment. Where do people learn to become good parents? From their own parents if they are lucky, but the more broken and invaded the home, the more a negative cycle perpetuates itself. Battered children batter their children. Many middle-class mothers and fathers today apparently don't feel they learned well in the home, because books, tapes, and seminars on parenting are all the rage. Most parents today focus so exclusively on just managing their lives that they cannot afford to think about schools. They give little attention to their children, who turn toward alienation and suicide if they're middle class and toward gangs and homicide if they're poor. Their consciousness is being determined not by warm human interaction but by video monitors and depersonalized street scenarios.

I hear a final objection: "This spiritual and psychological stuff is all well and good for social engineering, but what about the things schools are really supposed to be teaching—literacy, math and science, history, foreign languages, and practical things like nursing and economics?" Well, we try now to teach all these things insulated from street realities and the emotional life. What results is a dark comedy. As any veteran teacher can testify from unforgettable experience, youngsters learn subjects like that only in the measure that they can master negative feeling and feel good about themselves and the world. Creating a curative educational culture is in fact the only way they will ever learn the academic subjects.

Indeed, so ineffectual has it been to serve these subjects under glass amid the incoherence of students' lives that we have settled for a shockingly low expectancy in academic achievement. Doing things the wrong way gives a wrong idea of what can be done. A person who has spent twelve to sixteen years as a full-time student should know enormously more than we hope now even from our most successful students. Indeed, academic learning presupposes *more* emotional contentment and general serenity than other learning, because it is not as immediately gratifying.

I taught ten years at one of the nation's top prep schools,

▲

and even there you could easily see how most students were seriously underlearning because the highly competitive, single-sex, boarding-school culture focused much more on academic achievement than on the personal state of the learner. If a place as enlightened and humane as that, peopled by the most promising scholars, far removed at that time from drugs and other serious social problems, could not prevent such an imbalance from undercutting its goal, how much less likely is public education to succeed today in teaching the traditional subjects without generating a curative culture of its own?

Healing and Growth

It is impossible to distinguish healing from growth, "learning disabilities" from the various constraints of anyone's particular conditioning that may hinder growth. Much, most, perhaps all learning is unlearning things that are not so or not complete. What understanding is ever complete—the truth and the whole truth? Our knowledge is always partial (not impartial) because it is made conditional by our own conditioning, which is egocentric, sexcentric, ethnocentric, geocentric. Nowhere is this more evident than in trying to heal the human organism. To cure is to neutralize some conditions of the mind-body system that are giving rise to the symptoms. It may be helpful to regard this deconditioning as unlearning, wherever it occurs in this system.

This deconditioning amounts to reconditioning or relearning, because to cure is to *restore* health. Let's say that the pure, unconditioned life force is health supreme and that any impairment of it owes to some cramping or crooking that occurs when it is embodied in a particular organism *partial* to certain conditions of birth and growth. To be hale is to be whole, all glands, organs, and systems fully functioning and in balance among themselves. To be whole is not just to be all there but to be integrated, so that nothing is hyper or hypo. Healing is setting something right that has got out of kilter or balance, whether it's a bone or an endocrine ratio that is reset. Thus in healing as in other learning, we are reconditioning our organism in the direction of some original integrity. Holistic medicine and holistic education are both on the right track.

School reform can benefit enormously from our understanding of what getting well entails, because healing focuses directly, like growth, on changing ourselves for the better. Each individual literally embodies the life force in some unique combination of inheritance, environment, and personal spirit that must be taken into account in healing. Bodies of the same age and sex vary infinitely in their structural proportions, chemistry, and the strengths and weaknesses of their systems and organs. Minds and psyches vary correspondingly. Therapy serves as one good learning model because it tailors treatment completely to the particular conditions of the individual, who has the biggest stake in success and who can best assess results.

So-called physical therapy illustrates well the reconditioning and the integration common to both healing and growth. To recover from a stroke or an accident, patients often have to practice arduously some action like walking or talking until they either reestablish old neural connections or, in the case of brain damage, establish new ones. A coach is important to direct, inform, encourage, and sometimes assist the patient. Though called "physical," what impresses you about this therapy is the tremendous mental and emotional effort and the sheer will that the patient has to exert to succeed. Because the learning is indispensable to the patient's life, the whole organism mobilizes itself to accomplish seemingly impossible feats. Sometimes results go well beyond recovery; the cripple becomes a champion runner. In relearning how to walk or talk, patients discover their potential for learning to do far more of anything than they originally thought.

Public education should give youngsters the same proof of power that physical healing does. But how does one muster the equivalent motivation? You don't have to have had a stroke or an accident to need healing. Everybody is wounded. By the time most children arrive in school, they need physical or mental therapy, usually both, since trauma in one part of the organism affects all the rest. Conditions in today's world are extremely hard on the young. If the mother's body has not been an unhealthy environment, the ecosystem they are born into probably will be. Most parents themselves grew up abused, abandoned by one or both parents, neglected, or slighted and so perpetuate their own plight. Outside the home lies a soulless society that will wound them further. Without expecting ordinary teachers to take on healing roles appropriate only for specialists, it seems essential to include healing as a part of the total education being proposed here. Some ways to work medical expertise into the community learning network are suggested by certain of the observations and proposals elsewhere in this book. For now, the point is to include both the aims and the methods of therapy inasmuch as, like employment, healing is a lifelong and universal need. It is a prerequisite for, if not a concomitant of, other forms of growth and learning.

A common concept can bring healing and growth together with academic and practical learning. It can be stated as a basic goal of *getting better*, a handy term because it has three meanings. To get better may mean to *get better at doing something*, to acquire competence. It may mean to *get well*, to heal, perhaps simply to improve one's health. It may mean *become a better person*. In keeping with a holistic approach, let's say that this triple ambiguity signifies a basic unity among worldly competence, healing, and moral and spiritual development. Why not, since each furthers the other two? Besides raising food, gardening may heal or become a form of entranced contemplation, as fly-fishing served for the sons in "A River Runs Through It" (taught by their minister father).[1] When I taught yoga, I observed that people took classes to get better in all senses—to heal from an auto accident or a divorce, to get fit and look trim, to deal with stress, to relate to others better, or to deepen spiritual experience.

Schools have focused a lot on certain ills that seem to thwart academic teaching, like dyslexia, or that disrupt routines, like hyperkinetic behavior, but schools themselves seem implicated in these somewhat suspect categories of pathology, because their own institutional conditions generate or exacerbate problems. On the other hand, students suffer from a far greater range of physical and mental ills than educators have been able to detect or deal with in public education as we know it. At the very least, this makes for gross inefficiency, because people ailing in body or mind cannot simply skip over these priority needs to learn something having nothing to do with remedying them. Public education must first make sure it is not causing such ills and then arrange to take a curing role in ills students truly bring with them. This will not only increase learning efficiency manyfold but will help individuals mature enough to rehabilitate in turn the culture.

4

▲

Education to
Transform
Consciousness

Now let's add to culture the other half of the new framework
for education—consciousness. The special new educational
culture will need to generate the higher consciousness that can
regenerate the culture. The evolution of consciousness from a
kind of group mind to independent perception and judgment
puts tremendous stress on the individual, who is increasingly
less guided today by built-in cultural imperatives than by personal decision making. Our free society multiplies choices,
crudely epitomized by all the alternative brands in a supermar-
ket. Today's middle-class people have far more choice about
where to live, what occupation to enter, who to mate with,
what to buy, how to spend leisure time, and what to think
than any people in history. Choice both creates anxiety and
develops higher consciousness.

This critical effect of political freedom and technological liberation receives no attention in official discussions of social
problems and education because policy makers feel obliged
to avoid "philosophical" frameworks in favor of "practical"
matters like employment or abortion that are familiar voting
issues. But in the end even the most nitty-gritty problems—pov-

erty, divorce, pollution, addiction, poor health, crime, international conflict—are solved by higher consciousness, because solutions for them all depend on people developing more inner strength and relating to each other more maturely. Perceiving personal growth and interpersonal relating as the common denominator of problem solving is itself an advance in consciousness.

Overpopulation, for example, may well constitute the world's biggest single practical problem, from which many others emanate. Some parents have numerous children to increase income, to achieve status, or to comply with a religious commandment, regardless of consequences for the children or the society. People of more individualized consciousness tend less to exploit their children, use them to boost ego, or have them to obey some cultural imperative. Socioeconomic status interplays closely with development of consciousness.

In America, overpopulation mostly comes down to sexual relating, like the problems of divorce and broken families. Why is overpopulation a lower-class problem while divorce is a middle-class problem? Both concern the integrating of sex into the rest of one's life. In poverties of culture, channeling sexuality becomes a problem of the moment, of an impetuosity that overrides knowledge or the will of the partner. Sexual gratification may also take on for the destitute the desperation of those who have few other means of pleasure or expression. In dire poverty, divorce may be less an issue because marriage is less an issue—less practiced or less meaningful.

Parents in the middle class, on the other hand, are not having enough children even to replace themselves, but nearly half of their marriages end in divorce. The single-parent family is becoming as common in the middle class as among the poor. Middle-class people can control sexuality in the moment but not over a longer time. In other words, they can route impulses through the mind well enough to connect them to memory and reflection and can thus put sexuality on a longer-range basis. This sort of delaying or tempering of instinct may in fact define the middle class and account for its being materially better off in the first place.

At any rate, for better or worse, the middle-class mentality represents a certain stage of consciousness that generally spares people unwanted pregnancy but not the degeneration of the male-female relationship. Middle-class Americans rebel against their own self-control and change mates. They have a freedom to do this unparalleled in the culture before. But like other exercises of freedom, the culture has bestowed this one without guidance in how to use it, because that's now a matter of individual responsibility. A higher stage of consciousness would include inner resources commensurate with this freedom and would therefore integrate sexuality into one's total being. Such problems as unwanted pregnancy and broken homes could decline sharply in a society whose public education created a culture where good human relating was itself the main teaching method and where practical problems were part of the stuff of the curriculum.

Like the culture they imitate, schools make people feel alone and afraid, powerless to get what they need, desperate to feel good about themselves and just to feel good at all. Physical gratification then becomes terribly important, because whatever else one lacks, one still has a body that can feel, though it may take more and more stimulation to sustain sensation. People who feel ungratified gravitate toward drugs much more than people who get satisfaction from their work, their relationships, and their surroundings. Today, even many people in the middle class find their jobs a source of anxiety rather than pleasure, their relationships frustrating because everyone is too self-centered, and their favored environment encroached upon increasingly by forces like crime and pollution from which no amount of wealth can long buy escape. The new educational culture will have to take stock of such features of the parent culture and deal with their effects.

The biggest features of American culture are personal freedom and individual expression. These are good and right, but Americans have not yet understood all the unforeseen consequences that attend the liberation of the individual. When sharing and sacrifice are no longer enforced, as in authoritarian cultures, selfishness may result at first. The more society leaves the individual alone, moreover, the more isolation becomes a problem. Not told what to think, surrounded by a smorgasbord of ideas, what indeed is one to think? Not directed to behave thus and so, how does one behave? In the end one has to fall back upon personal understanding and judgment. The catch is that the culture has been too busy liberating its members from social and material restraints to show them how to develop such inner resources. In a way, we have been drunk with freedom, and only now are the consequences of this imbalance sobering us up.

A reaction has set in against freedom, as if freedom itself were the problem. All while celebrating their liberty, Americans seem to long for authority figures like Ronald Reagan who make a show of strong direction in return for which we are willing to cede some of our liberty. Alarmed by the self-centeredness of the 1980s, some people began to equate individualism with selfishness, as if the one necessarily brought on the other. Some, like the proposers of "cultural literacy," are calling for more conformity lest the society fall apart. Americans are throwing away democracy in alarming accord with psychoanalyst Erich Fromm's classic explanation, in *Escape from Freedom*, of why Germans turned toward Hitler's fascism.[1] Such backing off from freedom and individuality cops out on the real issue, which is to grow inwardly equal to the ideal of personal development. As the American Transcendentalists kept saying, highly developed individuals are more moral than are mere conformists.

Individuality must be cultivated to the fullest for its contribution of original thought but without the competitive intellectual pride of academic intelligentsia, for this sorely needed creativity will have to serve society. Indeed, to be original enough to help, our minds will have to attune well beyond ourselves and our personal conditioning and encompass a cosmopolitan perspective. Earlier in the evolution of group mind into personal consciousness, it no doubt made sense to treat individuals more collectively and hence to speak of educating for a *citizenry* or for *a work force*. But today's citizenry and work force call for people of more awareness, who can realize their own freedom without impairing others', who can take care of themselves, and who can think originally about today's problems—problems caused by freeing people enough for them to *want* for themselves but not enough for them to *think* for themselves.

We are now learning very painfully how to function in unselfish autonomy and seem to be making a terrible mess of it, judging from the widespread selfishness in business and personal relationships, the corruption in government, and the outmoded approaches to problem solving. Crime, poverty, addiction, poor health, overpopulation, and pollution cannot be eradicated by legislation or adjudication alone. The mind-set and soul state of those making and interpreting laws are paramount. Solutions require some shift in consciousness, or rather, a further development of individual consciousness, which will coincide with a curing of the culture. Human evolution may spiral, but it never merely circles. Public education has to go right on through the consequences of personal freedom and out the other side.

The evolutionary purpose of liberty may be to force human beings, through the very adversities it causes, into a more spiritual consciousness. Spirituality is connectedness. The more spiritual a person, the more he or she identifies with the rest of humanity and nature and sheds feelings of boundaries. The more we identify with others, the better we treat them. This explains how highly developed individuals become necessarily more moral. Selfishness merely indicates an early stage of individualism, and one outgrows it by going forward, not backward.

The process of expanding the self into a citizen of the universe can lead eventually to the famous oceanic or mystic feeling of being at one with the life force. Most of us might first settle for not feeling alienated and anxious. Older cultures bought security and harmony for the individual soul by keeping it submerged in the group soul. Oneness or spirituality was achieved by the suppression of individualism. But evolution seems bent on developing individual consciousness to the point where it can achieve *on its own* the unity with the world that it knew before only by virtue of being *unable* to distinguish itself from the world and unable to function independently of the group. People of higher consciousness feel their innerness, their essential being, as a solid reality independent of validation by others. All while *identifying* more broadly with people and things outside, they *depend* on them less. Self-reliance and self-esteem are fringe benefits of expanded consciousness.

Acknowledged or not, this framework occurs naturally at a certain stage of self-awareness, which is the key to higher consciousness. Beginning, at age eight to ten, with the consciousness of oneself as distinct from other people and things in the environment, people grow in awareness of themselves as a subject and an object and as an agent, a creator, who has choice and is responsible. The awkward self-consciousness of the adolescent—self-involved and self-entangled—matures by expanding the notion of the self to again include other people and things. The distinctness of oneself remains, but now one incorporates other viewpoints, other selves, gradually hearing out the world, broadening the repertory of empathy and identification, reducing the anesthesia, amnesia, and agnosia of initial conditioning.

The more consciousness comprises, the more it comprehends. It works toward omniscience by including as many viewpoints, angles, and considerations as possible and yet differentiates particular people within this pluralistic experience. Public education has to enable learners to entertain diverse points of view and to enrich their experience well beyond familial upbringing. Intermixing the learners themselves—of all ages and backgrounds—helps do this very effectively but must occur as a natural part of operating the communal learning system, not through coercion. Those who want school to merely reinforce the home under the guise of teaching "family values" are really fending off spiritual education, which depends on widening identity. Personal consciousness first developed when cultures began mixing and broke up each ethnic group's self-contained collective consciousness or race spirit. Not only a matter of ethnic equality, this multicultural process has to continue until personal consciousness subsumes both the individual and the group and becomes cosmic.[2]

The Primacy of the Arts

The arts heal, increase awareness, and realize individuality, besides developing the body and the mind. They should play a far more important role in public education than has ever been assigned to them. Huge numbers of people are taking classes for self-cultivation through the arts and other creative disciplines—ceramics, photography, dance, or writing but also aerobics, martial arts, discussion, gardening, and meditation. Most populous localities offer a prodigious array of learning activities out of school, usually for paying adults, that ought to be available to youngsters as well and ought to be part of a community learning network. Much of this comes across as dilettantism, but that's only because such efforts at cultivating oneself lack a spiritual framework.

If the basic method of healing is reconditioning, the basic method of the arts is making things, creating. But how different is remaking from making? After all, healing re-creates, and art deconditions. Painting, poetry, music, and dance increase our range of experience by exploring potentialities of life beyond the utilitarian. Generally, both extend personal capacity. The self-correction of healing and the self-expression of art give *full play* to one's potential. Both strike into the core of our being. Most shamans and many artists were initiated into or abetted in their life's work through a serious illness or handicap that forced them to learn to do things most people cannot. Artists consummate the free play of the child in a personal discipline that pushes back the boundaries of everyday experience. Both healing and art break open the ordinary through the extraordinary. In this and other ways, they share processes with spiritual disciplines, which in fact draw on healing and the arts for some of their methods.

It isn't necessary to reduce art to therapy to point out the role that painting or dancing or writing has served in enabling both artists and amateurs to cope with wounds or handicaps, even when they could not in this way wholly triumph over them. Treatments that do not cure a condition can still improve a life and enable one to evolve. Child therapists use doll play or painting as a means to diagnose and treat emotional disturbance. This parlays self-expression into self-understanding and self-correction. Practicing the arts helps prison inmates utilize their sentences to get in touch with feelings and intuitions, find gratification in creation, experience their individual being, and reorient their view of themselves and the world. The arts are transpersonal media into which people can project the deepest aspects of their unconscious being without scaring themselves, because the arts work obliquely and figuratively, through intuition.

Actualizing one's potential amounts to a kind of incarnation. We seem to need to manifest our inner selves in material reality, as if to imitate the general embodiment of the life force in the physical universe. As Maria Montessori said, "The real drawing teacher is the inner life, which of itself develops, attains refinement, and seeks irresistibly to be born into external existence in some empirical form."[3] Once out there, in any case, we can regard this personal artifact as an object—offer it to others for response, embrace it, analyze it, rework or play further with it, or dismiss it and go on to something else. T. S. Eliot regarded a metaphor or poem as an "objective correlative" to some element of the psyche. As a way to heal or grow, revising this outer creation seems to facilitate changing its inner counterpart in the way doing things to a voodoo doll is supposed to cause the same effects in the person of which it is an effigy. It doesn't take magic to affect oneself by doing something with one's artistic facsimiles of the inner life, so kinetic are the correspondences between the inner source of art and its external product. This reflexiveness induces self-awareness in artists, who at the same time give their audience creations in which to recognize themselves also.

Let's not forget that the arts educate the beholder as well as the artist. Just as the arts themselves originally formed a unity that later fragmented in the West into painting, sculpture, music, dance, and literature, at first everybody participated and only gradually split into composers, performers, and spectators. In recognition of this original sacred unity, Richard Wagner wanted to fuse the arts together again through opera, and Antonin Artaud wanted to return theater to a participatory ritual for all. Their successors today are legion. At any rate, we still must work with this breakdown, which characterizes our society.

If we regard literature and the other arts not just as works to be understood, as in the historical-critical treatment of them in schools, but as experiences to be undergone, then audiences or spectators can more nearly benefit from them in the same way that their creators do. The arts are meant to cast a spell, and that is what they should be allowed to do. This means subordinating history and analysis to response. The arts aim directly at the unconscious and at the soul. School usually intervenes by organizing and interpreting works of arts so as to format them into the cerebral mode that they are in fact intended to submerge within the whole being.

One of the main functions of the arts while still a unity was to induce trance, to alter consciousness. We can still see this in the performances of, for example, Balinese gamelan orchestras and dancers, during which some participants in the drama go into trance monitored by priests. The whole point of the Mevlevi Sufi whirling dervishes is to enter trance by revolving to music or chanting. So long as consciousness remained collective, as a sort of group soul, the whole community sang, chanted, danced, and made music together to entrance themselves into a reintegration with Spirit.

As the group fell farther out of unity with the rest of creation, and as individuals singled themselves out from the group, a split seems to have occurred. The majority of a group continued to use the arts as communal rites to regain attunement, while more evolved individuals underwent another sort of entrancement induced, for example, by being placed physically underground in a state of complete quiescence while being sent out of the body. Then apparently this initiation and the communal rites, both by then degraded from increasing loss of attunement, melded into spectacle experiences led by some sort of priests, probably accompanied by drugs, and limited to an elect.

From such "mysteries" at Eleusis near Athens, Greek drama emerged, replete with composers, performers, and audience. Later, medieval theater evolved from the liturgy when scriptural antiphony modulated into mystery and morality plays and moved from the church altar to the church porch to the marketplace. Similarly, music and dance, architecture and painting, began sacred and became secular. After a phase of royal patronage, Western art ended by going commercial as aesthetic entertainment for the middle class. In a secular society, people need to think of the arts aesthetically, because they have repudiated the sacred view. But as Soren Kierkegaard said, the aesthetic person represents only a stage of becoming the spiritual person.

The Waldorf schools founded by Rudolf Steiner make the arts paramount. "Artistry arises always and only through a relation to the spiritual," he wrote. "It was out of a spirit-attuned state that the artistic urge proceeded. And this relation to the spiritual world will be, forever, the prerequisite for genuine creativity."[4] Secular as John Dewey was, while making the case for art as experience he could say

> A work of art elicits and accentuates this quality
> of being a whole and of belonging to the larger,
> all-inclusive whole which is the universe in which
> we live. This fact, I think, is the explanation of
> that feeling of exquisite intelligibility and clarity
> we have in the presence of an object that is experi-
> enced with esthetic intensity. It explains also the
> religious feeling that accompanies intense esthetic
> perception. We are, as it were, introduced into a
> world beyond the world which is nevertheless the

deeper reality of the world in which we live our ordinary experiences. We are carried out beyond ourselves to find ourselves.[5]

In his William James lectures at Harvard in 1931, Dewey argued that art illuminates ordinary experience and makes it conscious by bringing out in it the tensions and forms it shares with the rest of nature. As opposed to *anesthetic, aesthetic* means alive and formed.

Writing during World War II, Herbert Read agreed with Dewey that art is a universal language that breaks down national and ethnic barriers. He also upheld it as "mankind's effort to achieve integration with the basic forms of the physical universe and the organic rhythms of life."[6] Ultimately, Read and Dewey assert, these forms of growth are mathematically expressed. Suzanne Langer was to say not long after that "expressive form is always organic or 'living' form. . . . art is the making of virtual forms, symbolic of the elusive forms of feeling."[7] She constructed a theory of mind based on forms of feeling corresponding to biological forms. In her view, the arts are not merely "affective" but cognitive as well and constitute alternative semantics to language. As Read says, "Art is the representation, science the explanation, of the same reality."[8] More recently, psychologist Howard Gardner has ratified this view in his theory of multiple intelligences (spatial, visual, kinesthetic, and social as well as verbal and mathematical).[9]

The fact that the arts are serious modes of knowing in the highest forms of play explains why someone like Read would advocate them as the basics of learning—the thesis of his *Education Through Art*. The key word is *through*, by means of. Art is the natural medium of growth for learning everything. It is not only the best avenue to avocations, vocations, and the so-called academic subjects, but, more than anything except spiritual disciplines themselves, the arts develop the whole person, precisely because they deal at once with correlated forms of feeling, thought, and nature. As Read says, "The general purpose of education is to foster the growth of what is individual in each human being, at the same time harmonizing the individuality thus educed with the organic unity of the social group to which the individual belongs. . . . In this process *esthetic education* is fundamental."[10]

Read cites Trigant Burrow's idea from *The Social Basis of Consciousness* that "the cultivation of consciousness has involved the development of 'separateness'—the individual has cut himself off from the collective unconscious." Modern neurosis owes to "the obstruction of man's tribal or congeneric life and to the consequent interruption of the creative expression of his personality as a social unit." The child is "tricked into complicity"; school is wrong to "prepare" students, to "substitute a mental impression of life for life itself."[11]

It is true that the evolution from group mind to personal consciousness has starved the individual of the knowledge and creativity of the collective unconscious and consequently caused neurosis. But the *social* basis of consciousness does not give the whole picture. From a spiritual perspective, the evolution of the individual trades off this deprivation and neurosis for an educational gain. It is teaching individuals to know and create autonomously, to access *at will* both the contemporary community and the collective unconscious without having to pay the price of automatic conformity to a herd mind. Doing without the *old* sort of social solidarity forces higher consciousness, which in turn allows communal reintegration on a new, more spiritual basis. Only those can truly unite who first become fully themselves.

PART TWO

▲

Reform by the
Right Means

Educational reform must occur not only for the right reasons but by the right means. If the main mission of education is to develop culture and consciousness so that they improve each other, the means also have to change. Even for the nationalistic and commercial mission, the means have been ineffective. Before trying to envision reform more specifically, we would do well to look at why schooling has miscarried so alarmingly despite strong public pressure and the best efforts of many dedicated professionals. To illustrate this I will sometimes draw on my own professional experience.

I would prefer not to dwell on the negative conditions of past and present, but any futuristic vision can seem entirely too cavalier if not grounded in current realities. It is essential to characterize the plight of today's schools in such a way as to indicate which means will succeed in building a bridge to a better future and which will not. The means now preferred in school reform will perpetuate failure and must be replaced.

Sorting good and bad entails taking sides. This is a polemical task. The stakes are too high, and the time too late, to go about this with a studied neutrality or well-bred indirection. Behind the need for educational reform lie moral issues and wrongdoing that should be identified as such. The course of both education and its reform is wrong, in more than a pragmatic way. In fact, it is ineffectual because it is unspiritual.

The first step in proposing solutions is to investigate how differently public education should be determined in the future. So we will look now at which forces actually account for its current state. This will indicate what might best determine it in the future and which means might best bring about such a change. Taking a hard look at what really goes on behind schooling also gives us a chance to define spirituality by contrast with what happens without it. Occasionally I will make this contrast, but I also count on readers themselves to refer the following description of things as they are to the previous spiritual framework and to their own vision of things as they ought to be.

5

▲

What Determines
Public Education

I have spent about thirty years working to change schools—a full-time career effort that began during the reform of the 1960s and has lasted into the reform of the 1990s. In order to focus single-mindedly on effecting practical change nationally, I have foregone taking any long-term institutional positions. Operating independently across the continent, I could do workshops and courses for teachers, consult with district and university staffs, conduct trials with students, do offbeat study to bring outside ideas into the field, write for the profession, produce learning materials, give talks to teacher organizations, and generally urge curricular innovation.

The main thing that has been borne in on me is that most schooling problems are not learning problems. They are institutional and political problems, many of which are the same that plague the larger culture. That is, most of what schools struggle with are not difficulties inherent in learning to read and write or do science and math. Their difficulties stem from the society at large and are merely reflected in schools.

Institutionalitis

First of all, school systems are bureaucracies, and second, they are *public* bureaucracies. Schools share some problems with many other large institutions, which tend notoriously to standardize, mechanize, and compartmentalize whatever materials or procedures they are dealing with. Institutionalism makes its own rules and tends to appropriate more and more resources for its own functioning. It's a parasite that feeds itself first. This is no more true of schools than of for-profit corporations, agencies of government at all levels, the armed forces, or even many not-for-profit foundations.

Public schools are more visible and vulnerable than many of these, however. Nearly all Americans attend them and later send their own children there. All taxpayers are obliged to pay for them. Because they are much more palpably bound into people's daily lives than most other institutions, schools are more carefully watched and more frequently criticized. As public institutions serving a constituency nearly as large as the population itself, they can be held accountable to the public for results.

Businesses and most government agencies, by contrast, generally account for themselves only to themselves or to superiors in their own system, seldom so directly to the public as schools do. Inefficiency, waste, and corruption are easier to mask when you can simply pass losses on to the consumer or pass the buck around within a mind-boggling complex of government agencies. Commodities and services, too, are much easier to produce and monitor than human development, the delicate business of schools. It is important to appreciate that schools have an extraordinarily difficult mission to perform under the same negative institutional conditions as other enterprises that don't perform any better but can better hide their inefficiency.

Schools play out a tragicomedy. Learning language and literacy, for example, are extremely personal, and yet schools are supposed to pull this off in absurdly public circumstances. Since the 1960s I have, along with other curriculum developers, advocated that the language arts curriculum move toward more individualization, interaction, and integration. This would make learning more personal, interpersonal, and holistic. Learning to speak is more difficult than learning to read and write, but it occurs successfully at home (unless the child is defective or totally ignored) without any failures or dropouts because those three conditions characterize the spontaneous verbal life of the family. Schools could find no better model for teaching literacy, but individualization, interaction, and integration run exactly counter to the standardization, mechanization, and compartmentalization that are the hallmark of large institutions.

During the 1980s, for example, an educational movement called "collaborative learning" arose that promotes peer-group processes for learning all subjects. Because I was known to have been advocating this since the 1960s, I was invited to participate in a day-long program allotted to collaborative learning at an international conference on language teaching. Though expected to endorse the movement, as I was certainly inclined to do, I had to say there that what should have been an innovation I could heartily welcome had already become so compromised to accommodate institutionalism and commercialization that it was hardly worth it. This sad turn exemplifies a critical reason why schools don't improve.

A perfectly natural human process requiring no commercial materials was proceduralized almost beyond recognition. Small-group interaction was ritualized fore and aft by so much goal setting and assessment, briefing and debriefing, that little time remained for the substantive collaboration itself, which was so formalized, moreover, that little choice or spontaneity remained. Defenders argue that without all this "structure" teachers and students will not be able to handle collaborative learning and administrators will not "buy" it. Some of the most strenuous advocates had also commercially invested in the movement by way of managerial systems embodied either in materials or in training seminars. Is it really true that a practical social process native to human functioning and widely practiced everywhere out of school can be established in classrooms only by first bureaucratizing it and running it through the market? If this is so, then removing such a necessity deserves top priority in educational reform.

Commercialization

Part of institutionalitis is the incorporation of schools into a commercial system very similar to the military-industrial complex. Education and defense are the nation's two largest industries and are, furthermore, tax-supported. The customers are governments, not mere individuals, which means that the stakes are high and that boundaries tend to dissolve between public and private institutions. In each case the "complex" consists of intricate interrelationships among commercial companies that want to make customers of public agencies, which in turn want to make suppliers of them. Each industry lobbies key public managers, who often pass back and forth, during their careers, between the industry and the government. By persuading policy makers and lawmakers that the public function requires their products, corporations can, instead of selling to individuals one at a time, collect from all of them at once from one source, the government agency, to whose tax collector they can leave all the nickel-and-diming.

The most direct determinant of curriculum is some form of commercial materials. The great majority of schools *buy* their curriculum; they don't create it. To this fact alone may be attributed a major portion of their ills. The curriculum-adoption conditions set by school districts and state departments of education constrain drastically what textbooks and other commercial school materials may contain or do. And the corporations who produce those materials for them should not be entrusted with anything so important as learning.

Most states and districts adopt only books, though some localities have started, too late, to include other media. This stricture has ruled out manipulatable and sensory materials that could accommodate other learning modalities and therefore individualization. Most software for adoption just shifts textbooks and workbooks onto computer. Even texts themselves have been limited to hardcover books in classroom sets, whereas a classroom library for individualized reading requires trading off a single set of books of the same title for a variety of titles, many of which would have to be in paperback. Typically, teachers who want to individualize have to scrounge on their own instead of being able to use state or district funds, which are allocated to adoptions they have little to say about.

In math, the arts, foreign languages, and the social and natural sciences, it is even truer that books are by no means always the best way to learn the subject. They favor memorization and student passivity over student interaction, initiative, and inquiry, as advocated today by specialists in these subjects. The best books, films, and recordings for science or history are rarely those made especially for schools. Since adoption usually occurs only about every five years at best, for one thing, informational textbooks are chronically out of date. Most seriously of all, publishers precensor the content of them to avoid controversies that would deter a community from purchasing them because some faction objects to some facts or concepts. The practice of adopting commercially produced school materials amounts to a form of mind control incompatible with free education. Learning materials for an open market of ideas should be bought on the open market of media merchandise.

The worst aspect of materials created to pass adoption is that they are expected to accommodate the standardization, mechanization, and compartmentalization that characterize institutionalitis. Thus they militate against the individualization, interaction, and integration that learning requires. This fits the assembly-line mentality of both the public bureaucracies that are the consumers and the corporate manufacturers that are the producers. Adopted materials are also expected to mesh with various standardized tests, which always shrink the curriculum to fit their extremely narrow measures. Testing itself is one of those scourges of schooling that adoption keeps firmly locked into place.

Most textbooks come in series and packages because they constitute entire courses and even whole programs spread over many years. These series and packages are in fact *managerial systems*, usually replete with teacher and student directions and with tests. They do not just contain information about the subject; they install certain methods and procedures in the classroom that preempt the curriculum and remove choice from both teachers and students. For example, they render group process and individual inquiry virtually impossible, though they may make pretenses of including these, and they displace some of the content itself with excessive procedure designed to make the materials "teacher-proof" and to establish tight control over student activities.

These commercially packaged curricula manipulate both students and teachers outrageously. It is *this* that makes them hopelessly boring even when the actual subject matter is not bad. Like other literacy consultants, I often advise teachers who have no funds for alternative books to just strip out the good reading selections from the adopted materials and ignore the system that goes with them. *Buying* a curriculum plays havoc with learning and impedes needed change as much as any other single factor.

Many textbook publishing executives I have known privately scorn many aspects of the books they are putting out. They send their own children to schools that don't use them. When in the 1950s and 1960s I taught at a top prep school, Phillips Exeter Academy, none of the fifteen English teachers would be caught dead using textbooks for literature, grammar, composition, or anything else. Teachers there in science, history, math, and foreign languages did use textbooks, but in many cases they or their colleagues were the authors! This was a school to which public secondary schools looked for guidance, but they usually weren't free to follow it. It is well known that the more experienced, creative, and successful public school teachers become, the more they ignore commercial materials and devise their own curricula. At a workshop on educational publishing sponsored once by the National Council of Teachers of English, I asked the audience if they felt this was so, and nearly all members raised their hands. The few who did not were probably the publishers' representatives in attendance that day.

Ours is a society that seldom values something that has not been run through the market. Anything free and natural is suspect. If it were any good, it would cost something and be advertised. We're a nation trained to solve problems by purchasing something, whether the problem is how to get relief from hemorrhoids or how to get along with your spouse or teenager, to the point that managers of institutions think just like other good consumers.

To exemplify, for decades I have been trying, along with some other English educators, to make the learning of speaking, reading, and writing more nearly resemble the actual ways in which they are practiced outside of school. Such authentic language activities must replace artificial exercises with particles of language such as isolated syllables, words, sentences, or paragraphs. Realistic learning, I have maintained, is holistic first, that is, takes place within whole speech acts and whole texts complete for their purpose. Within these language wholes, students can work on the parts—spelling, vocabulary, grammar, and so on.

Precisely because the particle approach breaks discourse down into artificial behavioral units that exist only in schools, it requires, both to teach and to test, materials especially made for schools. The holistic approach, on the other hand, can be implemented with trade books and other materials already available and can be assessed by no more means and activities than learning itself requires. One reason our society prefers the particle approach is that it costs a lot, whereas the holistic approach is too cheap. Our economy seems to depend on expensive solutions to unnecessary problems.

I once directed a commercial K-12 program for language arts intended to penetrate schools with what were really trade books and nonverbal media disguised to sneak past adoption committees as textbooks with "ancillary" materials. Since schools *buy* their curriculum, I thought, I'll give them something to buy that will for once be honest and practical, because it will fit the truth of language learning that other programs rule out for bureaucratic and political reasons. As the only major set of commercial materials for students ever created specifically to implement a full-blown holistic and individualized approach, *Interaction* provided a good test case.

Although it enjoyed a fair success among schools ready for it and helped establish a visible model for an alternative curriculum, I concluded from this experience that the kinds of books and other materials that schools really need cannot possibly survive the corporate practices of the big companies that alone can capitalize the large curricular packages that both schools and the companies prefer. Corporate bureaucracy being no better than that of public institutions, the simplistic military-like procedures of editorial and production cannot deal with the variety, flexibility, and complexity such a program requires.

Moreover, the salespeople don't so much sell it as sell it down the river in favor of one of the company's conventional, competing programs that they can more easily understand and pitch. As much as any other major factor, textbook marketing personnel exert a reactionary influence on education, because they want to push sure old winners. Today I recommend to schools that they compile and create their own curriculum materials.

The reason that I took this calculated risk and became a capitalist lackey was that I felt it was the only way to change curriculum. Most teachers were themselves raised on commercial programs when they were students, probably had these materials surveyed for them as part of their teacher training, and found some of them installed at the schools that hired them. So when the education industry says it just gives schools what they want, this is like the television industry saying that it gives the public swill because swill is what the public wants. Most people think they want what they were brought up on. These all-pervasive industries can't honestly claim to be merely responding to requests when they are profoundly influencing the very mental cast of the public.

In fairness to publishers, whenever they have gambled on a more flexible program, they have gotten badly burned because schools have not sufficiently supported them or because they have become embroiled in a nasty censorship row. Such debacles have set back the whole industry. If publishers retrench cynically into convention, school administrations and the public have to take some of the blame. It's truer than it should be that they give us what we want. At any rate, it will not be the manufacturers who break the cycle; it will have to be educators and parents, acting for the sake of those proxy consumers, the students. As we know from defense procurement, it is very dangerous to link a major, publicly funded endeavor so closely to private business, which has its own rules and goals and institutional limitations. Adoption tends to lock in the worst of the past. The stakes are too high, and the common denominator is too low.

There is another way in which public education has to be decommercialized. A major reason that schools look to commercial companies for the curriculum they should be forging themselves is that the very concept of public schooling in this country derives from industrial engineering and business. For at least a hundred years education has been thought of as akin to mass production and mass marketing, as if the job of schools is to turn out as efficiently as possible the reliable, quality-controlled products that the "consumers"—the parents and employers—are looking for. Much of the awful stuff that goes on in schools can be traced to this inappropriate analogy between learning processes and the procedures by which inert physical materials are manufactured and sold.

Few citizens have ever quite forgiven their own schools for treating them this way, whether they realize it or not, but their resentment betrays itself in everything from trashing the buildings to blaming schools for social ills to voting down tax levies for them. What this dehumanized schooling *does* prepare them for is to be manipulated like objects by governments and corporations as adults. Schools did not invent this materialism—the society thrust it on them—but it is impossible to understand why schools are the way they are and which direction change must take unless one grasps the full import of asking schools to function like commercial companies.

This unseemly metaphor equating education with business has adversely affected the curriculum, the administration, and the relationship of schools to the outside world. It is assumed that schools are in the business of certifying people for employment (or for higher education toward the same end), but employers should determine at their own expense who is qualified to work for them. The effort to certify students for the job market spoils education, which is swamped by all the rites and tests that this entails. People have to develop as human beings before they can learn objective skills and be of any great use to employers.

The citizens too look on schools as a business for which they are the consumers. They pay for public education through taxes and expect to get their money's worth. But it can't be a business. It is basically a community cooperative. Instead of tutoring our children at home we say, in effect, let's pool resources and do a better job of it. Unfortunately, large urban populations have made schools remote bureaucracies that are easy to think of as companies that take your money in exchange for a product. However, parents often object to teachers' unionizing on grounds that "Schools are not just a business; our children are involved." But you can't play it both ways. One of the sad facts of schools is that they have become increasingly alienated from the people in the community, who feel as injured by them as they do by any other company that they have overpaid for a bad product—except that the law requires them to pay for schools and to send their children there, a reminder that schools are not born from a commercial contract but from a *social* contract.

The Public Will

When I began my career I naively thought that bright ideas, good sense, and clear research indications would suffice to change curriculum. It was a turning point when I realized that the biggest obstacles to improving schools were political and mostly beyond the reach of educators alone.

The public has just the awful schools it "wants." Through the political chain of state legislatures and state and local boards of education, it controls schools much more than it admits and

▲

is therefore much more responsible for the negative results than appears. My own field of English education, for example, has been especially hard to reform because popular public prejudices about reading and writing often determine which methods and materials teachers may use. A book by some zealot can inflame the public about why kids can't read and cause a craze for one reading method at the expense of a balanced approach. And of course community censorship has increased dramatically in recent years, intimidating teachers more and more, even though the complainers almost never represent the majority.

Perhaps worst of all, the grammar mystique has for generations blocked serious improvement in literacy education. A public pet that many English educators have long since repudiated, the ticketing of parts of speech and the analysis of dummy sentences have substituted for real writing and have generally taken up curricular space and resources desperately needed for real language activities. As much as anything, this explains why writing is such a problem in this country. Formal grammar has taken up huge amounts of time and money, partly because it has been locked into "composition" textbooks that run as a series for many school years. The subject is not that big in the form given to students, but because it is nonfunctional and hence quickly forgotten, it has to be repeated.

Many lay people see formal grammar as upholding the pillars of civilization. I hope that a lot more is holding them up than word endings and word order, which is what grammar means to linguists. Strictly speaking, it never rises above the level of the isolated sentence. Both the public and some of the English profession, however, have equated the study of grammar with something grand like how to think or the command of language or even a good education. This exasperates those educators who know that the best way to learn grammar—and to think and to command the language—is to practice authentic speaking, reading, and writing, which the ticketing of parts of speech and the diagramming of sentences routinely displaces. The historical reason for this crucial discrepancy is that in the classical trivium of grammar, logic, and rhetoric derived from the Greeks and absorbed into modern pedagogy, grammar comprised far more than school grammar exercises today, having included literature, for one thing.

Only the rarest school superintendent would risk dismissal to take a stand against the modern tradition of grammar teaching and to expose the mystique, even if he or she knew, as many do, that this teaching has been proven ineffectual in improving speaking, reading, and writing and that the mystique is used to justify spending huge sums for fraudulent "composition" textbooks. As is so often the case, a mistaken notion in the public will play right into the hands of certain bad teachers, who can avoid, for example, the difficult business of mounting a real writing program in favor of being an usher(ette) in a grammar textbook series.

The public has schools in a double bind. On the one hand, it stays apart from them, complains about them, and expects them to do an important job for their children as if schools bore the whole responsibility for education. On the other hand, the public runs schools themselves in important ways by electing state and local officals who set policy according to popular notions about education and to political expediency. School administrators have to practice a lot of public relations. Teachers often complain to me that their principals try so hard to please every faction of the community that they make a mishmash of schooling. I know that many if not most teachers are doing many things they do not believe in and omitting much that they do believe in, because they are not free to make many of the decisions about methods and materials.

These decision are made over their heads and behind their backs by administrators following public mandates. Many parents think, for example, that it's a great idea to break down a subject into fine pieces and then to drill on these subskills until students "test out" on them one by one. To the laity the subassemblies approach can look very practical, because it proved so successful in industry. Professionals in English, math, and science tend to agree today that this has not worked and that schools will improve only if this particle approach is supplanted by a holistic approach that subordinates memorization to intellectual development. But most administrators are still buying large managerial systems for teaching in the old discredited way and saddling teachers with them, because this assembly-line model is lodged deep in the public psyche and because these tidy systems simplify administration.

The most important fact about schooling may be the unsuspected ways in which the more obscure motives of parents, managers, merchants, and teachers coincide to spoil education. Everybody uses schools for noneducational purposes of their own. For example, the profession and the public have favored what I call the particle approach for psychological reasons that reinforce the economic reasons. Public schooling evolved in parallel with the industrial revolution and tried to apply that successful mode of working with inorganic objects to the functioning of human intelligence. Small wonder that a bias so solidly built into the culture has become a personal mental block within us all. It makes organic learning through wholes seem wrong, unprofessional, and "unstructured" even though people clearly learn to do most things out of school holistically, by saturation practice in the target activities themselves, through which the subskills are learned in their place.

The holistic approach not only goes against the ingrained thinking of our society, it requires us to transfer to our students far more power than schools ever have before. To use literacy as an example, you can't plan in advance the subject matter students will talk, read, and write about and still expect them to benefit from the chief advantage of whole texts and complete speech acts, which is the realistic context of meaning and motivation. When curriculum is laid out far in advance, moreover, and in great detail, students are manipulated beyond any possibility of either spontaneity or responsibility. Nor can you schedule specifically which students will be doing this or that activity, because they don't all need the same things, at the same times, in the same connections. Nor will students get the massive practice required if you try to keep them abreast of each other, in unison. You can't teach good judgment and make all the decisions yourself, teach students to think for themselves and still control what they talk, read, and write about.

The teacher's personal fear of sharing power with students partakes of the community's fear of losing control over the young. A main goal of schooling has always been acculturation, to direct the minds of youth toward the ideas and values adults have in mind. The traditional curriculum is very much the way it is for the purpose of controlling content. Particles are perfect for this because they avoid real subject matter—and indeed most meaning at all. The smaller the language unit that is the learning unit, the less point and purpose it has. (Indeed, censors actually *prefer* phonics for teaching literacy because letters and syllables have the least meaning and therefore render texts innocuous.) In addition, schools select books that limit subject matter to what is regarded as safe. Since writing has traditionally been mostly about the assigned reading, controlling the content of the texts controls much of the content of the writing. Other writing is assigned by topics, which stipulate subject matter, rather than by types, which would leave subject matter open. The hardest activity to control, small-group discussion, was not until recently considered a serious classroom possibility although it had long been recognized in government and business as the most effective way to get things done.

The fact that so much of this resistance goes against common

sense and common learning experience gives some idea of the
strength of the fear of losing control. It also shows why
the public and the teaching profession have tolerated so
long the huge abuses committed in the educational-industrial
complex to maintain the particle approach. It's not only good
for business and bureaucracy, it safeguards our personal and
societal state of mind from disruption by youth.

The real learning goals threaten adults, because to attain
them schools would have to empower students more than they
feel is safe. Teaching children to think for themselves conflicts
with adults' need to control the young and is therefore unwel-
come in deed however much it is honored in word. This is a
sort of double-mindedness that unwittingly puts schools in a
double bind. Thinking for oneself entails more than either parents or teachers have ever sufficiently realized, for if they had,
they would not expect to teach it while forbidding students to
make decisions and while sedating them by prearranged lessons.

Control is the crux. If school is just a big day-care center
and holding tank to neutralize children until, one way or another, they go off on their own, it is doing its job and giving
parents just what they want. Supposedly, rather, we all want
children to learn to read and write and think for themselves,
but literacy is and has always been held potentially dangerous
to an establishment. For much of history it was forbidden to
the masses. Today governments foster literacy—but in order
to use it to direct the citizenry. Unless you control what people
read and write, they will get ideas and form plans you do not
intend.

With the approval of the community, schools have played a
fine game of teaching students to read just well enough to follow directions and write just well enough to fill all those clerical
jobs in government and industry but not to read so well as to
do it on their own, which is when reading becomes dangerous,

or write so well as to turn writing into a tool for investigating the world for themselves. Require literacy, but make it feel so negative that children won't want to read and write on their own. Show kids who owns literacy. This unconscious sabotaging of literacy, done with the tacit compliance of all the adults involved, is a major cause of the failure of our schools.

An innocuous curriculum is perfect. Parents and teachers, who both have the problem of controlling the young, both want them as tractable and unarmed as possible. School district administrators can fit this sort of literacy instruction to the managerial systems that promise to dispatch the mind-boggling organizational problems of today's schools and that keep teachers also from thinking too much on their own. The reading business loves a self-crippling literacy program because it seems to require all sorts of expensive special materials, and it drags on, sells on, forever. Harmony reigns. Failure pays off in some way to all parties except the students, who have nothing to say about what happens to them.

So despite its alienation from schools, the public is running them far more than it knows or perhaps wants. Typically, certain issues like phonics or formal grammar or creationism or discipline or accountability become associated with certain strong emotions and beliefs. These build into a veritable mystique that fixes the issue in the mind in a primitive, simplistic way. This blocks further thought and lends itself to sloganeering and exploitation. The citizenry is too far from the classroom to see the effects on it of their mandates as translated by administration and industry. Ordinary citizens still think they have nothing to do with school results and that educators are failing them on their own authority. The laity has got to quit blaming schools and work more with them. Again, the relationship is not that of merchant to customer.

All of this self-contradiction can be worked out, and it must be if education is to equal the occasion. But it will take an

honest soul-searching unprecedented in forums on school reform. We will have to go beyond what officialdom can afford
to pronounce upon and get into what human beings in the
world today really feel and do.

Accountability and Evaluation

The American public has wound up in the position of wanting
to hold schools accountable while at the same time telling them
how to do their job. This sort of double bind is indefensible
even in the business world from which the cost-benefit concept
of accountability issued. A company doesn't try to hold an
executive accountable without giving him or her decision-mak-
ing power commensurate with the outcomes expected! Of
course the public should control its schools, but a dangerous
game is going on whereby its will is being translated by administrators into terms congenial to themselves.

Accountability may be instituted in many ways, some of
which suit education and some of which can destroy it. Administrative training derives from business, and it was from Detroit
and the Pentagon that managers of school systems drew their
accountability models, based on production of automobiles
and delivery of weapons systems. You match the costs against
the benefits, which you measure by physical or fiscal means.
In school this amounts to looking for certain student "behaviors" to make themselves overt soon enough after the teaching
treatment to assume a cause-and-effect relationship.

The emphasis lies on *soon*, because the managerial mentality
fixates on those quarterly reports to stockholders. Schools
don't have to report profits quarterly, but then if appropriate-
ness were the point, they wouldn't cleave to a business model
in the first place. The fact is that managers today are generic,
are taught principles for running an enterprise that are sup-

posed to apply no matter what the enterprise. These principles are short-term and serve the managers first, the enterprise second, and the public last. In catering to personal drives for big money and status, business schools have emphasized how their clients can build successful careers, disregarding the consequences of this narrow perspective for the public or even for the companies that hire their graduates.

Parents and taxpayers just want, after all, to feel that their children are getting a good education and that their taxes are well spent. They don't have in mind a particular procedure to achieve this reassurance. This creates a vacuum some commercial and administrative interests can't resist filling. Like formal grammar, accountability becomes a blank check into which all sorts of abominations can be written because the public supposedly wills them.

Let me show by a true story how badly curriculum can be deformed through evaluation done in the name of accountability. In the summer of 1966 the national English-teacher organizations of the United States, Britain, and Canada brought together for a month at Dartmouth University fifty educators and researchers for the purpose of establishing future guidelines for language learning. I was invited to it as a former secondary teacher then based at the Harvard Graduate School of Education on a Carnegie Corporation grant to develop and write up a new English and language arts curriculum. Though sorely deficient in both multicultural perspective and representation by schoolteachers themselves, this Dartmouth Seminar in the Teaching and Learning of English proposed some important and much needed changes in the direction of more personal and more authentic language activities, as reported in two books, one by a historian and one by a British educator.[1] Just as the profession began to try to implement these proposals to play down rote learning and particle exercises in favor of such things as dramatic activities, small-group talk, personal response to literature, and authentic writing, the federal government was mounting a movement to render schools accountable for the unprecedented educational funds issuing from its Great Society programs.

These two initiatives turned out to be on a collision course. By 1969 I was invited to a very different conference of English educators. An unholy marriage had occurred in Washington between Detroit-Pentagon management by objectives and behaviorist psychological testing. The U.S. Office of Education had funded three midwestern universities to sponsor a project to create *A Catalogue of Representative Behavioral Objectives in English, Grades 9–12,* which was to be nationally promulgated as a basis for evaluating English education for federal funding. The handwriting was on the wall when we twenty-six consultants were asked to spend several days writing these objectives together under the very tight direction of two "major consultants" who had authored the bibles of the behavioral objectives movement[2] and who would, along with the resident behavioral psychologist, visit the schools where these would be field-tested and draft the final document.

Half of the consultants were staff members of these "experimental schools of the 1970s" and no doubt felt proud to be aboard a project with such potential for determining the American high school English curriculum. Others were sophisticated national consultants who satirized the project in asides to each other but felt resigned to this sort of governmental domination. "If we don't go along, they'll do it anyway without us. Better we're in on it." During plenary sessions, the two "major consultants" brooked no debate about their assumptions and responded to our reservations with hostility. We were to shut up, get out in those motel rooms, and produce those behavioral objectives, that is, endorse this movement on pain of being left out.

The only accurate name for this is extortion, which is how the federal government got its way. The proponents of behavioral objectives were manipulating us exactly as schools would manipulate the children having to undergo such a curriculum. So what was new? These were exactly the conditions that made schooling a candidate for reform in the first place.

After two days I told the university directors I couldn't stomach it any longer. We agreed that on the third day I would write a position paper explaining my resignation from the project and that they would disseminate it to all participants. I began the criticism: "What I see as negative in the formulation of behavioral objectives for English concerns three areas: the inadequacy of such formulation to do justice to the goals of English, the unintended mischief that will almost certainly result from publishing behavioral goals, and the bad precedent set for future relations between government and education."[3] I had in mind one thing that at the Dartmouth Seminar we had taken pains to denounce—the use of narrow testing that shrinks the curriculum to fit itself—because teachers teach to the test to protect themselves. Also, as a practical matter, the amount of testing required to monitor all students on all the small overt acts thought to comprise language behavior would so swamp the classroom that it would leave no time for serious learning. Finally, I said that "losing this battle means losing a lot more in the future."

In stipulating behavior externally visible soon enough after the teaching treatment to attribute this behavior to it, behavioral objectives raised a central issue of evaluation that has yet to be adequately considered—the time-space compass in which evaluation occurs. Any important, complex learning like writing well, solving problems, thinking critically, or judiciously interpreting texts will manifest itself only over many occasions, months or years apart and months or years after the "treatment," which will realistically occur also over months or years, since all of these activities require a long time to learn. To evaluate by behavioral objectives is to trivialize the curriculum by committing it to the particle approach. The double assumption is that language behavior can usefully be broken down into such small units and, if so, that testing them out separately amounts to the same as assessing the complete language acts they are supposed to comprise. In a landmark essay that has remained quite pertinent, Noam Chomsky roundly refuted, to the satisfaction of all but die-hard behaviorists, B. F. Skinner's doctrinaire effort in *Verbal Behavior* to explain higher language functioning as just a complex of small operant-conditioning behaviors.[4]

So at the very time that the English teaching profession was trying to reform its curriculum in the early 1970s along the guidelines worked out at the Dartmouth Seminar, policy makers at all levels were installing a management-by-objectives system of accountability based on the physically measurable behavior of automobiles and fighter planes. It was no match. The one aimed holistically at higher-level thinking, the other at unreal bits and pieces. The English curriculum of the future was not to be determined so much by educators as by legislators, who would nevertheless hold educators responsible for results. State legislatures, it is important to realize, ape the national legislature not only to get federal money but to invest themselves with the style, the aura, and the status of that ultimate power source, Washington, D.C., whose trends are just as irresistible today as when behavioral objectives locked into the curriculum the worst of the past.

About twenty years after the Dartmouth Seminar, in 1987, the National Council of Teachers of English, the Modern Language Association, and their affiliates sponsored its successor, the English Coalition Conference. The sixty selected participants, English teachers of all ages from kindergarten through college, convened for three weeks at a retreat in Maryland to draft some agreements and guidelines. Two books likewise reported the results of this conference,[5] which carried further the double thrust of the Dartmouth Seminar toward a language curriculum at once more personal and more social. The conferees proposed:

- Accommodation of individual differences in background and learning modality
- Active students making decisions and constructing their own meaning
- Considerable interaction among students
- Heterogeneous classes
- Integration of all the language arts
- Looser boundaries between ages and between subjects
- Shift of emphasis from memorization to higher-order thinking
- Assessment in full accord with the highest goals
- Learning of language particles via whole texts and speech acts
- Greater development of oral language, as in dramatic work

Most schools are still very far from actually implementing this excellent program, which was delayed twenty years because the Dartmouth recommendations were stymied by governmental determination to impose behaviorally objectized evaluation and accountability.

I don't believe that history repeats itself; *people* repeat history to the extent that they resist needed change. The same forces that determined curriculum during the reform era of the 1960s still do in the 1990s. The voices of those who understand learning best and work the closest with children are the last and least heard. Policy makers outside of education overrule them on grounds that schools are doing badly and need stronger external control, but the schools are always doing badly because policy makers want to control instead of enable educators.

Had the English profession been free to follow up the Dartmouth recommendations, literacy learning might very well have evolved so far toward the program outlined by the English Coalition Conference that the program would have been a reality for most schools by the 1990s, not a still risky experiment for a few. In order to put it across now, educators will have to struggle against the same overcontrolling of schools by government that leaves school reform still unfulfilled after two or three decades.

"Business Knows Best"

During the 1970s accountants took over accountability and quit fooling around. In a movement called Planning, Programming, and Budgeting Systems (PPBS) that spread from Washington in the wake of behavioral objectives, they said, "Make each program or subject in the curriculum an actual budget category so that you can directly match its costs against its benefits, instead of distributing operating costs across such categories as salaries, buildings, maintenance, and so on." Imagine trying to calculate how much of a school system's expenses go toward learning social studies or biology. Naturally, tying money so directly to scores puts even more pressure on schools to pare education down to those things the testing industry can easily and cheaply measure.

The California legislature set up the Advisory Commission on School District Budgeting and Accounting, which contracted with one of Wall Street's most famous acccounting firms—Peat, Marwick, Mitchell—to develop a comprehensive scheme for reorganizing California education along the lines of the "systems approach" then in vogue in Washington. Earlier, in 1964, the equally prestigious corporate darling Arthur D. Little Company, a management consulting firm, had submitted a report to the California State Board of Education in which we could read: "As we move toward such comprehensively designed educational programs, the teacher's latitude as an innovator becomes somewhat restricted. As always, the teacher may have ample opportunity to display ingenuity in fulfilling his or her role, but that role will be increasingly defined by overall program design considerations."[6]

On the following page we find: "An era of educational technology also adds new influences to the change process. In particular we see a growing stimulation toward change coming from manufacturers of various kinds of facilities and equipment that can be incorporated in integrated pedagogical designs. One can argue that there have always been companies selling . . . 'hardware' to the school. However, we suspect that educational technology will produce changes in kind as well as in degree of influence by manufacturers."

That is how it happens. State governments buy into glamorous national trends in the federal and corporate worlds and make way for these invasions into local schools, which are bound by the laws of the state and beholden to state funds, even though schooling in America is traditionally a community responsibility.

California schools were targeted as a test case for putting PPBS over nationally. If it won in California, other states would almost certainly follow. Accounting firms stood to make fortunes showing every school district in America how to convert its accounting to this very different and expensive system. Technology manufacturers would then lock into this well-prepared market. In 1970–71 California's Advisory Commission on School District Budgeting and Accounting was trying to implement PPBS as if, in the spirit of the Arthur D. Little report, such a change were inevitable. It was disseminating thousands of copies of its manual, training teachers in PPBS and behavioral objectives, running pilots in some districts, and urging other districts to start the system, although the California Board of Education had not, as required, ratified the adoption of PPBS. This dominance, incidentally, of a state board of education by a state legislature is all too typical.

Not by nature very political, I nevertheless joined a resistance movement organized by educators who felt that the combination of behavioral objectives and PPBS would utterly frustrate our efforts to improve schooling. Those of us who were proposing the integration of all the language arts could see that PPBS budgeting categories would actually *increase* the fragmentation of learning. Reading and writing, for example, would remain separate programs with separate textbook adoptions, since PPBS made learning programs themselves the budget categories and since the more circumscribed the programs, the more easily they could be tested so as to prove their cost-effectiveness. Here is where behavioral objectives would come in—to define a program so that it could be evaluated in this way. Both movements would by their very nature reinforce rote learning and drills with bits and pieces.

We dissenting educators arranged debates around California with representatives of the Advisory Commission, which could then say that all views had been allowed for in their deliberations, just as they made minuscule emendations in their drafts of PPBS to "incorporate" our objections. Significantly, my opponent in these debates was never another educator but usually the chairman of the Advisory Committee, who was simply a professional lobbyist representing the accounting faction, with no previous connection to education. State affiliates of the National Council of Teachers of English held conferences and put out bulletins to warn the teaching profession and the public that an accounting system untested in education, very costly to install, and educationally very controversial was being railroaded through the state to become effective by the very early date of 1972.

In July of 1970, the Central California Council of Teachers of English scheduled a presentation to the California Board of Education and asked me to represent it. The Board knew little about PPBS beyond the glowing reports of the Advisory Commission. Far from improving schools, I said to the Board, adopting the accounting procedures of this systems approach would increase the very bureaucratization and systematization that are education's major problem. I questioned the alleged success of PPBS even in the Department of Defense, where it had not prevented the wings from falling off the F-111 or other expensive debacles. I pointed out further that the emphasis on behaviorism implicit in PPBS would make it almost impossible to carry out the California English Framework recently adopted by the state Board of Education. The questions and genuine interest of Board members showed clearly that they had not heard this case and had not thought about the educational ramifications of PPBS. The Board was obviously letting itself be inched along toward approval by periodic positive reports from the campaign run by the accounting firm.

Here we have a typical conflict between state departments of education and state legislatures. At the same time that the California Assembly was passing bills to tie accountability to behavioral objectives, narrow testing, and such systems as PPBS, the English and language arts specialists in the California Department of Education were starting to publish curriculum guidelines that supported a student-centered approach, influenced by teacher experience, the proposals of the Dartmouth Seminar, and the writings of educators like myself. So just as the state educators were making way for individualization, interaction, and integration, the state legislators were making it extremely difficult for schools to implement such an approach by pushing them back toward standardization, depersonalization, and fragmentation. Trying at once to minister to the child and yet teach to the test, teachers are caught right in the middle of this chronic conflict between professional educators and the elected officials who overrule them.

California never adopted PPBS, and it soon died out. We may have won a battle, but we certainly did not win the war against managerial systems that exploit the public cry for accountability. As television and divorce broke down the hidden middle-class curriculum that had made schools look more effective than they were, the public began to blame the experiments of the 1960s, which actually never got off the ground. The "back to basics" movement set in as part of a general reaction to the whole progressive spirit of the late 1960s and early 1970s. Policy makers translated this outcry into their already preferred narrow accountability programs.

Another campaign coinciding with those for behavioral objectives and PPBS also promised better accountabililty on the grounds that for-profit corporations can teach public agencies how to operate more efficiently. "Performance contracting" was all the rage for a few years in the 1970s. Companies like RCA, Westinghouse Learning Corporation, and Behavioral Research Laboratories would contract with a school district to come in, take over the instruction of a certain activity such as arithmetical calculation or reading comprehension, and raise test scores by a certain amount at so much cost per head. Usually the funding came from one of the federal education entitlements. The moral of the story would be that if you really want to run an enterprise right, do it the way business does, because companies live by the laws of cost-benefit accountability.

For a while this seemed to work in the sense that the scores would rise for the targeted activities. Ironically, a performance contractor was allowed to do all the things that the district would not permit its own staff to do. The outsiders could set up and run their own learning environment in relative independence of the bureaucracy and yet with administrative support. They could use different materials, choose or train their own teachers, reorder the environment, and enjoy precisely that waiving of routines that an experiment requires. Not least among these privileges was an exemption from responsibility for the total learning process. All that counted in the contract were scores for a single activity—not any negative side effects in other areas of learning or in student attitudes. The fact is that *any* party, including the most unimaginative, can nearly always make test scores spurt up in one narrowly delimited activity by specializing in it at the expense of other activities.

Moreover, this looks good only *for a while*. Superficial learning notoriously backslides over the long haul, as evidenced by the declining scores of the same students on the same sorts of tests. One of the nice things about performance contracting was that the very time limit that looked so efficient allowed the company to cash in and check out before the long-term truth became clear. Some contracts included a transitional phase called "turnkey," which stipulated some process whereby this smart company showed how to perpetuate its success once this dumb school was no longer graced by its corporate presence. I called this "turncoat" instead because it represented a betrayal of schools by schools. To get federal money, they bowed to the principle that business knows best.

Suddenly the performance contracting movement began to rapidly unravel. Cases of fraud were appearing regularly in the press. Then it dropped out of sight like a shot. No less than a prestigious establishment think tank put out a report concluding that it was indeed not proving itself: "Generally the evidence indicates that performance contracting was not successful." "The attempt to use incentive contracting in the education area has thus proved to be rather inauspicious."[7]

Performance contractors were licensed to play to its extreme the absurd game of atomizing learning and then teaching to a behaviorist test for each particle. So they perfected one of the great errors of schooling itself as some policy makers determine it. Second, profit motivation simply cannot be locked so directly into enterprises for the common weal, as we should know well enough, God knows, from the examples of defense, energy, and medical care.

Tying test scores directly to money makes accountability boomerang by inviting rather than deterring corruption. Many students and teachers are tempted to cheat when tests are too closely linked to career opportunities or to holding a job. School staffs can make themselves look effective by teaching so insistently to certain tests that they all but give away the upcoming questions or by comparing pre- and post-scores on tests that are not really comparable. The more *particular* the tests, like those based on behavioral objectives, the easier it is for everybody to cheat and to turn accountability into a cover-up.

Most of the federal money for education dried up long ago, but like light from a dead star, behavioral objectives are still with us. It is understandable that a psychology in which people are manipulated from the outside should continue to appeal to some people in government. As funding shifted to the states, which had adopted federal evaluation to get federal money, state legislators perpetuated the practice of holding educators to objectives they were forced to write in an unfitting mode, then of requiring behavioristic tests to measure whether teachers had met their "own" objectives.

To the extent that educators' rebellions have given a bad odor to behavioral objectives, their name and complexion have changed. Like a virus mutating as it meets resistance, this notion of testing and accounting modulated itself into various other forms and settled into schools under names like "performance objectives" or "minimal standards," which assume that students can be tested out on certain "terminal behaviors" (!)

specific enough to establish the cause-and-effect relationship that will prove cost-effectiveness. Later the buzzword was "outcomes."

Behavioral objectives still thrive openly in some quarters, however. The senior editor of a major textbook publishing house, describing a current project to me in a letter of 1991, apologized that one of the company's compromises was to include behavioral objectives, saying that as a former teacher she sympathized with those who had to put up with them but that her company had to include them because virtually all state departments of education (compelled by state legislatures) require them for textbook adoption. This remark catches with telling accuracy the complex that I am saying determines curriculum.

This sort of accountability did not protect the consumer and the taxpayer from the arrogance of Detroit and the Pentagon. Only Japanese competition stopped the monopolistic American automobile industry from putting out uneconomical, deliberately obsolescing cars. Nor has this accountability system ever kept the defense industry from producing equally shoddy products or from outrageously overcharging and overrunning cost estimates. The fact is that such cost-benefit systems do not benefit the *public*, in whose name they are installed; if they benefit anyone, it has to be the managers who impose them and can use them to control an enterprise—or create the illusion of controlling results. The automobile manufacturers may have saved *themselves* some money but not their customers, who paid for more than they got. The question here is cost-benefit *for whom*?

The defense industry has never been interested in saving money, because the money is the public's, not its own, and because it knows that any accountability system is hopeless in a military-industrial complex comprised of various parties who don't want real accounting because it would expose how they are syphoning off taxpayers' money. In such circumstances, a strict-appearing accountability system serves the purpose actually of covering up fraud and waste. If the accounting itself is partially false, after all, how efficient can the accountability be? It may be argued that corruption can spoil *any* sort of accountability and that its existence does not invalidate the method itself. Put another way, if it is true that bad faith and fraud are the real problem—and consider here all the fines defense contractors have paid for fraud, and all the conflict-of-interest charges leveled at managers rotating between government and industry—then no kind of accountability will solve the problem. Only moral people will.

Actually, some kind of fraud is practically bound to occur in management by behavioral objectives when applied to social services. An easily quantifiable objective of, for example, an addiction treatment program is to increase the number of people who stop a certain behavior. It then amounts to a kind of fraud if the subjects merely trade one addiction for another or develop some other negative condition not apparently related to the addiction but actually stemming from the same underlying, still unresolved cause. Too narrowly circumscribing the problem ensures that we will treat the symptoms, not the disease. Tests on which students match like phonemes, choose correct spellings, define words correctly, identify metaphors, create isolated complex sentences, list the three main points in a reading passage, and so on, make schooling fraudulent by posting high scores for particle activities that do not add up to the real goals of actual reading and writing, especially when such tests are labeled "reading comprehension" or "composition."

Virtually all standardized school testing defrauds in this way, the more so as it is influenced by behavioral objectives. The poor performance of school graduates *in society* reveals the real fraud—that even good scores have not amounted to anything like a good education. Many of those youngsters who scored well on all those tests of phonics, spelling, vocabulary, grammar, comprehension, and composition are not functionally literate, and very few of them like or choose to read and write. It is painful to remember how many school superintendents or principals I have known or heard of who, embarrassed by their students' low scores in vocabulary or spelling, have driven their underlings until those particular scores rose while the rest of the language program went to pot.

All this is not mere history, because school reform today is still playing out within this complex of government and business playing to the anxieties of the public and to the weaknesses of a profession only too accustomed to submission. This submission partly obtains in the boss relationship between the makers of law and policy and the employees in the systems they establish. Another reason for this submission—significant but rarely discussed—is the preponderance of women in classrooms and of men in managerial offices from principal to district or state superintendents. Working as a consultant with schools all over the country, one becomes very aware not only of such an obvious constant but of its cumulative effect, which reaches far beyond the obvious. The predicament of schooling mirrors to an important extent the predicament of women, many of whom were raised to abide by male decisions even at the expense of their own ideas or perceptions. You cannot get the full picture of what determines schooling without understanding how traditional female submission abets governmental domination of public education.

Government and industry are no more to blame in this history than the rest of society. Our whole culture has reached a stage of materialism that, though perhaps necessary for evolution, it must also necessarily outgrow. It is in the nature of this materialism that we naturally look to the external life for both benefits and remedies—that is, to such things as law and commerce. Nonetheless, we have to see social and economic problems as also psychological and moral problems that require attention to the inner life. People created the negative conditions of education that we have been surveying here, and people can change them. But self-determination as a society depends on self-development as individuals.

The conditions we have been examining here result from shortsightedness, which we could break down judgmentally if we liked into various sorts of selfishness but which we would more usefully regard as the central issue of education itself, the need for inner growth. Individuals need to feel more connected with each other despite increasing self-consciousness and differentiation. This will not happen merely because it is the rational thing to do; by the time the sheer necessity for it has been borne in on us, it will be too late, because we all want to defer the shedding of selfish materialism, like dying, as long as possible. Only a spiritual impulse will prompt people to shed voluntarily, and this impulse arises from certain experiences of self-transcendence that occur when the inner life is licensed *by the group itself* to discover and fulfill itself. Selfishness and shortsightedness come from not having been allowed to find oneself, seek purpose and meaning, follow out one's own destiny, and recover the unconditioned state of being that makes for real freedom, including the freedom to act morally, a luxury we usually feel we cannot afford.

Selfish materialism is merely a second-best, make-do way of life that people adopt by default because they have not liberated themselves from their initial conditioning. The self-aggrandizing games of power underlying politics and economics parody the self-realization that people really want, just as the human burlesques the divine. We all know that we are fallen gods still bearing somewhere within an infinite capacity that seeks to actualize itself, but the fallen part tries to enact this potential by seizing and wielding power through the acquisition and achievement of external things. Were people to understand that what they seek is far grander than these grandiose dreams, they would make themselves and others far happier. I think it is indeed part of spiritual evolution that many people in government and business are beginning to shift from power *over* others to power *for* others as they perceive that the latter is grander and better fulfills what really impels them. But this perception requires more self-understanding than many yet have. Hence the limited framework of government and economics for education and its reform that we are in the midst of reviewing. Sometimes it takes exposure and even excoriation to help us break through our conditioning into the hardest self-knowledge and the fullest perception of what the lust for power is really about—finding out and living out our latent godship.

6

▲

Top-Down
Posing as
Bottom-Up

Now that we have examined how public education has been determined up to now, we are in a better position to assess the means by which national and state governments have proposed to reform schools. From this critique we can begin to understand what should determine public education in the future and which means might best effect its reform and eventual transformation.

The governmental school reform initiative of the early 1990s based itself on precisely two of the assumptions most responsible for the problems that reform aims to solve. One is that assessment is the instrument of change, because schools teach to tests. The second is that business knows best, because public education is really just another business.

Official School Reform

American educators began to speak of "restructuring" about the same time Soviet leaders began to speak of *perestroika*. Both had come to realize that when officials too far from the scene of an action make key decisions about that action, disaster results. So both embarked on a campaign of decentralization, the Kremlin by deregulating the market and granting autonomy to provincial governments, American school districts by instituting site management and parental choice.

When George Bush decided to become an "education president" and set goals with the governors, however, this decentralization of the local school district was surmounted by a new federal centralization grafted on to an old state centralization. The supporters of his initiative, "America 2000," claimed that a national assessment and a national curriculum would be voluntary, but this was not honest, for state and district school constituencies always clamor for their officials to get on board the Washington train, so strong is the fear of being left out and so great is federal prestige even when not backed up by federal money.

The token funding that America 2000 did pledge—$1 million per congressional district to "reinvent schooling"—was to go only to communities that in turn pledged themselves to America 2000's program for national assessment and national curriculum. The same was true for the school grants that the private sector was to generate through such "philanthropic," "venture capital" foundations as the New American Schools Development Corporation and the Next Century Schools, both of which were dominated by board members of the RJR Nabisco Foundation, which had close ties to America 2000 through another board member, Secretary of Education Lamar Alexander.

Most important of all, *state* governments were locked into the implementation of America 2000 via the governors' National Education Goals Panel and other activities of the National Governors' Association (a member of which was president-to-be Bill Clinton, who helped develop the initiative). Bush bypassed the Democrat-dominated Congress, which he didn't want to ask for money and with which he didn't want to share credit. He allied himself with the governors, because states have increasingly come to control schools. In my experience, the biggest single stumbling block to educational improvement are the state legislatures, because they wield far too much power in education for the little they understand about it. Since the U.S. Constitution does not empower the federal government to administer education, Washington cannot legally enforce national assessment or a national curriculum. So any proposal like America 2000 must depend on the states to carry it out.

Federal and state officials share a common investment in standardized testing: along with funding it constitutes the main way they can control or just get a handle on schools, since local school districts traditionally determine public education in this country. External exams mean external leverage, which elected or appointed officials can always justify on grounds that it is they whom the public is holding accountable for education. But the public usually blames school personnel, and state officials promise to reform schools as if their own decision making were not implicated in school failures. Not conversant with the actual processes of education, not involved in the means, politicians grab hold of the one thing that they can think about and speak to and that concerns their job—the bottom-line results, preferably in the quickly perusable form of test scores.

For little money and less thought, you can become an education president just by claiming to set higher standards. The broad goals that Bush and the governors fantasied for America 2000 constituted a wish list that everybody had been dreaming of for years—schools free of drugs and violence, drastic reduction in dropouts, all adults literate and able to compete in a global economy, all children starting school ready to learn, and all students of grades four, eight, and twelve scoring well on national tests. A press secretary can draft such a list in a half hour. How to accomplish these in the face of massive problems is quite something else. Such a proclamation implied, moreover, that schools had never thought about accomplishing these things and were simply waiting for the president and the governors to tell them what to do.

Unfortunately, this thoughtless initiative is not merely an insincere way of garnering votes but the principal way by which policy makers of good faith also propose to reform education. In 1993 the Clinton administration renamed America 2000 as "Goals 2000: Educate America Act" and asked Congress to enact it by passing into law Bush's national goals, federally chartering the National Educational Goals Panel, and creating a federal body to certify "voluntary" national curriculum standards and assessment. The last was immediately objected to by Janet Emig, chair of the English Standards Board, formed by the National Council of Teachers of English and the International Reading Association to write standards within their professions: "No federal body can legislate our success or failure."[1]

The Bush/Clinton initiative implied that schools had failed in large measure because their standards were too low. Good teachers have always had high standards but have been thwarted in implementing them by external testing. The initiative sacrificed *teacher* standards to standardizing itself, which requires referencing to some old "norms" or to some threshold criteria ensuring that most students will pass. If school standards need to be raised, it is because external testing has set them so low. It was managers, not educators, who saddled schools with "minimal standards," whose original purpose was to protect schools from malpractice suites and other charges of graduating illiterate and ignorant students. "Demonstrating competence" benefits the institution, not the individual, and constitutes more the problem than the solution. Citizens have no obligation to demonstrate their competence to the institution or the state.

America 2000 made much of choice, a magic word in a democratic nation of free enterprise. But committing yourself to a specialized school amounts to far less choice than making up your own personal curriculum in a learning environment that offers the possibility of studying anything, any time, anywhere in the community. The very specialization of magnet schools that makes them attract certain people actually limits choice all while seeming to foster it. You shouldn't have to pick a *school* in order to pick an *interest*. That's an old way of thinking that was fine for the beginning of school reform and looks good to families only if educators don't lay out better possibilities. In other words, really individualizing education *within* each school and *across* schools through a community-wide network of resources would be the only way to realize the ideal of choice. But by putting schools in competition with each other, a scheme such as America 2000 works against the pooling of community resources across schools and other facilities that would make real choice possible.

At the same time, by stipulating only certain "core" subjects—math, science, English, history, and geography—Project 2000 narrowed the concept of curriculum and therefore also limited choice. Arts and foreign languages, for example, were not included in the assessment planned at grades four, eight, and twelve. Nor would proposals to "reinvent schooling" that didn't echo such emphasis and priority be likely to receive development funding. National exams force schools to emphasize these "core" subjects first, the result of which, as all educators know, is that in order to cover themselves securely, schools will neglect other subjects like the arts and foreign languages. Actually, giving the *arts* high priority would be the best means to reverse the depersonalization of schooling that constitutes its largest single problem. Whether considering emotional issues such as alienation and low esteem or the intellectual and motivational difficulties of math and science, the arts provide the best growing medium. But state and federal government is not interested in the arts, because it is dominated by business, which thinks math and science will serve its interests best, along of course with literacy. And a bit of history for patriotism and "our heritage."

Furthermore, stipulating tests of *separate* subjects (a built-in assumption) showed how little authors of America 2000 had thought about the crucial issue of *integrating* learning across the curriculum. Such national exams discourage learning that cuts across traditional subject divisions, whereas the current thinking in professional organizations for teaching the various school subjects emphasizes interdisciplinary education. It's hypocritical to push a strategy based precisely on teaching to tests and still claim that educators remain free to integrate learning so long as students do well on the tests of separate subjects.

Prioritizing and separating subjects also militates against individualization, which requires organizing curriculum around learners rather than subjects. In fact, integrating learning naturally goes with individualizing it, for reasons treated in Part Three. By reinforcing the old subject-centered approach, America 2000 thwarts the student-centered approach that real choice and school reform require. Exploiting the appeal of choice aimed to realize the old conservative goal of funding private schools with public funds. This is why it defined choice merely as family selection among some competing schools, not as learner selection of daily activities from alternatives arrayed across many possible sites and situations.

Theoretically, however, according to the 1991 request for proposals of the New American Schools Development Corporation, experimental schools applying for funding might integrate or individualize the curriculum or even dissociate education from school sites and deploy it across a whole community, as I advocate. But, interestingly, the authors of this manual were inspired to say yes to such possibilities only after their consultants specifically queried about them.[2] Naturally the authors could not exclude such possibilities and still call for proposals to "reinvent schooling." But they either didn't see or wouldn't acknowledge the contradictions between this call and their ultimate goal of a national assessment and national curriculum. It was surely these contradictions that prompted their consultants to question how far they would actually go.

Phi Delta Kappa, the national education fraternity, did a special issue of its organ, *Phi Delta Kappan,* featuring the pros and cons of America 2000. Evans Clinchy and former commissioner of education Harold Howe II both pointed out emphatically there the contradiction between America 2000's rhetoric about futuristic experimentation "from the bottom up" and its insistence on nationalizing curriculum and assessment, which would mold the projects that America 2000 sponsored.[3] (For commentary on the projects that the New American Schools Development Corporation funded for the first year, see page 251.)

Rethinking Schools also critiqued America 2000 in a brace of articles in its issue of March/April 1992. The titles probably typify the view of most multicultural urban educators such as make up the constituency of this independent educational journal published by Milwaukee-area classroom teachers and educators and much consecrated to reform: "Bush's Testing Plan Undercuts School Reforms," "America 2000 is a Plan for Re-Election, Not School Reform," "Who Are These Guys?: Corporate Involvement in the 'New American Schools'," and "The Illusion of 'Choice'."

Whether duplicity or not, the fact is that reinventing schooling is not consistent with a national curriculum, which already dictates what the subjects shall be, nor with national assessment, which in limiting itself to these subjects and to standardizable forms of testing takes any serious meaning out of "reinventing." You can't have it both ways—choice *and* standardization. Enforcing *conformity* as a way to *innovate* characterizes this centralized approach masquerading as grass roots experimentation: "You are free to use any means to reach our goals as measured by our tests."

Testing, Testing, Testing . . .

The issue of *Phi Delta Kappan* featuring America 2000 also focused on accountability as a reform strategy in six articles summarized in a seventh and authored by experts in school reform and assessment. They all had strong reservations about standardized testing in general, the use of such testing to achieve educational change, and the compatibility of America 2000's goals and means with sound assessment. As summarized in the final article, these experts all reached a common conclusion: slow down on testing. But America 2000 had a notably short timetable. In her summary, Milbrey W. Mc-Laughlin framed five statements that the articles expressed in common:

1. It matters what you measure.
2. Don't confuse standardization with standards.
3. Tests constitute a limited lever for reform.
4. Test-based accountability plans often misplace trust and protection.
5. The process of setting standards is as important as the standards themselves.[4]

America 2000 did not arise in education quarters, conspicuously bypassed educators, and was heavily criticized for being pushed through with very little debate even among policy makers themselves. "Go Slow on National Curriculum, Tests, ASCD Warned" read the headline of the May 1991 issue of *ASCD Update,* which featured a report on the annual conference of its parent organization, the Association for Supervision and Curriculum Development, the chief national organization for school principals and superintendents, other district or state administrators, curriculum specialists, and researchers. "With remarkably little deliberation or involvement of practicing educators, the United States appears to be rushing headlong toward a new national assessment system and its implied national curriculum, speakers warned participants." Chris Pipho, an analyst with the Education Commission of the States, which represents governors no less, declared, "I feel very strongly that at this point it is unbridled, running loose, rampant, and so far undebated. . . . If you're opposed to a national test, now's the time to get in gear and head them off at the pass."[5] Other speakers "presented a number of potential problems with a system of common exams: that exams won't be made part of a comprehensive plan to improve curriculum, teaching, and textbooks; that the 'authentic' performance-based exams called for as part of a national assessment are unproven on a wide scale and will be costly; that exam results will not be used to improve instruction for students who do poorly; and that U.S. schools already devote too much time to assessment."[6]

In shifting its focus, between the 1960s and 1990s, from learning to the assessment of learning, government has had to come up with a new rationale for the relationship between the two. It sounds very practical: "If schools teach to the tests, then let's change the curriculum by changing the tests." While still begging the question of why *testing* should be the means of change, this places a premium on replacing old tests with vastly superior ones. A new generation of assessment experts has tried to make standardized testing look respectable again by attacking multiple-choice tests and by claiming that other ways of assessing can measure the highest, most complicated kinds of learning. This position is argued by Lauren and Daniel Resnick, who run the New Standards Project to help implement America 2000.[7]

Superior ways of assessing can indeed take place *in the classroom,* as some teachers have been showing. In other works I have recommended kinds of local evaluation for the language arts (which apply in large measure to other subjects as well) that could indicate to parents and administrators how well students are doing and how well their school is faring.[8] But it's impossible to carry out in the very limited circumstances of the examination room these preferred means of assessment. They are performances, portfolios, and projects, sometimes now called the three P's. Performances refer to authentic activities such as found out of school, not to piecemeal exercises.

It is not at all clear how the new assessors are going to work local portfolios and projects into a universal assessment that permits nationwide, worldwide comparison—that must standardize. The timed performance exams are closest to familiar testing and because of their far greater ease of administration and standardization will certainly overshadow portfolios and projects in any composite assessment. According to the Resnicks, "These exams might consist of substantial essays, laboratory demonstrations, or the use of multiple mathematical methods to solve a complex technical problem."[9] If one is to have exams, these would be laudable, but the more that performance tests might truly measure complex orders of learning that previous ones have not, the more difficult they would be to score and the more they would cost. Administering and scoring such exams would cost exorbitantly, and whichever level of governance wound up with the bill would certainly scale these laudable exams back toward the cheap old computer-scored multiple-choice tests that they can hardly afford now and that new assessors like the Resnicks repudiate. Lower levels of gov-

▲

ernment already bitterly resent having to bear the expense of complying with what higher levels of government require but don't fund.

If you test rarely, as the New Standards Project suggests, you decrease costs only by increasing the chronic dilemma of testing—that the fewer the samples, the lower the reliability. If you're sampling every semester, every year, or—as in America 2000—every four years, you're dipping a minnow net in an ocean and saying, "Here's what's in the sea." Or, as now, you just dam off a tiny tidal pool and dip the net there. The upshot is that even ridiculously few samples of the good sort of performance exams will cost far too much, and since portfolios and projects would be even more problematical and expensive to make part of a national assessment, schools will fall back on the old tests.

Furthermore, because "performance" can be construed more or less narrowly, it can lend itself to the old "objective" testing. Indeed, even the new assessors tend to fall back into talking about short tests demonstrating competence in a particular activity. The giveaway to how much the new performance exams may resemble the old is that, just as the behavioral objectives movement delineated five levels of increasingly specific performance evaluation ending in test questions, the Resnicks speak of four increasingly specific levels of assessment ending with performance tasks and rubrics for scoring them. After describing general standards of performance, "the next step is a task you expect a child to carry out. The standard must therefore be concrete enough to show what a child is expected to learn and to help the teacher know what she needs to do to help the child learn and to show the community the school's expectations. Scoring rubrics then substantiate the standards."[10] Note how the government initiative links up here with the testmakers' need for *standardized specificity*. But even this unwitting, inevitable drift back toward particle behaviors alarms me less than the old assumption that some entity beyond teachers, students, and the community will show these key parties what is to be expected.

Students and teachers don't need tests. Assessment for *learning* purposes is no problem, because the data can be as rich as the learning activities themselves. Teachers can easily monitor performance when they examine student products and witness their processes. Because they work with students over a long period of time, they can make *composite judgments* based on continuous observation across numerous occasions supplemented by periodic conferences. Portfolios and projects are best assessed on site, and no one has any idea of how to standardize the assessment of them for purposes of comparing results around the country or the globe. Good education simply does not require comparing students or schools with each other, the only point of standardized evaluation. The real problem is to get going the kind of *productive* classrooms where authentic performances, portfolios, and projects do in fact thrive. The right curriculum solves the problem of assessment. The reverse is not true, that the right assessment solves the problem of curriculum.

Everything in assessment depends on *how much time and space* it encompasses, on how big the arena of action is. For extremes, compare a problem specific enough for a student to solve in fifteen to twenty minutes on one rare occasion in exam room conditions with, on the other hand, continuous observation of a student's problem-solving abilities across numerous different circumstances. Advocates of behavioral objectives insisted, as we saw, on assessing acts specific enough to manifest entirely on one short occasion and soon enough after a lesson to establish cause and effect. But the higher and more intricate the mental activity, the more difficult it is to capture on one short occasion. Consider the many long-range projects out of school that best represent complex thinking and creative problem solving. Moreover, the accuracy of assessment increases with the number of samples, which is also a factor of spreading performance over time and space. Taking quick samples every four years as in national assessment, or even once or twice a year, makes for skimpy, shoddy assessment even for its senseless purpose of comparing scores around the nation or the world.

Tests are for outsiders, for *their* purposes, some of which are legitimate. In writing and consulting, I suggest that parents and administrators should assess how good their schools are by taking slice-of-life samples of what's going on there, that is, by examining performance for themselves as this manifests in portfolios and other products or as they can hear and see student activities in audiotapes and videotapes. In the long run, however, the laity judges schools mainly by practical outcomes—by how well graduates can handle their lives, their childrens' lives, their jobs, and their civic responsibilities. It is not by test scores but by real-life behavior that the public, including employers, is assessing education. Fair enough. Testing, on the other hand, really just provides fodder for a system of institutional self-monitoring that indicates cheaply and simply where teachers and students should be placed and when they should be moved on. This is a system of routing and promoting, qualifying and disqualifying, including and excluding that should itself be reformed.

Since the whole system of testing comes down ultimately to certifying graduates of all educational institutions for jobs, it is a colossal example of how the private sector foists onto the public sector, at public expense, something that it should be doing, at its own expense. Employers—and colleges too for that matter—should screen applicants themselves by their own means. If they did, schooling could in fact send them better-educated applicants. If that is not ironic enough, consider that school certification now indicates so poorly who to admit or hire that it serves badly anyway even the purpose for which this intolerably high price is paid. The real problem for colleges and businesses is that the education of virtually all applicants has been crippled by the very testing system that is supposed to do their screening for them.

In addition to being obliged to accommodate the College Board and various governmental directives at all levels, school districts *buy* their curriculum and most of their tests from national manufacturers, whose first principle is to sell what has sold. These and other uniformizing forces long ago combined to create a *de facto* national curriculum and national assessment. America *already* has what government is urging today as innovation.

Inasmuch as reason and experience fail to support the promise to measure in a standardized way the complex thinking and creativity that higher standards call for, the national assessment movement has invoked a concept of "calibration," equally unproven, to bridge this credibility gap. Since assessors like the Resnicks champion a national *system* correlating local assessments, as opposed to a single national examination, they have to find a way of mediating between one and the other. Sensing that the more nearly assessment fulfills their claim, the more nearly it will simply resemble what occurs naturally in good learning circumstances, the new assessors are hoping to draw on such local assessment by "calibrating" it to national standards. This way of thinking makes two unfounded promises seem to shore up each other. It promises to policy makers comparability among testees and to educators integrity of learning.

Advocates of calibration point to the high scoring agreement possible among teachers of different regions rating each others' student writing samples by their own rubrics. But by its nature writing eventuates in a distinct and immediate product, which is not true for all kinds of mental activity. Furthermore, for years now teachers all over the country have been learning to rate writing in such similar ways that high reliability in their scoring should occasion neither surprise nor a belief that this experience proves calibration, which for most activities would require comparing across much more dissimilar modes of assessing. The more that the evaluation of writing goes beyond issues of correctness, construction, and documentation and tackles ideas, expression, and originality, the less likely are judges to agree.

Most important, the conditions under which the performance occurs are critical. To continue with the example of writing that calibrators use: because plucking samples from local classroom portfolios would be virtually impossible to control for real comparability, we can be sure that writing samples will be acquired, as usual, by sitting students down in an exam room for a timed period under controlled circumstances. This is the way the National Assessment of Educational Progress, the California Assessment Program, and the College Board do it—all praised for their reliable scoring of whole writing. But certain important kinds of writing, such as investigative reportage, original research, and fiction or poetry, can't be done in a single timed sitting. Nor can most of the recent advances made in the teaching of writing be accommodated, because exam circumstances rule out this "process approach," whereby writing is staged over phases of prewriting exploration of subject and material, workshop interaction, one-to-one conferencing, revisions, and dissemination or other utilization of the product. For any kind of writing, finally, the context of a real purpose and audience drives this whole process. The decontextualized exam model has too long served as the curriculum model.

This raises the general issue that students have no honest motive to do well on exams that merely compare them with each other. In fact, one hears of students revolting against state and national tests by doing them badly on purpose or leaving the test booklets blank. This is even more likely to happen when student performances are not personally identified but merely sampled to monitor the curriculum. Since the main point of standardizing or calibrating assessment is to compare the effectiveness of schools or districts, as a kind of consumer's guide, such sampling, already quite common, will surely dominate testing.

There is no way to make good on the double promise to measure higher orders of thinking, on the one hand, so as to compare far-flung results, on the other. The rich data base of a good learning environment is unbeatable for assessment, which remains one with the learning process itself. As soon as some activity is done only to assess, we know already something is wrong. To claim that external, comparative assessment can measure as well as the classroom, can truly avail itself of the three P's, or can do justice to our highest learning goals is boasting at the risk of fraud. This is a moral issue, because policy makers want to gamble public education on these mere promises.

Of course the subject professions like math, English, and the social studies are invited to develop their own standards and submit them as a basis for national examinations. Educators can be part of the new game so long as they play by the old rules, which are to prepare students across the whole land to take exams permitting them to be compared with one another. Forcing educators to promulgate standards especially for the purpose of standardizing harks back to the behavioral objectives movement, epitomized by the project from which I resigned, although the new assessors believe they are repudiating it and eschew any assessment that decontextualizes and fragments learning. Despite their protestations, they cannot avoid doing just that all over again, because the new movement has the same wrong motive—to control education through standardized external evaluation.

It is the *users* who should assess schooling, not the state. This is the only pertinent and honest accountability. Since to assess is to control, user assessment would restore power to the citizenry. People using public libraries and museums don't take tests. They assess such institutions by saying what they want or what they want changed, by praising and complaining, by supporting them or not. Schools are public facilities that should satisfy their users. Admittedly, the problem is circular in that good public education depends on educating the public. Ignorant people may want some ignorant things. But the way to solve this problem is to educate for choice by helping learners make their own decisions, not to use their ignorance as an excuse to patronize them and decide for them.

Public accountability does not depend on centralized assessment. In fact, accountability loses meaning exactly in the measure that the public allows district, state, and federal governments to structure education from the outside and yet blame schools for poor results. When users set and assess their own curricula, moreover, whatever need there may have been for state and federal intervention to offset local bureaucracy is obviated, along with the need for *any* government to safeguard individual rights. A major purpose of the universal schoolhouse, as we will soon see, is to place control of learning so firmly in the hands of the individual users that the state can henceforward play *only* the role of their facilitator. In any case, future education will have to involve the community so much more than at present that the whole notion of accountability will itself have to be rethought along with the rest of reform.

But why should education be mobilized anyway around the question of national assessment? Why should we even assume that assessment of any sort is a major way to reform schools? Why not mobilize for things that experience *does* indicate, like personalizing learning, integrating the curriculum, renovating teacher training, or organizing community networks? Why not, in other words, focus on the learning environment and learning processes themselves? Why on *assessment?*

The only answer is that elected and appointed officials prefer this mode of operation and overrule educators, who if they support national assessment usually do so on the principle of "fit in or lose out." My observation over the years tells me that the farther people are from the classroom, the more they think standardized testing is the way to improve education. America 2000 was launched by the governors and the president with virtually no forum in Congress, the public, or educators. By the time most people knew what was happening, they could address only the question of how, not whether.

The national professional organizations in math, science, English, social studies, foreign languages, the arts, and other subject areas have since the 1980s been developing and promulgating new standards for the purpose of improving their respective curricula. They naturally want to cooperate with any federal initiative for school reform, despite their reservations, which I have heard strongly expressed by some of their representatives in meetings about standards. In any case, they can't afford to risk not being a part of such a political movement. So they are reluctant to see that they are being trapped, once again, into writing statements that government will use in ways they will find hard to live with once implemented beyond their control.

When you think of all the factors that enter into the success or failure of schooling—many intrinsic to mass public education, many inflicted on schools by an ailing society—to single out assessment seems so arbitrary as to be downright bizarre even without its long history of implication in school failure. Nothing in experience, research, or logic warrants this assumption. It exemplifies quintessentially how the main problem of schooling is still being used as the main solution.

Privatizing Public Education

It's impossible to understand the movement toward a national curriculum, which is not in the American tradition, or the railroading of national assessment, which is a wildly irrational way of dealing with the crisis in schooling, unless you realize how closely this initiative issues from business, state legislatures, and other noneducational managers. For example, the New Standards Project that works so closely with the governors' National Educational Goals Panel is co-directed by Marc Tucker, head of the National Center on Education and the Economy and author of *America's Choice—High Skills or Low Wages?* Business should indeed be served by a good public education, but the higher-order thinking abilities and creative problem solving that it correctly believes graduates now have to bring to the work force are precisely what have most suffered from testing, standardizing, and centralizing—that is, from an education driven by government and industry.

The assumption that comparative testing is the best means for changing schools rests on the equally unfounded assumption that public education will improve if schools operate by free-market competition as businesses are alleged to do. Corporations that were forced to reform themselves to meet the crisis of foreign competition now come on like born-again revivalists: "We did it, so we can show you how to do it." Chrysler's president Lee Iacocca became a folk hero for saving his company when in fact it was taxpayers' money that saved it through a bailout or subsidy that, had it been paid out to a single mother living with her children in poverty, would have been called welfare. Had Chrysler's cost-benefit management by objectives not arrogantly exploited its monopoly with the rest of the Big Three through such practices as deliberate obsolescence, it would have been able to cope with real competition when it finally came—from abroad. Ford would *already* have made "quality job one." Thus endangered, American corporations have indeed had to make some practical changes, true, but not in the direction of a moral conversion.

During recent decades, leading companies in every field—pharmaceuticals, chemicals, defense contracting, automobiles, brokerage, savings-and-loans, insurance—have been convicted or indicted for breaking laws, to the point that industry analysts are saying that even the oldest and most revered names can no longer be trusted. Criminal behavior aside, what about just plain moral behavior? How much honest public concern can we expect from corporations when they fire older employees to renege on paying retirement, keep secret their own unfavorable findings about their products, and mount massively expensive campaigns, paid by the consumer through increased prices of goods, to lobby against environmental protection?

Douglas D. Noble, the author of *The Classroom Arsenal: Military Research, Information Technology and Public Education,* did brief profiles of members of the board of the New American Schools Development Corporation as a way of asking, "Are these really the people we want to have shaping our children's schools?" *

> Norman R. Augustine, CEO of Martin-Marietta, formerly served in six positions at the Department of Defense, including undersecretary of the Army. According to *Business Month,* he has "played a key role in the shaping of the modern U.S. arsenal," and remains a "consummate insider" in U.S. defense policy. . . .

* This extract is reprinted with the permission of *Rethinking Schools* (Douglas D. Noble, "Who Are These Guys?: Corporate Involvement in the 'New American Schools'," March/April 1992, p. 20), 1001 East Keefe Avenue, Milwaukee, WI 53212.

James K. Baker is vice chairman of NASDC, CEO of . . . Arvin Industries, and a founding member of Commit, Inc., a business group involved in Indiana school reform. According to *Education Week*, Indiana Teacher organizations are currently engaged in "all out war" with Commit, whose adversarial agenda "confirms the worst fears public educators hold about their new and powerful partner. . . ."

Frank Shrontz, vice chair of NASDC and CEO of Boeing, . . . a major defense contractor, served in the 1970s as both assistant secretary of defense and assistant secretary of the Air Force. In the past year, Shrontz has been battling Washington state teachers to prevent "fair tax" legislation that would increase Boeing's taxes by $500 million, with much of the money targeted for the state's beleaguered schools. . . .

Kay Whitmore [is] CEO of Eastman Kodak, . . . which has been reeling in the past few years from [among other things] huge fines for patent infringements and environmental pollution. . . .

Louis Gerstner, Jr., vice chair of NASDC and CEO of tobacco-food conglomerate RJR Nabisco, is known for his marketing genius. As former president of American Express, he . . . exploited an elitist image with the slogan "membership has its privileges." Gerstner was hired as CEO of RJR Nabisco by the firm whose leveraged buyout of RJR was called by *Time* magazine "the worst display of greed since the . . . robber barons." The buyout has also been immortalized in such books as *Barbarians at the Gate* and *True Greed*. Since taking charge, Gerstner's top priority has been to

stem the erosion of cigarette sales, which account
for over 60% of the firm's operating income.
Under his leadership, the company has recently
been hit with several scandals: its targeted marketing toward poor black youth and young, white,
working-class females; its aggressive cigarette ex-
ports to Third World populations; and . . . its exploitation of young people through its "Old Joe
Camel" advertising campaign. Meanwhile, the
RJR Nabisco Foundation has channeled $30 mil-
lion into its own Next Century Schools program,
a prototype of NASDC that funds model ventures
stressing extended schooling, productivity, and
strict accountability.[11]

America 2000 proposed that, under such people, the New
American Schools Development Corporation should fund and
guide the research and development of experimental projects
to reinvent schooling.

Behind this federal sponsoring of partnership between public
schools and for-profit companies lies tremendous anger among
businesspeople that their efforts to survive in global competition are being thwarted by poorly educated employees. Their
efficiency experts have convinced them, as they did earlier regarding company alcoholism, that remedying employees is
more cost-effective than turning over employees—in this case,
to find ones who can communicate, collaborate, and cogitate.
Companies are furious about having to pay both school taxes
and the costs of running their own schools to do what public
education should be doing. They have a just complaint here.
The best way to respond to it, however, is to reform schooling
the most effective way, considering *all* educational goals.

Business does not know what is best for schooling, and it is
suffering no more from poor education than the rest of the

society, including individuals. As a stakeholder and as a possible learning resource, it should indeed participate in school reform, but it has too narrow a perspective and too limited a motive to guide it. Results would be skewed and not even in its own interest. Many local businesspeople who chat with the high school principal every Monday at the Rotary Club do feel genuinely concerned about the common welfare of their town and may indeed want to help its schools do more than merely shunt them the kind of employees who will enhance their profits. But in any profession there are few minds as big as that of Edwin Land, the inventor of Polaroid, who not only founded one of the most successful companies in entrepreneurial history but also set up within it a school for the personal development of employees, decades before efficiency experts were advising it for more self-serving reasons. He apparently agreed with what I tell schools: staff development is self-development. Anything else is shortsighted shortcuts. There do exist other business executives who, like Land, have fulfilled their own humanity enough to try to help others develop in both schools and corporate life. Unfortunately, they are yet too rare to place business in a mentor relation to schools. Both the corporate model and its money are dangerous.

The government's conviction that business can show schools how to set their house in order derives not only from a concern about the employability of the populace but from the old false analogy that running schools is like manufacturing and marketing commodities. When Lee Iacocca addressed the Association for Supervision and Curriculum Development (ASCD) at its annual convention in May 1991, he said, "Your product needs a lot of work, and in the end, it's your job." His tough attitude on the problem of the increasing numbers of children in poverty was that "your customers don't want to hear about your raw materials problem—they care about results." So children are raw materials. After complaining that Chrysler spends $60 million for school taxes and still has to teach basic skills to many workers, he likened graduating a student who can't read to selling a car without an engine: "It's massive consumer fraud." (How good it must have felt to be able to level against another "industry" the charge that has so often been leveled at his.) He pursued the theme of consumerism: "Right now, American education has a lot of dissatisfied customers."[12]

Comparing children to metal, rubber, and plastic is hard to forgive. Comparing human growth to factory production implies the putting together of inert parts into subassemblies that eventually go into that final assemblage, the product. This applies an inorganic, particle approach to an organic, holistic process. But what irrational thinking anyway to compare students to products when these "products" are also the "consumers," both as students and later as parents and taxpayers. Furthermore, these consumers are tax-paying voters who also *run* schools—much more, as I've tried to show, than we admit. Chrysler's customers don't run the company. What possible sense can this analogy between school and business make when the raw materials, the products, and the consumers are all one and the same—the citizens?

Unfortunately, it is part of current executive thinking to lump all large enterprises together from a purely managerial viewpoint and thus to ignore the actual nature of each enterprise. Managing is managing, it is thought, regardless of whether the organization is a foundation, a government agency, a for-profit company, or a public institution. Manufacturing executives think they can tell an education system what it ought to do because they look on schooling as just another outfit to run. But what the outfit *does* is critical.

A politically conservative educational initiative, both Republican and Democratic, classifies education with other consumerism in order to push privatization, which is the real goal of its "school reform." At his ASCD talk, Iacocca also said, "Peo-

▲

ple are not just going to settle for an inferior product—they
want to shop around."[13] There it is, the free-market concept
of education whereby the parental choice among public magnet
schools is extended by vouchers to private schools. Thus conservatives can graft privatization onto school restructuring.
After all, wasn't free enterprise the way for *perestroika* to cure
the ills of the Soviet Union?

In the same month that Iacocca addressed ASCD, *Harper's*
ran an article describing Britain's national curriculum and national assessment, quickly installed by the beginning of the
1990s at Prime Minister Margaret Thatcher's behest by her
education secretary, Kenneth Baker, whom she later made
chairman of the Conservative Party and then Home Secretary.
"Thatcher and Baker chose to see education as an enterprise
that could be made more efficient by making schools subject
to market forces."[14] The British appear to be unembarrassed
by privatization of their educational system, which has always
combined both public and private schools, but their teachers
are now complaining that they can't teach for testing. In America the advocacy of vouchers incorporating private schools into
public education remains controversial. The privatization of
schooling thus proceeds unannounced as such but clearly
marked by proposals to encourage business to fund school
projects, to extend parental choice to private schools, and to
throw all schools into free-market competition.

A full-page ad in the same issue of *Harper's* that contained
the article on Britain's national curriculum bares the strategy
of parlaying school restructuring into privatization: "A well-
established practice from the business world could do wonders:
management by exception. . . . Deregulate and decentralize.
Encourage teachers to design and implement teacher coopera-
tives or collaboratives. Give principals the authority they need
to run schools without red tape. Permit parents to choose
the public school their children attend. In short, permit

schools—some of them at least—to be market-sensitive."[15]
The company paying for the ad was a prime defense contractor,
Rockwell International; one author of it was a nominee for
deputy secretary of education, and the other was coauthor of
*Winning the Brain Race: A Bold Plan to Make Our Schools
More Competitive.*

National assessment and national curriculum contradict this
call for deregulation and decentralization, which are being used
here to justify competition among schools considered as businesses. Decentralization of education need have no connection
whatsoever with "free-marketing" it, since education could
perfectly well decentralize and remain totally public. What enables the ad authors to modulate from the now popular idea
of decentralized schools to their ultimate idea of "market-sensitive" schools is precisely the deceptive confusion between the
public and private sectors. For *business,* decentralization of
government does mean deregulation, which can indeed create
a free market. But it is not just the false analogy between the
two sectors that, once again, misleads. It's also the boast that
business holds the patent on "management by exception,"
which presumably means creative thinking that waives bureaucratic rules. Since when does business practice this in an exem-
plary way? And for whose benefit if it does?

It's of course true that, since government regulates business
far less than it does education, business is freer to develop and
exercise creativity. That freedom defines, in fact, much of the
difference between the public and private sectors. This should
give business a reason to help liberate schools from regulation,
which the ad purports to do, not prolong it, as national assessment and a national curriculum will certainly do in providing
the score comparisons on which free-market schooling would
be based. The ad argues for freeing teachers and principals
from *school district* centralization but not from control by *state
and federal* government, with which large corporations are

more naturally allied. School districts respond more to local businesses, which are more apt to include total community welfare in their aspirations for schools than Rockwell International.

In both Britain and the United States, the nationalizing of education through testing is a move to cut money for social services, the biggest of which is schooling. The ostensible motive is accountability, to get more out of schools while putting no more into them. Conservative constituents want to get their children out of public schools and send them to private schools without paying for both, or at least to get them out of the worst public schools into the better ones. Teachers of English to Speakers of Other Languages (TESOL), which tends to look from the viewpoint of minorities or poor people much more than other educational subject organizations do, spotted immediately the bias toward more affluent families: "What about children of parents who don't have transportation options? Who can't pay the difference between their voucher and the private school tuition? Who can't read the brochures comparing the schools they may choose from? Who are so busy with two or three jobs that they can't visit the schools to make a choice?"[16]

The article in *TESOL Matters* in which this comment appears cites 1991 Teacher of the Year Jeffrey L. White, who asserts that school choice presupposes good and bad schools and therefore favored and unfavored children. The article continues: "Providing seed money for innovative schools is an exciting concept, yet the New American Schools are limited in advance by the requirement of consensus on World Class Standards and the focus on scoring well on the 'National Achievement Tests.' Bush's recommendations for leadership in this process muffle the voices of educators, parents, and students while amplifying the voices of business officials and politicians."[17]

In the issue of *Rethinking Schools* cited earlier as focusing on America 2000, one article reports that the Pennsylvania legislature rejected a plan to provide a $900 voucher to attend either a public school in another area or a private school because the amount would discriminate against the poor, $900 being too little to pay tuition at most private schools.[18] Another article says that the 1991 Massachusetts choice plan "flatly encourages students to leave poor districts for rich ones" since "the 'home' districts are charged a 'tuition' roughly equivalent to the per-pupil expenditure in the receiving district."[19]

In the lead article, "The Illusion of 'Choice'," Robert Lowe makes similar charges of inequity and cites a host of other reasons why vouchers for private schools will not work as claimed. Reminding us that conservative economist Milton Friedman first proposed this voucher system in the 1950s, and citing the results of the Milwaukee Parent Choice Program, which the Wisconsin superintendent of public schools opposed, Lowe refutes point by point John Chubb and Terry Moe's *Politics, Markets, and America's Schools,* the bible of the free-market movement in school reform.[20] As Lowe points out, "This market ethos ignored any responsibility for other children's education, any obligation for community control of education, any commitment to schools as sites of democratic discourse."[21] (When California placed a proposition for school vouchering on its ballot in 1993, this issue of *Rethinking Schools* was reinforced into a sixteen-article special booklet that included Herbert Kohl, Jonathan Kozol, and Deborah Meier among the opponents of vouchering. This proposition, opposed by both Governor Pete Wilson and President Bill Clinton, lost decisively.)

Comparing schools, which otherwise seems irrational as a way to improve them, makes perfect sense when viewed from the standpoint of a constituency of businesspeople and conservatives. In theory, test scores will expose ineffectuality, spur the bad schools to shape up, and permit parental choice by identifying the good ones. Only hidden motivation can account for such sloppy thinking. It is obviously not mere dereliction and the need to be exposed that cause school failure. In any case, comparative testing cannot possibly be a fair way to sort schools for efficiency because too many local factors determine success and failure, many of which—such as population, local history, and material resources—schools have no control over.

This "market-sensitive" approach will simply increase the differential between good and bad schools, not improve overall quality, because nothing intrinsic to better learning will necessarily have occurred. Most private schools to whom some ghetto students have been admitted on vouchers run essentially the same curriculum as do the public schools from which the students have been rescued, but they have smaller classes, little bureaucracy, and a more serene atmosphere—all attributes that reform should bring to public education. Were these private schools to be incorporated into the public system or enlarged enough to make room for other lucky refugees, they too would come to resemble regular schools unless the whole system were reformed. A few havens for the favored prove nothing.

In other words, we can't afford to have *any* bad schools. There is nothing efficient or cost-effective about polarizing an educational system this way. *All* schools must improve. In the gloating about the superiority of capitalism over communism, we are glossing over some nasty unresolved problems of free enterprise, most of which amount to this: capitalism is a system of winners and losers, and the number of losers is growing in America, whether measured by unemployment, poverty, crime, addiction, or the many other social ills. Losers in business may be acceptable and necessary but not in education.

Such conservatives don't want to accept that being a winner means paying for the losers that the system itself entails. Applying free-market thinking to education sacrifices some children to others. Inefficiency becomes an excuse for inequality. Public education should offer choice among alternative ways of learning and alternative things to learn *within* each school or *across* schools, not choice merely between good and bad schools. It should never be necessary to shop for a good school or send your child way off somewhere or pine for a private school. Actually, many voucher systems, like the one proposed in California, allow private schools to reject applicants, which encourages them to screen out low-scorers and other problem cases who will make them look bad. In this system, schools choose, not families.

And how far are you going to carry free enterprise into education? Will the failed schools file for bankruptcy? What do you do with them? And the children still stuck in them? Imposing the rules of the private sector on the public sector destroys the point of the public sector, which is to act collectively for the benefit of all. The failures of both communism and capitalism should spur us to think beyond both and to draw our educational models from other realms than politics and economics, whose models play all too easily into the hands of the less-evolved elements of any society. Only the spiritual perspective truly gathers in everyone, as communism claimed to do but as its very materialism prevented it from doing.

The idea that business knows best and that education should imitate the secret of its "success"—competition—underlies the movement toward national assessment. This approach to reform is faulty from one end to the other—from the initial assumptions to the consequent strategies. If rationalization were not standing in for rationality, and were it not backed by government and business, this line of thinking would not even have to be refuted. It is simply not true that educators have no idea of how to improve learning unless their dereliction is exposed and they are forced to cast about for something better.

The Right Means Are Right Here

The real truth about school failure is that we educators aren't doing what we know to do. To take the example of my own field of literacy and language arts, the profession has periodically pointed out and tried to rectify fundamental problems.[22] The right things to do in literacy have been around for decades and could give us a nation of readers any time we could succeed in *implementing* them. For nearly a century language educators have cyclically proposed integrating the language arts and putting the productive activities of speaking and writing on a par with the receptive activities of listening and reading. I had been crusading for such changes some time before I realized that my counterparts of earlier generations had also done so—and also failed. In *The Struggle to Continue: Progressive Reading Instruction in the United States,* Patrick Shannon traces through examples the strong advocacy of progressive or alternative literacy education in America for more than a century.[23]

We have to ask why the changes that educators themselves propose for literacy never happen. The reasons are systemic. Listening and reading suit bureaucratization and politicization better—textbooks and testing, compartmentalization and standardization, the control of student behavior and thought. Authentic speaking and writing are much harder to control and centralize, precisely because they are *productive* and thus shift decision making to the learner. Yet learning to read through writing is one of the most promising roads to literacy. In the 1920s and 1930s some educators championed other badly needed practices such as individualized or free reading, which would likewise have greatly improved literacy learning but also never became more than marginal methods, especially in secondary schools. It too challenges centralized control, like individualized learning generally, whether that control is wielded by the state or the teacher. Yet individualization may more nearly meet the needs of reform than any other single practice.

One of the most oft-repeated slogans of today's reform effort in math and science asserts that "Less is more"—meaning that instead of mistakenly trying to incorporate all the new knowledge in these fields, schools should cover more thoroughly fewer topics selected for their representation of the field. In 1913 Alfred North Whitehead wrote, "Mathematics, if it is to be used in general education, must be subjected to a rigorous process of selection and adaptation. . . . It must . . . deal directly and simply with a few general ideas of far-reaching importance."[24] On the broader question of curricular integration, which educators likewise advocate repeatedly, Whitehead wrote in 1916, "The solution which I am urging is to eradicate the fatal disconnection of subjects which kills the vitality of our modern curriculum. There is only one subject-matter for education, and that is Life in all its manifestations. . . . Unless quadratic equations fit into a connected curriculum, of course there is no reason to teach anything about them."[25]

In *What Are Schools For?: Holistic Education in American Culture*,[26] Ron Miller brings out a powerful continuity across two centuries of American educational reform movements, which keep reasserting a holistic, person-centered learning based on spiritual rather than on merely economic or academic concerns. Miller founded the *Holistic Education Review*, which recounts and critiques both past and present efforts to integrate the learning of all subjects around the total growth of individuals, as pioneered in the Montessori, Waldorf, and certain other private schools. Only in late 1991 did the educational subject organizations for English, math, science, social studies, and the arts ever form a national organization (the Alliance for Curriculum Reform) to work together toward a coherent curriculum. This welcome though belated coalition faces the wrenchingly difficult task of remagnetizing the lines of force in the learning field, across subjects and around the learner, a job that should have been done generations ago, as many educators proposed. Don Glines of the Educational Futures Project in Sacramento has described many highly experimental educational projects of the past that died out but that advocated or attempted school reforms still not implemented or supported today.[27] We have to understand the real reasons why the efforts of educational innovators from the eighteenth century to the present day have consistently failed.

It is simply not true that educational change awaits new ideas or higher goals or more information. What we know to do far exceeds what we are free to do. Neither more research nor assessment data nor bright ideas will improve public education if we can't act on what we already know. The blockages are the key. Thus I have dwelt on *why* known good things do not occur. Unless you analyze and remove the obstacles to the good ideas we have, educational reform is impossible. Some blockage is built into professional thinking, namely, the division of learning into traditional subjects. Even though it's true that defending their respective academic turfs prompts some educators themselves to oppose curricular integration, this thinking itself is systemic, because, as students themselves, educators were compelled to observe these boundaries and later to invest in an academic specialty in order to pursue a career in education.

From years of working with educators in the classroom, in district and state offices, and in the university, I know very well what constitute obstacles within the profession, but the more deeply I've been forced to consider the roots of professional inadequacy, the more I'm led back out into the society. From a shallow critique of schooling we could easily blame poorly qualified teachers. But until schooling begins to metamorphose into a humane, creative garden of learning, public education will continue to attract too few of the best people into the profession and thus force itself to accept many who are poorly qualified. It takes hundreds of thousands of people to staff the nation's schools. In order to recruit the bulk of such a large corps from among top-choice people, the society would have to drastically reform the negative conditions of schooling that repel many such people today. This means changing how public education is determined. Many heroines and heroes do go into schools, and some of the more saintly among them even stay, but too many of them burn out and leave or sell out and resign themselves to doing a lot they do not believe in and to not doing what they know to do.

Merely blaming school people will change nothing. They need help from a society that will take responsibility for what they cannot control. Current cries for reform appear to them as "teacher-bashing," as not only ascribing educational failure entirely to them but as also demanding that they penitently shoulder the burden of reform *in addition to* an already impossible set of responsibilities. When leading teacher workshops on innovation, I am very careful to make clear that school reform has to be part of a bigger social reform going beyond teachers' jurisdiction and that innovation must solve the problems teachers already face, not merely add a new level of difficulty and frustration. Successful reform will work in the measure that it so changes educational conditions as to attract more of the people who will *make* it work.

The assumption that educators are nonplussed and that schools have to be remedied from the outside not only generates a tremendously negative feeling among teachers, who already suffer from being political footballs in a top-down approach, but it stymies still further the implementation of what school people do in fact already know to change. The mandate to reinvent schooling does not mean we have to scrap everything and start from scratch. Most of the desired reform could be achieved simply by throwing out unjustified practices now filling the curriculum and pulling together into a unified learning field the many excellent practices that generations of educators have advocated, a few of which certain schools have already managed to implement in bits and pieces, often under special circumstances. Imagine the exasperation of those educators who *have* begun successful changes only to have government announce with a flourish of trumpets that it is going to reassert even more strongly the standardized testing and other centralization that such experimental enclaves have fought to waive in order to succeed.

Formalization and centralization may have served a worthy purpose before teaching became a serious profession, in the Prussia of Frederick the Great or in the Massachusetts of Horace Mann. Considering, however, the sophisticated operations of today's professional educational organizations like the American Federation of Teachers or the subject organizations like the National Council of Teachers of Mathematics or the International Reading Association, it is no longer necessary, and downright destructive, for government to continue to insist on uniform standards for teachers and students, to define the curriculum subjects, and to decide for schools what evaluation and hence, de facto, what methods and materials they should use. Government officials should ask teachers, "What can we do to help you?" And listen. But at the same time, they should urge communities to generate forums to discuss their total educational needs and resources.

The best ways of learning are not recondite exotica. They are taking place all around us all the time, if not often in public schools, then in some private schools. But if not in any schools at all, then everywhere else—at home, in the workplace, on the playground. People are learners, and they are learning all the time. We already know what works. More practical evidence exists for effective learning than special research could ever tell us. The prospect for reform is much more positive than it looks: find out how to act on what we know about learning, and don't let politics and economics obscure this obvious practical knowledge staring us in the face from the whole environment.

PART THREE

▲

The Universal
Schoolhouse

The first step toward creating a community learning network for all ages and all purposes is probably to convoke a fully representative long-term forum among public agencies and private parties to describe what its common education must be capable of doing today. What characterizes the community and the larger society of which it is a part? What are the personal and social needs? What would a learning system have to become to meet these needs? Next, the community can brainstorm about what learning resources it can muster toward the needs it is identifying. This book itself is meant to serve such a forum and in this section I offer particular suggestions for making a whole community and the world itself a schoolhouse.

This school without walls is universal in several senses. It is truly a common school in giving everybody access to everything at public expense. Through this self-directing, self-assessing learning process people may pursue any and all educational goals because, on the one hand, it adjusts infinitely to individual needs and, on the other, it draws on every available resource outside the individual. It takes place everywhere feasible in the community and elsewhere when possible, if not physically then at least electronically. It takes place through inexhaustible permutations of individuals of different age and knowledge. Such a system cannot fail anyone, simply because it is endlessly tunable and correctable for the benefit of and at the behest of the learner, who is constantly helped by a variety of advisers to determine what she or he needs. Part of what is universal about this schoohouse is its *pluralism*. It offers God's plenty and leaves selection to the learner.

This schoolhouse is universal in order that it may be not only democratic but also spiritual. Individualization is inherent in spirituality, which requires developing all levels of one's being toward self-realization and self-transcendence. If learners are to practice decision making of this order, everything has to be in the repertory of choice, bounded by nothing less than the metaphysical and the cosmological. By requiring nothing, this schoolhouse makes everything possible. The consideration of nonmaterial realms, of alternative realities, is thus kept open, not ruled out of education because the state is barred from sponsoring religion. In this common, open learning field, minds are thereby licensed to integrate practical and academic learning with the quest for ultimate purpose and meaning in life. The schoolhouse is the cosmos.

Obsession with immediate material problems may dominate forums if participants don't maintain this broader spiritual perspective. Too often community deliberations arrive at something little different from what already exists, because they are too cursory and are dominated by ideas and factions from the past. Keeping up with what other educational experiments are thinking and doing should help offset this, and special efforts should ensure that a forum utilizes advanced thinking from all sources. But advanced thinking within limited frames of reference can simply make some wrongheaded avenues look more attractive. It is crucial to enlarge the framework to the fullest, as treated in the first two parts of this book.

What I will propose now are some ways a community learning system might come into being and operate, with the understanding that all while using these guidelines, local people will have to work things out in different ways. As an old troubleshooter in harried schools, my inclination is to make suggestions as specific as possible in order to help the most. But since community learning systems will have to evolve from different particular circumstances, it's unwise to try to specify measures below a certain level of generality that can apply to most communities. And some important issues cannot be clearly enough foreseen to decide on until implementation is under way. In fact, educational reform as societal and personal transformation will have to last indefinitely.

7

▲

Good Methods
Already Known

Consider now any desirable educational practices that once existed in and out of school or that exist in and out of school now. The methods of the new educational culture will not so much be new in themselves as new to schools, or to schools in our time, or to those schools that have striven to implement them but never succeeded. A starting point, in short, is to catalogue all the ways that we know people learn.

Universal Learning Activities

Certain basic and universal activities are natural learning methods. We all register realities directly, for example, by *witnessing* what is going on, whether adventitiously as children imprinted willy-nilly by the environment or deliberately as adults seeking experience (through travel, for example). A related way of learning—*attuning*—goes beyond merely registering. Through familiarity or affinity or a developed sensitivity, one empathizes with, tunes in to, a person, place, or thing.[1] *Imitating* moves learning from receptivity toward action and is thus enormously important. We also learn a great deal about things and how to do things by *helping* someone more experienced. We can take an even more active role and learn by *collaborating* with a co-worker or co-player. We learn social and material realities simply from *interacting* with other people and the environment. Witnessing, attuning, imitating, helping, collaborating, and interacting occur so spontaneously, just as part of living, that we seldom think of these six basic learning activities as education. Most often they occur in some combination, as in play and work, which are major and composite ways of learning.

It may be useful to distinguish these unplanned ways of learning from deliberate efforts to acquire knowledge. If, for example, we manipulate the environment so as to cause something to happen just so that we can witness the results, we are *experimenting*, a learning activity not only of scientists but of children, whose play frequently consists of doing things to see what will happen. Children don't necessarily think of this play as learning, because such exploring is instinctual, as with lower animals. Experimenting brings together several of the spontaneous learning means, such as witnessing, attuning, and interacting.

A major deliberate learning method consists of *transmitting* knowledge through language or other symbols. Oral cultures transmit through talk, usually combined with witnessing and imitating, or through other symbolic media such as drawing, modeling, and constructing. Ancient peoples built into their friezes, steles, statuary, megaliths, mazes, gardens, pyramids, and temples their knowledge of astronomy, geometry, biology, or history. Literate cultures add to physical and oral transmission the passing on of knowledge through books, and high-tech cultures add to both the storing of knowledge in computerized data banks and in archives of audio and visual recordings. *Investigating* makes use of all means, from witnessing and experimenting to interviewing other people and researching the symbolized information transmitted from the past.

Various societies have combined some of these basic learning activities into organized educational practices that we will look at shortly as assets that can be further combined into a total and universal learning environment. One such practice, for example, is *apprenticing*, which brings together witnessing, imitating, transmitting, helping, collaborating, and interacting. Informally, we all grow up apprenticing to various activities that we more or less master. But it is clear that a method like apprenticing can fulfill itself only outside of a classroom or schoolhouse. Different methods befit different arenas or, at any rate, will benefit more or less from arenas of different scope.

Concentric Learning Arenas

Along with the *how* of learning we need to consider the *where*. Change will continue to occur concurrently in arenas of varying scope:

- The self-contained classroom
- An enclave or department within a school
- Throughout a whole school
- Across a school and its feeder schools
- Throughout a whole school district or community
- Across far-flung networks, national and international

These concentric arenas of learning encompass not only different extents of time and space and numbers of people but also different jurisdictions ranging from the sole teacher to a teacher group to the principal and on to district staff, superintendent and school board, state staff and legislature, and so on. Restructuring consists partly of changing this hierarchical jurisdiction, and certainly the goal I have in mind is to merge these arenas so that the community becomes the classroom. But during the transition, changes will have to occur at all levels simultaneously until they all coalesce. Each arena will act as a model for the others up to a point, but the smaller the arena and jurisdiction, the more limited the changes that can occur there without changes above.

What a community is may itself be defined by various scopes but would presumably be some continuous living area. Once organized as such, this community might then see itself as part of a more extensive community not contiguous but technologically joined aross time and space. The limits of any community can be extended through electronic networking. The isolated sheep stations of Australia have long used radio for schooling, but now fax mailing, conference calling, and electronic telecommunication via modems and satellites enable small and remote communities to become part of larger ones. Thus individuals might program their education within a local community that was concentric with broader learning networks. It is important to keep in mind the concentric, as contrasted with hierarchical, nature of these successively broader arenas, especially when considering how various governments or other organizational jurisdictions may relate to each other.

The smallest arena that public education has come up with is the one-room schoolhouse. It naturally fostered cross-age teaching and small-group learning because it contained a broad span of maturity levels. The teacher could not work with all students at once, but they could offset this problem by passing on what they learned among themselves. Having to differentiate lessons for different ages, the teacher enlisted older students to tutor younger, and it was natural anyway for the younger to seek aid from the older because the teacher was often occupied with others. The age diversity prevented the teacher from lecturing and forced the dispersal into small groups who had to work independently until the teacher came around to them. The one-room schoolhouse was not a bad model so far as a self-contained classroom goes. It made maximum use of the human resources on hand, but it had few resources from outside except the occasional visitor or class visit outside. It did set a precedent for collaborating in small peer groups, for younger students buddying up with older ones, and for the teacher as roving consultant—methods regarded today as innovative when in fact they are reactionary.

The main problem is how to facilitate these and other learning dynamics across the expanded space and time of a whole urban or rural locality where the number of people, and their age range, will be much greater. Schools did not quit mixing ages for educational reasons but because they got bigger. Size led not only to segregating students by ages but also to segregating subjects, to specialization, for as the number of students increased in a school so did the number of teachers. Just as the students were divided into grades, teachers were specialized into subjects.

In upper elementary school, students increasingly have separate teachers for reading, social studies, math, art, and science. In the middle grades these teachers are set off in different classrooms where students meet them only for certain periods in the school schedule. Finally, in high school and college, the classes become so specialized into courses that only a few are required and most become elective. Courses, furthermore, are tailored to fit students of different standard abilities and so are usually sequenced into separate tracks such as academic and vocational or simply fast and slow. Of course students have gained from access to more specialized teachers. The trick of the future is to expand this advantage while offsetting the compartmentalization that greater numbers also brought on.

It is useful in this regard to notice how schools have tried to overcome the disadvantages of increased population. Students were, and often still are, assigned several years running to a homeroom, which anchors them to an island in the flux of changing subjects and teachers. In this home, one has a family, a group of students and a teacher who remain together for several years and relate to each other more personally than academically. Students often help each other there with homework, however, or discuss school problems, and the teacher advises individuals about their program of activities.

The larger and more complex the school becomes, the more it tends to build up a special counseling staff—the second resort—expert in advising students on how to get around in the bureaucracy and make best use of the resources. School families will be of great importance in the expanded learning network, to help individuals capitalize on the network without getting bewildered by it. Young learners need a secure people base from which to venture and return and which will always help them navigate. Homerooms and counselors can provide surrogate siblings and parents, but the conception of their role has to expand along with the learning network.

A third resort in dealing with a large student population is simply to break it down into smaller organizational units that reduce the amount of counseling needed and allow staff to remain teachers. Often today a large school will be subdivided into alternative subschools, different organizations sharing the same site. The problem here is that the smaller these become, the more they approximate the limitations of the one-room schoolhouse. Fewer teachers means fewer subjects. For this reason many alternative schools specialize in the arts, say, or in math and science. By attracting students from different neighborhoods and socioeconomic groups, such magnet schools may be employed also to achieve by this voluntary mixing a degree of racial integration. Though necessarily limited so far by the fact that other schools and the whole community are not available to them, some alternative schools have at least begun to solve some of the practical problems of how to organize for multiple learning opportunities and for personal decision making.

During the 1970s, when several cities received special federal funding to experiment with alternative schools, my two daughters attended several in Berkeley, California. Thus, while consulting as a curriculum developer around the country, I was also involved in the movement as a parent. Both daughters attended at one time or another both a subschool on a traditional campus and a separate school set off on its own site. For some time I served on the parent-teacher governing board of one of the off-campus schools. Even where many alternative schools existed in the same district, they had massive problems trying to function very differently in a system that itself remained unchanged and therefore unaccommodating.

Some of the schools, content to be self-contained, specialized in a certain kind of student—urban minority or white liberal, for example—or, like the later magnet schools, in a certain content—performing arts, social or environmental activism, or traditional academics. The more general alternative schools floundered because the staff had no training and little experience in personalizing learning. All the alternative schools competed for money, space, staff, and materials, instead of generating a network of educational resources available to all, which would have required restructuring the district itself. Today there are regional and national organizations for alternative schooling, some of which put out publications,[2] and much has been learned from earlier efforts. But any individual public school chartered or contracted to experiment still suffers, as in the Berkeley alternatives, from being merely grafted onto a traditional school district operation. The lack of a community-wide learning network keeps them from realizing their goals.

Thinking across all arenas at once should help us considerably to make the transition from classes, courses, and schools as we know them to this total learning environment in which all learning practices are put into play for everybody to learn anything at any time. To consider how to get from one to the other, let's now join the concept of concentric learning arenas with the universal learning activities while also examining current practices in or out of school that can be assimilated into a community educational system for all.

Good methods are simply practical arrangements for utilizing the spontaneous ways of learning enumerated earlier—witnessing, attuning, imitating, helping, collaborating, and interacting—along with the deliberate ways that combine them, such as apprenticing, experimenting, investigating, and transmitting by symbolic media. Many public and private schools are already either implementing or contemplating various practices that utilize these ways of learning. Besides general notions like decentralization, family choice, and student and teacher empowerment, strong trends have developed toward individualization, collaborative and cooperative learning, active learning, integrated learning, heterogeneous grouping, nongrading, nontracking, team teaching, peer tutoring, cross-age tutoring, paraprofessional aides, the "integrated day" or scheduling of large, flexible time blocks, full-time use of schools, dropping of textbooks, replacement of standardized tests by on-site assessment, merging adult education with regular schooling, apprenticing, mentoring, and community service. This growing repertory represents a great deal of valuable ferment occurring within the education profession well before recent government initiatives. It shows that good sense and practical experience have never been totally destroyed but only await liberation.

Rippling

Constrained as they have been, however, schools have not availed themselves of what may well be the most powerful learning method of all, because age grouping works against it, and because the managerial systems built into curriculum packages would eliminate themselves were they to accommodate it. I will call this method *rippling*. Basically, it's an informal, continuous tutorial of some knowledge or skill that everybody is at once receiving from the more experienced and transmitting in turn to the less experienced.

It's perhaps best defined by illustration. In the long central farm valley of California, the San Joaquin, most males grow up cathected to automobiles or, more precisely, to pickup trucks. The culture is mostly agricultural, and distances are large. Wheels are important, and so is self-reliance. Many youngsters teethe on farm tractors and off-road vehicles then graduate to cars. Flat land is good for racing, small strip towns good for promenading on the main drag, and pickups good for picking up girls. The movie *American Graffiti*, set in and around Modesto, showed how the rites of that culture take place in or through the automobile. At any rate, gasoline vehicles figure significantly in the culture. Consequently, these young males are all at some stage of becoming an auto mechanic, whatever job they end up in. If you have to break down somewhere, hope to do it between Sacramento and Bakersfield; you'll probably get plenty of help.

This substantial, nearly universal body of knowledge about how cars work, how to take them apart and repair or alter them, is passed down from the more experienced to the less without benefit of classes, special learning materials, professional teachers, or scope-and-sequence charts. Everybody is both teaching and taught and constantly progressing. You enroll simply by being inserted into this culture. Just by participating in it, you learn not only a considerable quantity of factual information about a limitless subject but you learn how to do some very difficult and intricate kinds of thinking like troubleshooting ambiguous symptoms or customizing a standard vehicle.

This way of learning works consistently well across a variety of learners and subjects. Literacy could be entirely passed on in this folk fashion from those who read and write to those who don't. It's the main way many people have learned outside of school to do all sorts of arts, crafts, or sports or to operate everything from machines to offices and whole complicated businesses or other enterprises. Most adults learned how to do their jobs this way. It's the ripple effect.

Working with people who know more than you do and with those who know less can hardly be surpassd as a way to learn. Everybody benefits from and contributes to collective knowledge. Rippling is by nature individualized and interactive. It fits the learner and stays spontaneous, alive. It spiritualizes learning because everybody is giving to everybody else and helping each other realize themselves.

Tutoring and apprenticing constitute more organized forms of rippling. Usually, however, rippling is spontaneous and simply passed down through conventions of behavior that make up the culture itself. The younger unconsciously imitate the older, who are usually not slow to correct and otherwise exert influence. Most learning occurs through this socialization, which goes on so continuously as hardly to resemble education. In the more flexible schools of today it can occur whenever adults and students visit back and forth, whenever peers exchange knowledge, and whenever younger and older students work together on projects. Mixing ages and mixing levels of experience within the same age is what sets ripples going if participants are free to choose what they do and to interact while carrying out what they choose.

Rippling is essentially cultural, as in the example of the central valley towns of California. Rippling transmits the culture, and the sorts of things transmitted through it are features of the culture—automobile lore, in the above example. It may enable or cripple individuals. What rippling will transmit are not just skills and factual kowledge but qualities of life, ways of relating, and ways of being in the world. Once again, it's critical that transitional schooling and the future communal learning network it leads to should generate a warm and spiritual culture. The *ways* learning takes place, the climate and process, will ripple down through the population and greatly influence for good or ill the quality of the whole society—as they do today.

Tutoring and Coaching

Tutoring represents the most individualized form of social teaching. The tutor utilizes a one-to-one relationship to elicit, explain, converse, demonstrate, coach, and so on. So it may involve many of the fundamental ways of learning. For content subjects, the tutor may orally transmit a lot of information or concepts. For developing skills, the tutee may witness demonstrations or make repeated trials of an activity and receive feedback in the form of coaching that reflects and corrects his or her action. As in all individualized learning, the teacher plays to the traits of the learner, and together the two create a personal curriculum.

This model goes back before public schooling to private tutorials in a family setting. How do you teach when numbers are simply not an issue? In the eighteenth century, country-squire households hired their own teachers to live in and tutor their children. Insofar as the values of the period permitted, subjects were chosen and lessons tailored to fit individuals. If the student had trouble understanding a point in math, the tutor could dwell on that point longer and devise explanations or practices especially for that student. Ideally, education would be equally individualized today but, unlike the old tutorial, would also enjoy the advantages of numbers. A good learning system arranges for both.

Unfortunately, the teaching methods of private tutoring were transplanted more or less directly to public school classrooms without allowing for the great difference that numbers make. For example, a whole classroom full of learners was treated like a single person that could be talked to in a single way, assigned the same lessons in the same order, and expected to perform the same when assessed. A group was simply averaged into a mythical grade-level personage. What carried over from tutorial to schooling was not the concept of a different curriculum for each person but of a single curriculum for whatever number. No doubt also, the nineteenth-century press in America to meld immigrants into a single nation also ruled out a pluralistic curriculum.

Even in today's conventional classroom, a measure of tutorial can be set up. One teacher cannot answer all the tutorial needs of twenty to forty students, but in a decentralized classroom, the teacher can tutor one party at a time while peers tutor each other. The same change in classroom management that enables peers to interact in small groups makes tutorial possible. The teacher has only to drop the role of emcee, performer, or nervous hostess to become free to circulate around the room coaching, consulting, and counseling as small groups and individuals pursue their tasks on their own until it is their turn for teacher attention. In workshops, I show teachers how to reorganize the self-contained classroom so as to convert numbers from a curse to a blessing. You help the class form small working parties that you can then circulate among. While acting as a model of interactive learning yourself when you sit in on groups, you disseminate your expertise among the working parties, who also pool their own collective knowledge to parlay learning beyond what each participant could do alone.

So far as it can go, this partnering or small-group process helps a great deal to offset the unfavorable teacher-student ratio and turn numbers to advantage by setting up cross-tutorials among peers. I encourage teachers to let undeveloped students read and write with partners, collectively, and then, as learners acquire competence and confidence, to use partners to discuss reading and writing they have done separately. Or they devise and carry out other projects. The efficiency of small working parties to do a great variety of tasks has for decades been well appreciated and applied in other organizations but, typically, not in schools. It empowers the young and therefore fits neither school materials nor teacher training, which emphasize control.

Tutors should not always be peers, because the knowledge among participants does not differ enough to spread the most benefits. But schools segregate students by age and then again within age by scores on a couple of standardized tests. Placing like students together into tracks, classes, and classroom subgroups isolates one age or level of maturity from another so that the natural passing down that occurs plentifully outside of school cannot take place. Learners need to have examples of what they have been and of what they may become. This gives them not only new knowledge but developmental perspective and people with whom to work out issues of their past and future, even in a therapeutic sense.

The longer the continuity across ages, the more powerfully it works. This need breaks the limits of the self-contained classroom. I advise schools that cannot simply mix grades as most alternative schools are doing to at least arrange for older students in the same school to work routinely with younger ones. Having, say, fifth or sixth graders buddy up with first or second graders to talk, read, and write with them never fails. Everybody loves it and benefits from it. Some of these tutors have written movingly and reflectively of this experience. They naturally compare their younger charges with themselves at their age but also show a touching pride or solicitude worthy of any parent. Once literate themselves, older students can pass literacy on by writing down younger children's stories and reading to them if in both cases the learner is looking at the text. Reading and writing could definitely be much more effectively transmitted in this way than through commercial materials and teacher-directed methods—as could much math and knowledge in the various subject disciplines.

Older students from other schools, senior citizens, and other adults can come in and tutor if the school itself is not self-contained, but clearly the scope of the learning network determines the limits of tutorial. In the fullest learning network, people specialized in all sorts of subjects would be coming into local learning centers to work with younger children, and older students would be circulating around the community to gain access to such people. Cross-community tutoring could include current adult education programs like those for literacy, whereby volunteer tutors go to the homes of illiterate adults or work with them in informal community settings. Sometimes these programs arrange the concurrent tutoring of the parents and their children so that the parents can take over the teaching role.

In some other projects, lonely seniors with nothing to do now come into elementary schools to work with children mastering literacy and arithmetic. The special skills and knowledge of many talented or well-educated seniors can be tapped by older students, who can go to them and perhaps help them in exchange for tutoring. Some retired people, on the other hand, want to learn an avocation so that they can pursue an interest for which they never previously had time. Like other adults changing careers, they should be able to avail themselves of the same learning resources mobilized for the young—including tutoring by the young, who often master new technology first. This sort of reciprocal giving typifies how social problems may be used to solve each other and how a community can knit itself into a warm and spiritual web. What it takes is a comprehensive organization of people that brings needs and resources together.

Apprenticing and Interning

While tutors were coming into the homes of the landed gentry to teach their children Latin and history, geometry and astronomy, drawing and music, working-class children were being sent to apprentice with master craftsmen in carpentry, masonry, metalwork, and so on. In both cases, interestingly, learners and mentors usually lived together. Apprenticing is a kind of tutorial specialized toward particular trades, which one learns by observing, imitating, and helping a master. Guilds formally organized this education into strict procedures, and the apprentice joined a craft community with something of its own subculture.

Apprenticing may apply to learning any sort of vocation, even the most mental, but the term *internship* tends to distinguish the head work of office professions from the hand work of crafts. Also, apprentices often stay where they train, whereas interns usually move on. Both learn on the job in circumstances enabling some kind of master to tutor and coach them and immersing them in the subculture of that occupation. Internships do not entail as much commitment as apprenticeships and tend therefore to have the more general educational goal of sampling a certain vocational environment. In the future such distinctions could be kept as alternatives for learners and their counselors to consider.

Few people in our society do not have to work, so apprenticing or interning in some sort of vocation or profession makes sense. But it need not monopolize an individual's learning nor commit one for life, as in the past. Indeed, given the long period of twelve to sixteen years that our society allots to education of the young, and given the necessity for many adults to change jobs, there is time to combine a number of internships or apprenticeships with plenty of so-called academic education such as the live-in tutors used to supply. Not only would this pluralistic education make students flexible enough to cope with a changing workplace, it would benefit democracy and help balance the learning process. Preparing for employment should never narrow this process but rather interplay with a host of other learning experiences that fulfill the spiritual goal of developing physical, emotional, mental, and moral levels at once.

A classroom teacher can do very little alone about setting up apprenticeships or internships, since learning in the workplace generally has to be arranged between schools and other parties in the community. Also beyond the teacher's jurisdiction is the creation of students' total programs, including requirements and credits. Indeed, apprenticing and interning involve so many issues of general policy and community relations that often only a school board or other district administrators can make the decision to incorporate them into the overall learning environment. Some public high schools, however, already have set up some apprenticeships with the blessings and aid of their district administrations, and a number of private alternative schools have for some time arranged apprenticeships one by one as students sought them and as businesses could be found to cooperate.

It is essential that individual learners decide if and when to apprentice. Government should not track students into apprenticeships, nor should business be allowed to exploit apprentice-ships. Learning in the workplace simply becomes an option for anyone of any age at any time, arranged through the community learning network, whose function is precisely to match up learners with fitting situations. Actually, businesses will benefit considerably. Though the free or cheap help may well be offset by the time that experienced employees spend teaching the apprentices or interns, business will gain an opportunity to recruit and train young people before they enter the job market. Companies always have to spend time anyway training new employees in their particular business. Furthermore, this whole reformation of public education will spare them the expense of setting up their own company schools to teach incoming graduates how to communicate, compute, collaborate, and solve problems. Apprenticeships should be able to focus on learning that is unique to the enterprise.

Visiting

People have always learned enormous amounts simply from visiting some location where they can experience the subject or action directly. Travel to other regions or countries has always been a popular learning method. Exploring seems less important today because virtually the whole world has now been visited and recorded by outsiders, but specialists still study certain ecologies or societies, and some college students go abroad to learn foreign languages and ways. Most such learning takes place during short visits to nearby places in the tradition of the British ramble or of the modern drive, just to check out and get to know some part of a city or countryside.

Efforts to institutionalize this sort of learning comprise school field trips, which imitate adult guided tours through cities or countries, as well as zoos, museums, art galleries, and other exhibitions especially organized to simplify traveling to learn. Schools underutilize even these obvious learning facilities. Today specially arranged class trips introduce students to them and perhaps occasionally bring them back, in the case of museums, for a special exhibit. Some students may return individually at times to work on a research project, and the most personally motivated may visit both routinely. But except for the occasional field trip to the fire station or animal farm, most private and public enterprises or facilities have seldom been regarded as educational resources.

A sole teacher can take a class to visit a site or facility but has to make special arrangements for absence from school, for transportation, and perhaps for parental permission. Trips take extra time and money, but the teacher doesn't control the schedule or budget. The usual secondary school class period is rarely long enough to include a visit, which may also be regarded as an extravagant way to convey information that competes with "coverage" of the subject via more economical means such as books, lectures, or films. To take full advantage of the value of visits, schools would have to conceive of them as much more important and incorporate them into schooling as a much more common experience. This can be warranted when we consider that visits may at the least make possible such important kinds of learning as witnessing and attuning and, at the most, imitating, helping, participating, and transmitting as well. Of course the more participatory and the more repeated the visits, the more visiting resembles apprenticing. Visiting can in fact allow students to learn enough about an enterprise to know if they would like to apprentice there.

Indeed, reconnoitering career opportunities is only one of many investigative projects that require legwork. Most kinds of knowledge that we cannot get entirely from books or other sources of stored information require going somewhere to observe or to interview. The three main sources of information are what the environment shows, what other people know, and what public data bases store (in books, disks, films, and so on). In short, like good journalists, we go and look, go and ask, or go look it up. Being free to visit is being free to investigate. By keeping students penned up in classrooms, schools have failed to teach them how to investigate on their own and have taught them instead how to depend on others for knowledge, mostly through books and mostly through outdated, overly synoptic, and biased books.

Frequenting a courthouse and following various sorts of trials is an excellent way to learn about not only the system of justice but also typical social problems. Consider other public enterprises like county health departments, agricultural stations, senior centers, and building inspection departments. Laboratories and other research centers are prime resources, along with farms and factories. Shops and offices may offer a lot too, since commodities and services range over a myriad of interests.

Directors of private facilities and businesses will often tolerate or welcome visits for the sake of public relations, advertising, and recruitment. We shouldn't necessarily think of the visitors as large groups like classes that have to be steered around; they may be individuals or other small working parties who might come often enough to become familiar with the place and even help out. Developing standing relationships is better than taking a tour once. The best time for a visit, of course, is when a learner is working on a project or pursuing an investigation that includes the subject visited.

Many splendid educational projects require letting youngsters out of school, and indeed individualized, project-centered learning hardly stands a chance without considerable circulation of learners throughout the community. Traditional schools are commonly bound by district regulations and the terms of insurance policies not to leave students alone in a classroom, much less allow them to foray into town or country unaccompanied by staff. But if projects are done by learners of mixed ages and often involve adults in public life, then this problem may solve itself precisely by removing boundaries. In a communitywide learning network, all parties will have to share responsibility for the safety of students. Any serious reform will require a new such covenant between the citizenry and educators.

Reciprocally, professional people may come to the students to speak about or demonstrate what they know. Programs of writers and artists in the schools have become widespread, successful models for similar arrangements with other specialists or professionals in many fields. These artists and writers show or read their work, discuss their experiences with students, and inspire and coach students in their own efforts. Police, health experts, or reformed addicts often come into schools to warn or inform students about some widespread problem. These occasional precedents can be built up into major ways of integrating schooling into a broader learning arena.

Community Service

Solving some problems by means of other problems can happen more the more that people of different ages, occupations, and socieconomic status are interconnected through a network. Let barriers down, and empathies and energies will flow across. Many children show great concern for the homeless or hungry or mentally retarded, perhaps because they identify more than adults do with people rendered dependent. And because children want to act on what moves them, they can mount projects to actually help those they sympathize with. But to carry these out they will have to inform themselves much more fully and so will educate themselves while doing service for others. The inherent connectedness of doing and knowing ensures that service will develop not only the heart but the head as well.

Many alternative schools already build service into the overall curriculum the same way they do apprenticing and investigative projects, all of which entail community networking to facilitate students' working away from school sites. All the various social problems such as unwanted pregnancy, hunger, addiction, crime, pollution, mental illness, neglect of the elderly, and so on interest young people once they have seen some realistic samples. For each of these problems an agency and some funds probably exist locally but are overwhelmed by the problem. No society can afford to staff and fund such programs adequately. In fact, the problems can never be solved that way. People have to learn how not to become the perpetrators or the victims of these problems (and how to help themselves if they do). This they can do partly by working with the people already enmeshed in them. Service not only bolsters what the agencies are trying to do now to alleviate the problems but helps students prevent themselves from becoming part of the problems in the future. As student community service becomes integrated into schooling, allocations to social service agencies can be shifted into public education as so reconceived.

Playing Games

Among the ways that people transmit learning are games, which are an ancient folk form of education. Before public schooling was instituted, much learning routinely occurred through games passed down from generation to generation. Some, like tossing jacks, develop the sensorimotor skills. Others are more mental, like cards and dominoes, which are ancient, cross-cultural games based on the whole-number series up to ten and exercising memory and logic. In the case of the standard modern card pack, derived from the old Tarot deck, the number series carries the concept of 'more than' and 'less than' into social ranking—jack, queen, and king. (Ace seems to represent a sort of divine Oneness, above royalty, but also, coming full circle, playable as the first item in the number series.) The strategies of many games played with tokens on a board or in arrays of holes (like Wari from Africa) also exercise reason, as does a verbal game like Twenty Questions, based on the logical process of elimination.

The possibilities for learning through games have been hard to appreciate in a society bent on commercial competition and prejudiced against play. School is serious and prepares for work. Adults work, children play. Of course, this is not really true and merely exemplifies again the sort of fencing off and segregating that ruin public education. Both adults and children work and play and frequently cannot tell the difference. Defining work as what produces income has confused the matter, as commercial thinking typically does. Though most of us will admit that children learn a lot through play, we fail to realize just how far and how late it may go. Let's look at some card games to see how play can teach even academic subjects like math and science.

Most card games embody two main kinds of logic—classification and seriation. Poker, for example, is based on both. You play it by putting together either cards of the same suit or number—hearts or tens—or cards in succession—eight, nine, ten, jack, queen. Like much of logic, poker is a matter of going for flushes and straights—categorizing things as like or unlike each other or rank-ordering things as above or below each other in some kind of hierarchy. The "royal flush" combines both—the ten, jack, queen, king, and ace of the same suit, hearts.

As a boy I used to play Authors, which consisted of cards bearing the names of book titles that one made into hands according to author. For better or for worse, I learned the names of many classics and who wrote them long before I read them. A card game can be based on any category or series whatsoever and is an excellent way to learn both established classes and how to classify itself. Most kinds of information can be presented to some extent through categories, and many kinds of subject matter are ranked as well. Biologists group plants and animals, for example, according to similarities in form and function, subdividing groups successively from the most comprehensive—phyla—down to the most particular subspecies. Such a taxonomy is an information system, meaning that the classifications are placed in relation to each other—hierarchically, in the case of biology, where broader classes include subclasses. The creating and ranking of classes characterizes much knowledge. Classes can be added, subtracted, and multiplied, which is indeed a major part of set theory in math.

As part of the language arts program *Interaction* (referred to in Chapter Five and now out of print), some colleagues and I created a couple of dozen educational card decks and some board games for students of all school ages that taught a number of different subjects. Primary pupils played Clock Wise by making hands of cards that expressed a certain time in four ways—as the digital reading "11:45," as a position of clock hands, and as the English phrases "eleven forty-five" and "a quarter to twelve." Older elementary students likewise matched cards that stated the same number different ways—8 + 9, $(3 \times 5) + 2$, 51 divided by 3, and 17. Next, students played a similar game called Equivalents by making hands of cards bearing various expressions of the same quantity, such as equivalent fractions and percentages or equivalent English and math statements.

In other decks the cards depicted various animals that were named on the other side. These too could be played by both classifying and ranking. A simple biology deck included only familiar wild and domestic animals. Another ranged up and down the zoological scale of classifications. Another treated just one group—arthropods—and its subdivisions into crustaceans, arachnids, myriapods, and insects. Pictures were accurately drawn to show identifying characteristics, and each deck was accompanied by a chart arraying all the cards in order. In fact, a card deck is really a chart made modular by cutting it apart, having the advantage that players can manipulate the modules—cards—and thus learn more thoroughly the relationships of the items to each other and to the whole array.

In making the decks we found that game strategies can be devised to fit the facts. Whereas suits in a regular deck all have the same number of cards, our arthropod suits—crustaceans, arachnids, myriapods, and insects—occur in nature in unequal numbers. To represent this fact, we put more cards into some suits than into others and built into the game rules that the rarer suits scored higher.

Content is not all that players learn. They have to think—categorically and hierarchically to match and rank, but also strategically, as in bridge and chess. They have to figure out how to play the cards they have or which other cards to ask for. They have to make deductions and decisions. We devised decks so that each could be played by a half dozen or so different sets of rules, that is, as different games, often traditional ones like Old Maid or Fish or Concentration. While working over the same material, this approach varies not only the play and the thinking strategies but also the number of players, the difficulty, and the mental faculty featured.

Some decks were designed for students to develop their own categories and to figure out those of other players. At the elementary school level, the cards bore pictures of dragons having different visual traits such as horns or fire and, at the secondary school level, pictures of human faces showing or missing certain traits. Players make up a category by choosing certain traits only and try to deduce each other's categories by successively trying out cards they think will yield the most information. We built into these games the logicians' *conjunctive* categories (dragons breathing fire *and* having horns) and *disjunctive* categories (dragons either breathing fire *or* having horns) by making cards without certain traits and by writing the rules to call for both kinds.[3]

Perhaps these examples will give some idea of how facts can be mastered and logic exercised through games. Card decks are only one format or medium. Computers are another. Most sorts of content and many kinds of activities can be learned entirely by playing games, which might be solo or social. In fact, inventing or making learning games should itself become a major learning method. To make the game, you have to think through the material, as we teachers did in making the card games. But play has to be taken seriously, once again, as a prime way to learn. Education should be the place where play and work become bonded for life.

The playful approach goes with an emphasis on the arts and nonverbal development. And on social relating. Not all thinking occurs through language, which may well prevent some thinking. We think while doing all sorts of social and physical activities, as we interact with other people and with the materials and circumstances of various environments. Thinking is relating. It has counterparts in social and material exchanges, which become internalized and structure our thought. Such is the connection between dialogue and dialectic. These exchanges should be rich, pleasurable, and spontaneous.

People play for play's sake, gratuitously, rather than for specific utilitarian reasons. True, games exercise inborn human faculties like sensorimotor coordination, the play of the mind, and social interplay, all of which stand us in good stead some time or other. The immediate impulse behind gaming seems, however, to be primarily expressive, to flex our muscles or other capacities in order to feel and savor them as an affirmation of being alive and human. This self-expression and this freedom from more mundane motives make play kin to the arts. As such, both reach deep into a part of our essential being that enjoys some autonomy from our conditioning and is therefore relatively free. In games and arts we play for pleasure, and this enjoyment presages the ecstasy possible if we're released from determinism and necessity into the unconditioned state called spiritual freedom.

Therapy

Healing involves some of the most difficult and important learning one can imagine, whether the therapy is for emotional or physical trauma. This may seem most obvious in psychotherapy, where the main medium is language and a one-to-one relationship like tutorial predominates. The patient is presumed to get better by understanding things differently, by reinterpreting past and present so as to reintegrate them. Psychoanalysts were first called alienists, because mental illness was thought of as alienation of one part of the self from the rest, a state captured well also in the term *dissociation*. Treatment consisted of making the unconscious conscious through hypnosis, free association, and dream analysis. Whether or not these techniques work well as practiced, we know that emotional healing involves some such learning process.

This consciousness-raising can also be effected through certain body work like Rolfing, which releases buried memories or feelings along with chronically gripping muscles, in keeping with Wilhelm Reich's notions of muscular armoring, or through acting out or role-playing, as in J.L. Moreno's psychodrama and Fritz Perl's encounter therapy. At the micro level of cells, psychotherapy becomes chemotherapy; at the macro level, group therapy. Today mental, emotional, and physical healing tend to blend in a synthesis of approaches aimed at neurolinguistic reprogramming, that is, a kind of rewiring of circuitry that amounts to unlearning one's conditioning at all levels of the organism.

Classical group therapy was led by a psychotherapist who tried to orchestrate the various problems members expressed so as to allow each to enlarge consciousness through sympathies, antipathies, and other resonances set vibrating by each others' experiences and viewpoints. Such group interaction arose to offset the frequently disappointing results of much one-to-one therapy, which suffered the limitations of one participant being up and the other down. Also, a dyad, modeled on the old doctor-patient relation, is only one sort of human dynamic, and others were clearly needed. Just as the teacher-led class has in some schools given way to peer groups doing collaborative problem solving, group therapy led by professionals has evolved into self-directing groups of people helping each other to heal or mitigate some affliction, be it the aftermath of abuse by others, congenital disease, or addiction.

Alcoholics Anonymous set an example in its peer groups based on the practical therapy of exchanging experiences with others similarly afflicted, who alone really understand the problem. Peers in this sense support, teach, and inspire each other. Collectively, they generate an understanding and a power to change that each has not achieved alone. Similarly, paraplegics, cancer sufferers, bulimarexics, incest and rape victims, children of alcoholics, recent divorcees, or convicts seek each other and meet. From professionals and from the example of other groups, as well as from the media, many people have learned what you do in such groups and what the benefits are.

The populist, self-help "recovery" movement marks a significant cultural shift from authority to autonomy that characterizes also the workplace and that corresponds to the evolution from collective to individual consciousness. True, the medium is the group, but members make use of the group to become self-sufficient. (The Center for Independent Living helps paralyzed people learn to get around and get jobs.) Recovery groups spread the expertise of specialists, who often launch them or sometimes still run them, come into them periodically as consultants, or provide remote leadership by writing and talking, sometimes on television. Many of these experts became such by leading groups as workshops until they could generalize about the affliction in question and about ways that work to heal it. This is populist in that people take over from the experts and collaborate to heal each other. Surely, it will only be by some such process of spreading specialty expertise that America will ever solve its problem of health care and treatment—or of public education.

Practicing the Arts

A parallel model was developed, interestingly, in the arts. For generations, in studios or other institutions where students are headed toward actual practice of the arts, the workshop has supplanted the classroom. Like *seminar*, the term *workshop* has recently been so loosely used to designate all sorts of how-to sessions, from flower arranging to financial investing, that it is necessary to recover the original concept. Individuals who want to get good at the same thing—dance, photography, pottery, sculpting, acting—share their efforts and their growing skills in order to help each other get good together. A leader, a master, may be important, but some groups have none or, again, spread this expertise through their own interaction. They present works in progress, respond as sensitively and usefully as possible, rub off on each other, pick up techniques, and find inspiration in peers. Critique and tact develop together, because each participant understands how exposed you can feel and how easily you can be wounded or discouraged by harsh remarks.

Like health, aesthetic self-expression concerns some personal core of ourselves that is at once vital and vulnerable. As in the recovery groups, the common goal, the empathy and identification, the agreement to use each other for personal progress, the esprit de corps, all combine to create powerful bonds. Since the 1960s I have worked, as have other educators increasingly, to bring the workshop into schools as a way of learning to write, do drama, and practice reading. The times I have led summer workshops in writing for teachers, they have kept their sharing groups going even after the session was over and they resumed teaching, a common experience that others leading such writing groups have reported. Workshops represent a kind of spiritual learning: not only do people help each other to develop personally, learning through reciprocating and identifying, but in the very process of getting better at *something* they become better *people*.

Arts connect with therapy not only in their sharing of a peer-group process but to some extent in their function. Like play, art is a great teacher as well as healer. What is its method? Making things. Crafts teach too, not just how to make something but all the things one learns in the process of making that something. We learn a huge amount from creating anything. (Maybe that's how God became omniscient.) Crafts represent a bridge between artistic creation and utilitarian manufacture. For full development we need to practice this whole range from aesthetic to useful and to discover how, spiritually, these kinds of making are not different. In fact, the notion that the arts are aesthetic is modern. They originated in sacred functions that, in the West at least, degenerated into rites and spectacles that in turn secularized into self-expression for the artist and entertainment for the consumer.

Spiritual Disciplines

Healing and the arts come together in the basic method of spiritual disciplines, which is to transform experience by some raising or expanding of awareness. Spiritual disciplines employ some particular means of awakening people so that they can read reality more comprehensively. I enumerated some of these means in the first chapter—meditation and attunement, intellectual concentration, devotion, service, and discipleship. It remains to elaborate and extend these.

Devotion and discipleship are almost bound to be misunderstood today even by religious people, because these practices grow up around highly evolved individuals so rare that few of us will ever encounter (and recognize) one. The point is to experience the mere presence of such a realized or awakened person, on the same harmonic principle that causes a more slowly oscillating body usually to shift to the frequency of a faster oscillating body to which it becomes entrained. Given the presence, we tune *upward*.

Disciples experience something quite different from others who merely hear or read about a spiritual master. In its original meaning, for example, a blessing was not merely a sacred phrase spoken over the disciple as ritual but a transmission of spiritual energy directly imparted to the disciple by touch, look, or mere presence, to raise the recipient's vibration rate. The Hindu word for this is *shaktipat*, the awakening in this way of the disciple's own *shakti* or potential super-energy, which in turn alters consciousness. The master also teaches by example and by saying or showing things that decondition.

Devotion is the receptive focusing of the disciple on the master, which is aided by emulating and identifying with the master, bringing offerings, and meditating on him or her when not present. The more one gives oneself over to this relationship, the more it works, but of course the devotees take great risks if they misgauge the personage to whom they surrender in total trust and faith. The process compares to that of worship, the reaching up of the aspirant toward deity, which reciprocates by extending grace. The master or guru acts as a mediator—or broker, as my teacher once called himself—to bridge the seemingly impossible chasm between pure Spirit and one's present state of material involvement. Spiritual leaders intercede in this sense, not because some personification called God is wrathful or cranky but because, unmediated by some mid-frequency, the jump between lowest and highest frequencies seems hopeless to most of us and can destroy those who try too hard alone.

Strange or even repellent as this devotional risk may seem, its secular counterpart occurs all the time as hero worship, role-modeling, relationships, and so on, as we acknowledge in saying someone idolizes or adores someone else. Frequently we are mightily hurt if disenchanted. Children and parents enact the classic case of discipleship, through which much power and knowledge may be transmitted at the risk of misplaced trust and faith. Bemoan the costs if you will, but everyone takes such risks instinctively or deliberately, because they want to grow and know.

I could have simply called this process *mentoring*, a respectable and harmless-sounding concept familiar in school reform, but the purpose of a spiritual approach is to treat education in the greatest possible depth. Finding and working with mentors should indeed figure prominently in a communal learning network, but let's note that although the process may function at many levels of knowledge and intensity, the ratio between risk and gain remains. From a mentor you learn by presence, both theirs and yours; otherwise get your expertise from a tutor, computor, book, lecture, or demonstration. You're undergoing a devotional discipleship for which the model derives from spiritual discipline, even though the subject be a scientific discipline.

Another spiritual method of learning corresponds to the common practice of "taking stock" in a business. Periodically you look over what you have on hand at the store, size it up for quantity and quality, and on the basis of this appraisal make decisions about the future. The fourth step in Alcoholics Anonymous consists of a "fearless moral inventory" of oneself. All spiritual traditions seem to include ways of reviewing one's life from time to time, whether through confessions to a priest or a confidant, exchanging experiences in close discussion groups, keeping a journal, or rehearsing before sleep each night the feelings and events of the day. Frequently this stocktaking occurs as part of practical action, to purge the past or take counsel for the future. Habitually replaying one's life in a reflective mode also raises consciousness, because events appear differently after the fact and in the long-range perspective of the whole continuum of events. Holistically taking stock for the purpose of making decisions is central to personalized learning.

The spiritual methods of sacrifice and asceticism have been much misunderstood, partly because many of their practitioners interpreted these in a fundamentalist—that is, physicalist—fashion or abused them for obscure personal reasons. In a pure spiritual discipline, you sacrifice something to break attachment to it, to free yourself from it. Kicking an addiction would be an extreme example. We are all addicted in the sense that we have desires and dependencies that enslave us because they are compulsive. Sacrifice helps offset habit so that we can stay more in control of our lives. It is a form of nonattachment. This does not argue for doing without for its own sake or for taking cold showers to build character. Jehovah ordered Abraham to sacrifice Isaac as a way of asserting that blood attachments must not be placed ahead of the spiritual life. A spiritual person is not one who despises the physical life but one who is free of it enough to perceive what else there may be. Denser matters obscure rarer. The feat is not to avoid relationship or committment for fear of attachment but to engage and *still* stay free. As T.S. Eliot put it, "Oh Lord, teach me to care and not to care."

Whereas sacrifice and asceticism are themselves regarded today as unnecessary limits on happiness, the real purpose of fasting, vigil, celibacy, silence, or isolation is to liberate. Doing for a while without food, sleep, sex, speech, or sociality is a learning device to find out that you *can* suspend these and to find out what happens when you do. You discover how much these mean to you, *what* they mean to you, what you are like without them, your whole relationship to each of them.

Children understand this and incorporate the principle into their play in the form of rules. In blindman's buff you do without eyes; in hopscotch, you do without one leg. It's all part of experimenting to learn. What happens if I suspend this normal capability? Young people also like self-discipline, because it represents power. Doing without something means you can control yourself and therefore exert some control over your life. It goes too with acquiring competence. Getting good at something usually requires sacrificing some things in order to focus on others.

Sacrifice is also involved in service to others, another method of achieving spiritual growth. Serving others sometimes instead of only oneself accords with the natural idealism of youth—not so much belied by their tough cynicism today as underscored by it, since we all know that the worst cynics are disappointed idealists. Young people want to feel they are expanding outward from childhood and growing into the bigger world, and they have an instinct to improve that world that's going to be their home for the rest of their lives. They want to act, take charge, not just endure. They want to see themselves as mature and capable of magnanimity. Community service goes beyond just being good to people close to you whom you depend on. Helping people you don't know represents the spiritual impulse to embrace eventually the whole world.

Contemplation and attunement constitute the part of spiritual discipline that seems least natural or familiar to people today as a deliberate activity, and yet we practice them all the time in various forms. Rapt concentration is the key. The process is powerful and may be directed at the meanest or most sublime objects, inner or outer. One can distinguish *what* we focus on and in *which* circumstances, but intense focus always causes some loss of self-consciousness and some release from other preoccupations. Developmental psychologist Burton White reported finding in one study that those children judged in school to be the brightest, happiest, and most charming had spent as much as 20 percent of their preschool time "staring" at some object or another.[4] I take this activity to be what in adults would be called some sort of meditation. It exemplifies, I believe, the first meaning of contemplate, which is 'to gaze attentively', from which the secondary meaning of 'to think about' naturally derives, since observation produces observations. Interestingly, the underlying idea of contemplate is to stake out a temple, an arena for sacred learning identified with the human head, which is frontally bounded by temples.

From rapt gazing we learn much of what we know. This is direct knowledge based on attunement, not on conceptualization. Elsewhere I distinguished five forms of contemplation, which I related to education.[5] All assume a still person in a quiet place and represent some stage of entrancement. *Gazing* may become visualizing by closing the eyes and imagining an object. *Visualizing* may lead to thinking everything one possibly can summon about the object, drawing on all faculties and all levels of one's being, as is done in religious meditation on a spiritual subject.

One may approach such *topical meditation* from quite another angle; let the uncontrolled stream of consciousness flow by and merely look on like a spectator. From this *self-witnessing* one learns what is on one's mind and under one's mind. As in psychoanalytic free association, one eventually discerns patterns that characterize one's thinking, usually restrictive or even obsessive from a spiritual viewpoint. By narrowing the focus to a selected subject, blocking out all else, witnessing may become topical meditation.

Finally, instead of witnessing or focusing inner speech, one may try to suspend it altogether by *stilling the mind* (the principal definition of yoga, by the way, in Patanjali's classic *Yoga Sutras*).[6] Achieving at will this consciousness without an object seems a prerequisite for awakening or enlightenment. Healer Edgar Cayce may have hit on the reason for this in saying that prayer is talking to God whereas meditation is listening to God.

Suspending inner speech and the entire *stream* of consciousness is tantamount to suspending discourse, the culture it speaks for, and hence all the conditioning of our organism that both together account for. Ceasing thus to transmit, becoming totally empty and receptive, makes possible heretofore unknown attunement to realities beyond ourselves, as Cayce implies. Of itself, this state alters consciousness, because when else is our consciousness not streaming and not *about* something? Zen (itself a word meaning meditation) teaches that in ordinary consciousness reality is reflected with much distortion, as in a perturbed lake, but that when the lake becomes perfectly still, its surface faithfully mirrors reality. Monks and yogis practice silence because quieting outer speech facilitates quieting inner speech—a sacrifice with high payoff.

The ancient and universal spiritual practice of quieting and emptying oneself, which need have no connection whatsoever with any religion, opens the way to intuitive revelations from within and without. It should be respected for what it is, a supreme and indispensable educational method.

Home-Schooling

By 1993 the number of families in America teaching their own children was estimated at 350,000. National networks, organizations, and publications for home-schooling have existed at least since the 1960s, when some parents began to give up on schools instead of trying to change them. Holt Associates, founded by the late reformer John Holt, acts as the nucleus of a national network of organizations in all of the states and publishes *Growing Without Schooling*.[7] Home-schooling is not any particular way of teaching but a taking of education into one's own hands. Parents as dissimilar as rural fundamentalists and suburban radicals object with equal vehemence to public schooling. Still others have no ideological concerns but simply believe their children will suffer from the poor quality of the education there. However much homemade educational programs may differ in content and method, they all share, for better or worse, a greater family influence on the learner and an opportunity, whether exploited or not, for more personal interaction and self-direction.

The home-schooling movement has become more sophisticated as parents have cast about for aims and means and have pooled their increasing know-how and understanding. It constitutes an important kind of alternative education inasmuch as it throws us back on some of the fundamental out-of-school kinds of learning at the same time that it creates some of the conditions that would characterize a communal learning network—freedom to utilize any human and material resources without being limited to those certified by a central authority.

Some parents attempt to teach the traditional school subjects to their children, whereas others arrange for unorthodox kinds of learning based on a child's interests and available resources in the environment. Still others band together with friends and neighbors to home-school together so that they can pool their collective abilities and resources. In this way, their children can benefit not only from the knowledge and diversity of other parents but also from the companionship of each other, one of the great disadvantages of home-schooling being the risk of social isolation.

Home-schooling, in other words, takes us back to the original purpose of institutionalizing education—to take advantage of numbers and to launch the child into a world beyond the foyer. Coming at just the time when we most feel the disadvantage of numbers and the overwhelming of the individual by the institution, it can remind us of why people communalize in the first place and show us how to make it worthwhile. Many home-schooling families will eagerly rejoin some new organization of education if it avoids the drawbacks they fled, and they will bring valuable experience to it.[8]

Some school reform has included parent education in the form of programs to teach parents how to teach their preschool children at home or how to supplement and reinforce what the school is trying to do with their children once enrolled. Some such programs encourage parents to read to their children or aim to instill in them basic understanding of good learning conditions and attitudes. Others may show parents how to help with homework in math or writing or try, through a particular project, to involve parents more with their children's work and engage them in collaborating with the school.

The eventual coalescing of all parallel activities into a community learning system would surely gain if home-schooling parents were invited to help run parent education programs, since they have obviously taken initiative in that direction for themselves. Then too, all preschool parents are home-schooling and could come together through such school programs. In fact, some conventional schools already work with home-schooling parents, if only to monitor them and prepare for the children's reentry into the system. One way or another, parent education programs can provide a way for home-schooling families to reintegrate with public education as it changes in the direction of self-education.

Self-Teaching

A significant number of autodidacts (to use an old term current today in home-schooling circles) have always taught themselves outside of institutions and still do. A research team analyzed the lives of twenty famous experts in various fields who had no formal higher education, such as Virginia Woolf and Frank Lloyd Wright, and found that they focused early on a life theme and pursued it with great drive but were also helped by a strong family base and key supporting individuals.[9] Self-taught people typically don't bother much with school or get much from it, but the researchers list over a dozen ways in which schooling could foster self-education. It would, for example, help students to:

- "Internalize control over their own learning"
- "Identify and become expert at the activity or activities that may become central in their lives"
- Integrate "theoretical studies with technical training and practical application . . . for specific use now rather than learning for possible use years later"
- "Generate their own goals rather than . . . pursue goals set for them by others"

- "See themselves successfully experiencing very desirable attainments . . . and plan an effective way of making that vision a reality"
- Engage in "patterns of exploration" and "try out a wide range of fields of activities"
- "Develop a personal learning style"
- "Identify themes emerging in their lives, to build on those they choose, and to create new themes they desire"
- "Not only master some knowledge or skill, but also . . . develop a healthy attitude toward themselves, others, the world, and their activities"

Teaching for self-education involves:

- "Promoting drive rather than passivity, independence rather than dependence, originality rather than conformity"
- "Training in the process skills, such as reading and remembering, especially at the moment students urgently need to gain access to information"
- "Creating an active environment in which a student's self-directed activities are warmly supported and there are many opportunities to form close working relationships"[10]

The double emphasis on self-direction and social grounding accords well with my own recommendations. Indeed, all of these conditions for self-teaching would naturally be a part of the communal learning network, since they feature individual opportunities to find and develop oneself and to gain timely access to all available human and material resources. "Learning how to learn" often appears among the lofty goal statements of school districts, but setting the conditions for real self-teaching means transforming public education from a standardizing hierarchy to a pluralistic, lateral organization of resources that can put into play at once all the ways of learning that we have been surveying and that are proven by experience. How people learn is no mystery. What is mysterious is why we have not set up public education to accord with this massive practical knowledge.

Now that we have enumerated the many learning means at our disposal, let's try to put them together into a practical and spiritual educational system capable of transforming culture and consciousness along with itself.

8

▲

Rethinking Courses and Classes

In the education of the future, everyone is learning about everything all the time. One does not suddenly encounter a new subject in a compact, logical presentation of it lasting months or a year—unless one chooses such a course for its special pertinence at some stage of a personal pursuit. One grows with all subjects all the time—progressively filling in detail downward and pushing upward into more comprehensive perspectives. At each stage each learner is benefiting from sources of varying expertise. Peers cross-teach by pooling what they know. Older students are passing down their knowledge. Simultaneously, one is also learning directly from specialists through tutorials, projects, apprenticeships, and their presentations via texts, disks, and films.

This totally open knowledge system repudiates the secrecy, competition, and exclusion of government and industry and the mechanical controlling, the slow doling, of bureaucratic schooling. It is based on learners giving and sharing and identifying with each other across differences. Differences are valued, because you learn most from people unlike yourself. This principle of total access carries over into learning resources other than people—the natural environment and man-made materials. The media, materials, and settings should be pluralistic too. Students would spend a lot of time in the countryside and in town. They need to explore nature and society for themselves and not know them primarily through predigested presentations designed just for school.

Academic subjects would be learned all the time and in mixture with each other, as aspects of a problem or project. They would not ordinarily be pre-organized in courses, the way specialists might lay out their fields. Only advanced students working with such specialists might study physics or psychology in that self-contained way (but they would be rippling this knowledge down to the less advanced). It has been a huge mistake for schools to restrict academic intake to certain times, places, and persons, especially when the main sources are commercial presentations purveyed by teachers whose expertise is often limited to a comparatively narrow range of what is known in a given field.

The main teaching method has been memorization, and the material has been scheduled logically rather than psychologically—biology by the classes and orders of its taxonomy, for example, math more or less deductively by subtopics, and literature by periods, movements, and genres. When homogeneous groups of students are herded through the same material at the same time, even in "electives," with everything laid out in advance, the amount of content that can be thus "covered" is actually small and ultimately arbitrary, given all the knowledge available. Furthermore, this self-contained material is poorly remembered and applied.

Individual, Modular Courses

Until multi-aged rippling has gotten well under way, however, the oldest students may need some formal presentations in order to make sure that those at the top know enough to prime the pump. Once a generation has grown through this seeding process, it will probably not need courses like those with which we are familiar, having learned more from their predecessors than their predecessors did from the old systematic presentations. The purpose of any courses for them would be different from now, since only a pulling together of the subject would be required, not a more basic and comprehensive presentation. Any such courses would be chosen by the learner to fit into his or her program of projects. The best metaphor for this process is a culture, of either the biological or social sort, through which something spreads because the culture constitutes a growing medium.

Let's say, for example, that students are constantly learning biology and geometry from projects done with older students, who for their part are also doing projects with older students. These students know many facts about a lot of plants and animals and how to grow and care for them, and they have learned how to use figures and figure relationships to solve many practical spatial problems. Some of this would have been learned not only from doing projects with older students but also from reading and seeing films and from playing and building with geometric shapes and volumes. If, when older themselves, these students still did not have a grasp of the hierarchical classifications of plants and animals and the principles of form and function underlying the taxonomy, or still lacked comprehension of the whole system of interlocking theorems of plane and solid geometry, then a course could pull these together for them, in which case they would find it much easier and would remember the material better.

Furthermore, these courses in geometry or biology would probably bear little resemblance to today's classes. There are simply better ways to bring learners and means together for discursive learning than having thousands of modestly specialized teachers trying every day to explain the same facts or concepts of math and science, relying on textbooks and other commercial materials that are dumbed down to accommodate the negative circumstances of mass standardization. Those people who know the subject best should be filmed giving presentations that accommodate learner interaction and can be intermixed electronically with supporting text, sound, and graphics. Students can use these alone or create with other students a seminar or workshop in which they help each other learn, calling on specialists to consult occasionally and to afford live one-to-one interaction as tutor or mentor.

The new courses might consist of individual, interactive electronic activities of a self-teaching sort or of social games such as those described earlier for learning biological taxonomy through card decks. These means might be mixed with films combining some lecture, some animation or other graphics, some live demonstration, and some footage of actualities in human affairs or nature. Multimedia compact-disc programs operated through regular television sets or personal computers allow users to combine video, stereo sound, and text, all drawn from multiple sources that will increase exponentially as more and more material is stored in data banks available across international networks of "information highways." These sources include encyclopedias, collections of art and photos, atlases, educational programs, and games and will eventually consolidate virtually all of the world's printed matter and audiovisual archives. Special software such as Hypercard enables users to summon and edit this wealth of multimedia material so as to create, for example, the kind of collage of imagery, sound, and text that Ken Burns and crew assembled to make the acclaimed film series *Civil War*.

In other words, aside from tutorial, physically placing learners together with a teacher at a certain time in a certain room is unnecessary and inappropriate for most subjects. Exceptions include laboratories and other situations where a specialist may be needed and those activities such as arts, crafts, sports, or spiritual disciplines where personal coaching can be very useful.

Thus the transition between conventional schooling and the community learning network will no doubt see a phasing out of academic courses as *classes* and a phasing in of projects benefiting from rippling, accompanied by these new sorts of modular courses, which will be formated for individuals or small groups, individually scheduled at home or at appropriate community facilities, and closely interwoven with an individual's learning in other subjects.

A strong case can be made that the pre-organization of curriculum into courses accounts for much of the ineffectuality of schooling. Having taught beginning and intermediate French for three years in secondary school, I feel the feebleness of *classes* for foreign languages. Individual practice is the most important way to learn either to read and translate or to converse and write, but in group work where only the teacher knows the target language, any one individual gets too little opportunity to practice or receive feedback, and peers cannot help each other as much as in most workshops. Foreign language classes are either serial tutorials in a group, which is grossly inefficient, or unison marches through texts, which is hardly better. Clubs or other social groups for the foreign language can be very helpful, especially if fluent speakers can mix with learners, but otherwise a combination of live tutorial and work with tapes will get the best results. A file of fluent speakers in the community willing to tutor should be created. Many schools simply do not have enough foreign language teachers to offer classes anyway, or to offer much choice of languages, but this sort of tutoring can go well without any real pedagogical training because it is essentially a form of rippling adaptable to individuals. If not meeting singly with tutors, learners can at least share them in very small groups so that each person can actually practice enough conversing or translating to get good at it.

One can rather easily imagine how history and literature might be studied without formal courses, through guided reading, discussion, and media archives, since they constitute in large measure a textual corpus to become familiar with, interpret, and interrelate. But history is also a discipline with rules of evidence that should play a significant part in discussion and original research. Artifacts exist that may be correlated with primary and secondary textual sources to generate and document assertions. Tutors or teachers may help considerably in working these into individual programs or group projects. Any in-depth study of history almost has to overlap with the physical and social sciences—geography and geology, archaeology and anthropology, sociology and economics. This knowledge complex is so large, and the choices within it so many, that it is best to let these subjects cluster ad hoc around individual interests and pursuits. As story, history makes a fine lead-in to the higher abstraction of science, and as discipline, it also prepares for the necessarily more rigorous proofs of the physical sciences and math. This sort of crossing of fields is awkward to standardize into set courses, because of the close relation between integrating learning and individualizing it.

Literature is an art as well as a body of texts, best discovered as such by experiencing plays, poems, and fiction and by creating texts in these forms oneself. Reading and writing workshops are better for this than courses, which have encouraged teachers to lecture and interpret for students and to convert literature into history or the generalizations of critical theory. All of this has spoiled and misrepresented literature and prevented learners from personally responding to it, as intended by authors. The same is true for the nonverbal arts, which comprise both a body of previous work and a repertory of activities to do oneself. Though the history and analysis of the arts can be valuable and interesting, for different individual reasons, classes as we know them almost invariably emphasize these at the expense of experiencing and practicing the arts. These are only some examples of how the formulaic nature of broad subject courses seriously interferes with real learning.

Problems of Math and Science Courses

Since math and science embody logic and inquiry, respectively, they most seem to require set courses. But efforts to get tough about math and science in the 1960s failed and will do so again today if they merely depend on requiring more courses and setting "higher standards." Such administrative measures don't reach the real human problems that account for most Americans' ignorance of and even avoidance of these fields. If the problems are psychological, what good are higher standards? Start first by asking why virtually the whole populace has a math block. Math as presented in school courses is too abstract, which makes it not only hard to understand but to care about at all. To a lesser degree, science as a school subject suffers from the same remoteness from common concerns and feelings.

The "new math" developed in the 1960s failed because in restructuring math to show students *why* the operations are done the way they are, curriculum developers unfortunately made it even more abstract and inaccessible. Students quit electing math when they had a choice, but schools couldn't require courses most students would fail. The problem lies in trying to make a one-shot course out of algebra or physics and to can it in a textbook or other fixed format, especially if that course is required.

This may work to a limited degree in some societies where the authority of family and state can drive the young to repress their personal wishes and swat away at an arbitrary-feeling course during most of their hours out of school, including weekends, regardless of whether they can relate to the material or understand why they should make such an effort. A startlingly large proportion of the people in the United States who do fill the needed positions in math and science are immigrants—oriental, European, or Middle Eastern people who studied just this way. We can draw from this the moral that American students should simply be made to do more homework and to stop wallowing in self-indulgence, but the matter requires more thought.

Research has well documented the extraordinary success of Southeast Asian refugee children in American schools, even to the point of suggesting that the schools are fine the way they are; it is the bad attitudes of American parents and their children that need changing. It is indeed true that, even when they are unbroken, few American families have dinner together every night and then do schoolwork together for several hours afterwards, as many Asian families do, siblings helping each other and the parents reading to, working with, and encouraging them all. Such family coherence, such unity with school, and such intense belief in education as salvation rarely exist any longer in this country except among people recently arrived from a less individualized culture and highly motivated by the challenge of adopting a new culture and overcoming the traumas of the old. I doubt that it will ever again be possible, for better or worse, to both drive and support American children like that. Their challenge is different.

It's foolish to pine for bygone authoritarianism and envy it in nations still depending on it. The extraordinarily homogeneous culture of countries like Japan, moreover, isolated until the last century, represents an earlier stage of cultural evolution in which people are driven more by a collective imperative or group mind than individually from within. America evolved into a mosaic of cultures, some of which already included a relatively individualized consciousness and all of which together *induced* yet more individual consciousness. It should not try to revert to the authoritarian stage, which will not last even in countries like Japan as their cultures become increasingly cosmopolitized and their consciousness correspondingly individualized.

Besides, the cost of such driving to physical and mental health seems not to be worth it. Some of the adult foreign scholars have testified to the emotional problems that this extreme stress and their ensuing resentment of it have wrought by the time they have won jobs in engineering or research. Even if American students could be flogged through these courses, the payoff would probably not equal the price. People in such jobs have got to be just as whole as people in other jobs. Indeed, it might be dangerous if they were not. Not only must engineers, physicians, and researchers be whole people who care about the uses to which their work is put, they must be more creative problem solvers than students who were force-fed.

In any case, not enough students, no matter how hard they worked, would ever learn and retain enough from even very good conventional math and science courses to serve the nation as hoped. The most damaging evidence against such self-contained, one-shot, logical presentations stems not from the large numbers of students who failed such courses or scored low on standardized tests, or who avoided the courses in the first place, but from the equally large number who did well in the courses. My wife and I both took four years of math in high school and always got A's, but we have not truly integrated math into our lives, seldom remembered and applied it when needed, never learned to think mathematically, and never became what math teachers today call mathematically literate. We were temporarily trained monkeys. Most good students not especially gifted or interested in math can give the same testimony. High scores merely mask this failure.

New Ways for Math and Science

Elsewhere I have argued for making math once again a humanity, as it once was, and for thoroughly integrating math and science with all other learning, including the arts, humanities, crafts, and vocations, instead of treating them merely as technological tools.[1] As educators are coming to understand, self-containment of subjects is self-defeating. To make themselves understandable, math and science need the concrete particulars of personal experience and purpose, the realism of problems drawn from other subject matter, and the working over of mathematical and scientific concepts and procedures within the contemporary social contexts that establish their fuller meaning.

By the beginning of the 1990s the national professional organizations for math and science teaching, like other educational subject organizations, had published descriptions of how they would like to see their subjects taught in the future.[2] Although the math and science educators were still assuming courses in the old sense of classes with a self-contained subject, some of the practices they advocate will in fact by their nature break out of these old forms.

The very good scenarios for future math, for example, emphasize realistic problem solving based on experiences familiar to the student, collaborative small groups that work on problems and projects together, and building on the learner's intuitive concepts of number and measurement. The more fully math education realizes these scenarios, the more nearly will it depart from the whole-class, teacher-directed, self-contained, textbook-driven course and the more nearly will it approach an individualized, interactive, interdisciplinary project-centered system of learning. It is as if the old asssumptions about courses and subjects prevented the authors of these scenarios from realizing the implications of what they are advocating.

To a lesser extent the same is true for the also promising but less methodologically explicit statements for science education, which still emphasize core themes and concepts for all students but also call for more realism, relevance, group work, integration of topics, student initiative, and open-ended inquiry. These trends in all subjects owe much to the recent constructivist theories coming from research in cognitive psychology, according to which learners *make* knowledge by making sense of what the world presents. Because this knowledge is built on intuition, personal experience, and previous learning, constructivist research and theory strongly justifies the individualizing of learning.

Although educational reform has to dissolve the old curricular organization around subjects in order to allow for both personal and integrative organization of learning, students will actually be learning more science and math than they ever do in a forgettable course or two taken once in a lifetime. They would be studying these subjects throughout their youth, if not their whole lives. Nor does this change mean that the inherent inner organization of a field or discipline ceases to exist. Any subject can still be presented in all its disciplinary integrity whenever individuals and their counselors agree that it's appropriate to do so.

It really makes little sense, by contrast, to require a semester-long class in trigonometry when any individual who knows something about right triangles and basic equation-writing, and who sees a purpose for computing sides and angles, can grasp it much more expeditiously through a film, computer presentation, and/or some live spot-tutoring. *Applying* trigonometry is the key; the calculations mostly just require learning to use the tables of sines, cosines, and so on, which can be practiced alone or with a partner, perhaps using interactive software. Similar mini-courses in algebra and geometry might consist of a few students forming with the help of a counselor a workshop in which they teach themselves the subject through visuals, instruments, software, discussion, and even books, consulting a math specialist as needed. In the new proposals for math education from within the profession, the role of the math teacher already approximates that of a specialized counselor who helps students arrange the best activities at the right time to facilitate internalizing the subject.

Most math teachers recognize today that people best understand geometry, algebra, calculus, statistics, and other forms of math when the needs for them arise in practical situations or, in the case of something like chaos theory, when curiosity is aroused by its connection with some topic already of interest. Historically of course, arithmetic, algebra, geometry, and calculus were invented *as they were needed* in agriculture, astronomy, architecture, commerce, and physics, just as new forms are invented today to solve new problems or to exploit new technology. Ideally, students would make the kinds of things and do the kinds of activities that would make them feel the need to invent the necessary math for themselves—but naturally they could then avail themselves, through counseling, of what others have already developed for similar purposes. They don't need to reinvent math, but it helps to arrive at the point of *feeling* the need.

Most science can best be learned through direct observation, sensory films, laboratory situations, some reading, and encyclopedic audiovisual data banks that learners can access interactively through progressive menus. Employing slow motion, freeze-framing, microphotography, time-lapse photography, computer enhancement, and a host of other rapidly evolving techniques, films today can teach far more and far better than books or lectures about plants and animals, the inner workings of the body, cellular life, atomic physics, or chemical reactions. The more all these films become organized centrally for universal computer accessing, along with other forms of stored information such as charts, graphs, arrays, formulas, data maps, texts, and so on, the more students can pursue interests endlessly across scientific topics through various menus and networks of videodisks and data banks (the use of which they will be learning at the same time).

Again, practical projects will also entail finding out about scientific topics in the realistic way these come up in making things, growing things, or trying, say, to improve the local environment. Becoming naturalists and activists is the best way to study the physical and social sciences. These lead inevitably into laboratory and library but presuppose some purposeful access to nature and society, however one can come by them in one's locality.

Subject-Centered and Student-Centered

Realism and relevance, individualization and integration, problem solving and projects, collaboration and consultation are not mere buzzwords. Look a moment at the old geometry or biology textbook. Its feeble way of trying to contextualize or "apply" its contents was to pose "story problems" at the end of a chapter, like how you could compute the amount of paint you would need to coat a certain building or tank. You knew you could solve the problem by drawing on what that chapter had just presented about plane surfaces, which means that at least half the problem was done for you before you began. Even knowing a problem is soluble through *some* form of geometry starts you off with a big boost. But so often in real life you don't know if the problem is soluble at all; if so, whether by math; and if then so, which form of math; and if by geometry, which form of it.

Likewise for the biology textbook. A real-life problem in pollution or medicine will often mix kinds of science with each other and with kinds of math mixed also with each other. We educators have forgotten that the more we lay out discrete subjects by their discrete subtopics, the less learners can practice the realistic problem solving that both educators and employers are crying for. The main argument for mixing academic subjects with each other and with practical actualities is that life mixes them this way.

Obviously some balance has to obtain, however, between the integral nature of each subject and the integral nature of an individual's particular pursuit or project, which will in most cases cut across the bounds of both mathematical strategies and scientific knowledge. Formerly, learners were supposed to assimilate and accumulate self-contained bodies of knowledge organized according to the structure of each given field or discipline. This preserves frameworks and important central concepts like figures and functions in math or form and function in biology that can easily be lost in a purely pragmatic approach. But this very subject-centering makes it more difficult to understand, remember, and apply the subject. Educators in all subjects agree that learners can only assimilate new knowledge to their previous knowledge structures and to the rudimentary and intuitive understanding they already have about, say, numbers or plant life. It's impossible to install the new knowledge intact as conceived by its specialists.

So individualizing education does not merely cater to the desire for choice in a society preaching personal liberty. Individualization recognizes the inevitable inner negotiation that occurs as people digest new knowledge. Materialistic frameworks always slight the inner life; by insisting on it, a spiritual perspective actually fosters more effectively the acquisition of material knowledge. Gradually shifting, over the grades, from a child-centered to a subject-centered curriculum has been the schools' crude way of acknowledging that the younger a mind is the more it needs to contextualize knowledge in some personal way. Practical or playful activities that embed or entail the unknown open the learning pathways. Since learners digest objective material in their own way, even to grossly deforming a subject if this isn't allowed for, it is best to plan for personal assimilation at the outset by letting the learners determine consciously how they are to incorporate previously organized subjects into their personal agenda. In short, don't pit the integrity of a subject against the integrity of the individual; instead, arrange for learners to find out when the integrity of a subject becomes a means of furthering their own integrity.

9

▲

Whole Learning,
Personal Choice

In 1990–91 I had the illuminating experience of participating
in the founding of the Alliance for Curriculum Reform, which
brought together for the first time as an ongoing consortium
all the national organizations for teaching the various subjects.
The general purpose was to envision a coherent curriculum
that would do justice to the integrity of each subject and also
bring each to bear on all the others.[1]

I expect that as the national subject organizations continue
to collaborate toward a unified education, they will be forced
to work out the contradictions between their own calls for
change and their very division into separate educational organizations as demanded by the university models they follow.
Once each subject no longer constitutes the total field of vision,
but only one element of it, all will have to search for a whole
great enough to contain all subjects at once. This whole will
turn out to be, I believe, a new conception of the learner and
the learned as inner and outer aspects of the same phenomena.

The effort to imagine a coherent curriculum that is subject-
centered for all disciplines at once will cause all educators to
refocus on the learner, not merely as a willful individual but
as the only possible unity or unifier. Each learner represents

the prototypical knowledge-making creature whose mind alone can integrate all these subjects, because they are creations of fellow minds. If education is not organized around subjects, it has to be organized around students. But this is not a dichotomy. Minds and subjects correspond to each other through the same affinity by which creations resemble their creator. Math merely manifests logic, as science does inquiry. In this sense, subjects are not foreign objects; they are external equivalents of inner human faculties.

Neurophysiologist and cyberneticist Warren McCulloch once asked, "What is a number that a person may know it, and a person that he may know a number?"[2] We have to ask what are the sciences, arts, mathematics, languages, and vocations that people may know them, and people that they may know the sciences, arts, mathematics, languages, and vocations? Reconceiving the subjects as a unified learning field will cause us to perceive how all subjects integrate at a level more comprehensive than any of them alone. This will in turn redefine the subjects, which will then have to be understood not only in relation to each other as knowledge but in relation to the knower.

As I tried very tentatively to sketch elsewhere, I believe the sciences, arts, mathematics, languages, and vocations all have undeveloped (and even unsuspected) relationships among themselves that interdisciplinary teams need to think through and bring out for educational purposes[3] and that counselors need to know when guiding learners. These relationships between, for example, math and ordinary language, math and the arts, science and history, science and art will serve mightily to facilitate a system of education based on individuals putting together their own learning programs. Once more fully worked out, these epistemological connections will illuminate how people may integrate their own knowledge structures without violating the integrity of each discipline. Thus integrating learning and individualizing learning come to coincide.

The Arts, Avocations, and Vocations

Whereas conventional public schooling relegates the arts, avocations, and vocations to the periphery of education, compelling reasons suggest that in the future they should play a much more central role, not in competition with the academic subjects but as a major means of access to them. Math, history, and the various natural and social sciences have been formalized and codified by specialized practitioners who define the fields for purposes of research and advanced study. Young people and lay adults have to find or make points of entry into these fields. Once involved in a discipline they can begin to give themselves over to the integral structures of that discipline, in the same way that once we trust a person to have our interest at heart, we tend to value what they say and follow their guidance.

The arts, avocations, and vocations not only cut across academic fields—a fact that has integrative value in itself—but cut across them at a personal angle. That is, one gravitates toward music, nursing, or stamp-collecting for personal reasons that one works out in the terms of those activities, which have codes and conventions of their own amounting to subcultures like those of the academic fields. The arts, avocations, and vocations are disciplines too but are by their nature more personalized because we select them in order respectively to create things, to express ourselves, to play, and to find gratifying work.

Naturally, people choose academic disciplines for the same personal reasons but usually only after their motives have been mediated through these less formal disciplines, like the botanist who as a child just loved to watch and make things grow. Or the minority youth who becomes a historian trying to trace her roots. Or the child who loved building and becomes an engineer. Arts, avocations, and vocations constitute a natural bridge from childhood to adulthood, play to work, private to public life. They can aid our thinking about education if we regard them not as stepping stones we leave behind but as an accumulation that enriches the present.

Through these less formal, more personal disciplines one not only becomes involved in the academic disciplines but actually begins to learn some of the facts, concepts, procedures, and integral structure of math, history, and the natural and social sciences. One also acquires some competence in ways and means—the technology, foreign languages, or social networks that may be entailed. Anyone who goes far into music or filmmaking, computer programming or journalism, biking or rapping begins to come out somewhere else, especially if they're following out these interests in an educational network of opportunities and counselors especially designed to parlay anything into anything else that realizes the learner.

Through play and recreation—meaningful pleasure—the arts and avocations allow young people to find themselves and what they want to do. As mythology scholar Joseph Campbell was fond of saying, "Follow your bliss." This leads people to vocations that will fulfill them and that they will fulfill in turn. Roughly speaking, it makes sense to steep small children in the arts as an organic entrée into everything else, including literacy and math and science, because they are the natural growing medium in which children will generally thrive as human beings. Actually, the arts, avocations, and vocations are not easily separable in practice, which is part of the point.

The architect who loved to draw as a child, who now knows a lot of physics and math, has simply found a way to make a vocation out of an avocation grounded partly in the arts. Both architecture and engineering exemplify how careers can encompass the spectrum of aesthetic to utilitarian, play to work. The urban, natural, social, and technological environments that we inhabit in the future can be both beautiful and practical if created by people who have arrived at the technical via the expressive.

This does not mean that the arts should *precede* the sciences anymore than that they should continue to be shouldered off into limbo by the sciences and other subjects. The arts are humanities, along with languages, history, philosophy, and literature (also one of the arts). Child development or human growth may require some sequence only in needing to proceed roughly from the personal to the technical, the playful to the utilitarian. This would seem to argue for moving children from the arts through the other humanities to the sciences. But this would perpetuate the false split between the humanities and the sciences that has already done untold damage to society. *The sciences are humanistic also*, or should be so regarded, even though the tendency since the seventeenth century has been to divorce them from the humanities, which were regarded as polluted by superstition and subjectivity, and to wed the sciences instead to technology and commerce. So just as a humanistic *context* for the technical does not imply a *sequence*, it does not imply a dichotomy between humanities and sciences.

Art is no more fundamental than science, play than work, beauty than utility. The desire to know is surely as basic as the desire to create and express. Inquiry is as fundamental as play, hardly distinguishable in fact in the child. The humanistic and artistic nature of the sciences has to be fully recognized, since, after all, the motives and means are human and since knowledge is a human composition based on the same capacity to *pattern experience* that makes the arts artful. For its part, the scientific nature of the arts and humanities has to be fully recognized, since the arts too are modes of knowing, as Suzanne Langer documented in her monumental work, *Mind: An Essay on Human Feeling*, in which thought includes feeling.[4] Math has to be understood on the one hand as a special language that extends ordinary language into a more abstract or decontextualized realm where logic can operate more accurately. On the other hand, math begins with the weighing and counting and measuring of things of the material world and continues on to the manipulating and visualizing of volumes and shapes. So it is discursive like other languages and yet sensory like the arts. Like both discourse and art, math patterns experience.

Thinking is making. It is an art, an act of creative composition. This is what relates math and music, the rhythms and patterns by which thinking informs experience. And here we come to the primal force that unifies the learning field—the capacity of the human mind to put reality into ratios and rhythms, equations and similitudes, periodicities and proportions, and other mental forms that resonate with the forms of nature because the human being is attuned to the larger cosmic being of which it partakes.

Arranging for Student Choice

In consulting, leading inservice workshops, or writing for preservice methods courses, I propose that teachers who are still running a self-contained classroom counsel their students how to choose among a gradually expanding repertory of activities. The most primitive way is just to write on the chalkboard two or three things that children can do today, indicate where needed materials are for each, and say you will circulate to help. These choices might be to play a numbers card game together, improvise a two-person scene, or write a limerick. Change the activities each day until the class builds up an extensive repertory that students can usefully repeat and can teach each other. Better yet, set up learning stations around the room, each of which bears a poster with written directions and illustrations and contains necessary materials, such as a display of photos about which to make up stories, or a book, audiotape, and headset for listening to a text while following it with the eyes.

Some elementary teachers have for a long time used learning stations, and if the activities are authentic and interesting, they are an excellent way to launch individualization and a project curriculum. But a classroom can contain only twelve to twenty stations. How do we expand beyond this the array of choices, the learning repertory? This was the problem that beset the team of us who created *Interaction*, the K-12 language arts program referred to in Part Two. My colleagues and I wanted to introduce into the self-contained classroom several hundred activities ranging over every sort of natural use of language that we could think of, but we repudiated textbooks or other materials that would lock activities into a certain order and oblige all students to do the same things. In pooling our activities we realized that we were often raiding old shoeboxes of cards onto which we had written "assignment" directions.

But instead of assigning these activities one at a time to a whole class, why not put the cards into the hands of the students, let them decide when they would do which—decentralize the system? This way, the students would end up doing more activities, do them in a better order for each individual, and take charge of their own education. After all, they couldn't and needn't do *all* of the activities, which overlapped in what they taught. Part of the secret of pluralism is not just abundance but redundance—learning the same general things through different specific activities.

So we wrote hundreds of activity cards, clumped them into six main categories of action such as drama, reading, fictionalizing, or investigating, then had the publisher illustrate them, laminate them on sturdy stock, and package them in file-type boxes for browsing according to the categories. Since many activities required certain texts or tapes included in *Interaction*, we had to refer to these on the cards, which also suggested certain other activity cards, books, games, or tapes for possible follow-up activities. In fact, all materials were cross-referenced to each other so that students might enter the repertory of things to do by starting with a book or game or tape as well as an activity card. Following these optional routings, they could enter the web at any point and travel anywhere else. Thus someone who selected a book of fables while browsing would find at the end of the book not only suggestions for related reading via cross-references to, say, books of parables, folk tales, legends, and animal stories but also optional routings to decks of animal cards and to activity cards for writing fables or for dramatizing brief stories.

A decision about what to do next hinges not only on such inherent connections in form and content but on human connections and on chance. Someone reading fables alone, for example, might afterwards search for partners to act out or write fables with. A group reading fables together might agree on a follow-up activity or break up so that members can make different choices. In other words, people are not only choosing activities but choosing each other. Working parties are forming up and breaking up all the time and of course cannot possibly start and stop at the same times. A party pursues a project or a continuity of projects till it finishes, consulting with the teacher and perhaps others along the way.

Each individual makes decisions, then, under the influence of the total learning field, which includes the arrayed repertory, inherent connections, other students, and the teacher or other counselors. This is a mini-environment mirroring the interaction of the larger learning world.

Learning stations provide an easy entrée into a full-fledged activity card system of choice. But there are other ways to make the transition. A teacher can do one activity card at a time with a whole class until the class feels confident about breaking into groups and either redoing this set of now familiar activities or choosing new ones. Or the teacher can break the class into groups, give each a card, circulate among the groups, and have them report results to each other. Groups trade cards until all have done this small repertory and are ready for new activities. Or for a while the teacher can set up some groups of students who are ready to work independently while she continues to work with the rest of the class as a single body. Generally, the teacher gradually increases student choice and independence by feeding more and more activities and materials into the repertory and moving from whole-class to small-group process.

Learners putting together this way their own personal curricula need counseling about how to make good decisions. To facilitate this, both learner and teacher keep some sorts of records of what the learner has done. Periodically they chart past and future together. Looking at the pattern of a student's choices and of other experience she or he has accumulated, the teacher may suggest good ways to follow this up or balance it out—certain activities, materials, subjects, or people. If the student already has ideas of what to do next, the teacher can respond to these by helping the student think about ways and means of carrying out the ideas.

Any person counseling should give reasons for recommendations and show consideration for both the student's immediate interests and long-range education. This includes keeping before students some picture of all the kinds of learning and means of learning there are, and of the myriad ways these all intersect, so that students can pursue particular interests without losing perspective about what else there is and where else these interests may lead. Good counseling not only enables individuals to make up personal curricula but teaches them how to develop good judgment in making decisions on their own. While bringing a broader and longer-range perspective to bear on an individual's pattern of choosing, counselors show their charges how to take command of their life.

This mix-and-match system based on individual logging and counseling can in some ways be usefully computerized. Programs of menus and submenus can replace activity cards. These menus can convey both illustrated activity directions and rich cross-referencing among themselves and to other resources. Computerized menus cannot be lost, mangled, worn out, or temporarily taken out of circulation by one user. They don't have to be purchased but can be created and revised right within the school, without loss of sophisticated graphics. Breaking dependence on publishers is essential. The quantity of such activity menus can be far greater than the amount of physical activity cards schools could normally afford anyway, because collating makes cards far more expensive for publishers to produce than books. (But of course it is precisely the loose-leaf, modular aspect of cards that befits a mix-and match system of choice.) Students of any age can browse across a huge range of electronically arrayed activities without being limited to a few boxes placed in their proximity.

Computerized data bases lend themselves splendidly to keeping track of what each individual has done. In fact, relegating the burden of record-keeping to machines would no doubt encourage teachers to individualize and would ensure fuller records, which can be called up for charting conferences and gone over together to pick up on past patterns and future possibilities. Such records could much more easily be transmitted from year to year. Activity-direction menus, furthermore, can be so coordinated with individual record-keeping that records can cite the activities and resources a student has worked with in the same way they are named and referred to in the menus.

Some of the disadvantages of computerizing activity directions are the same as for any use of computers—that it confines people too much to monitors, with possible physiological and psychological risks, that it displaces much needed socialization, and that the more learning depends on computers, the more of them you have to buy if learners are not to be forever waiting on each other. Often, furthermore, it's more practical or just more pleasurable to be able to hold, manipulate, and transport physical objects. Playing card games on computer, for example, may be less desirable than for a pair or quartet just to get a deck and go off in a comfortable corner somewhere. For a great many activities the computer will be in the way, because one wants to keep any activity directions and illustrations at hand as one works.

Once, while I was conferring about an individualized activities approach in a junior high school with some teachers engaged in a project for the National Endowment for the Humanities, the staff decided to take a break and give me a tour of their building. The shop class illustrated beautifully what I had been trying to get across. On the walls were hanging handy wooden paddles bearing directions for how to make a metal sugar scoop or book ends or a miniature solid airplane. A student would just take down a paddle telling how to make the desired object, carry it around wherever needed, consult it occasionally, ask the teacher or someone else about questions it raised, and so on. The shop teacher was there to help decide what to do next and to explain further how to operate a machine or otherwise proceed. He was already doing, early in the 1970s, what I was advocating to his colleagues in language arts, social studies, and the other arts.

Combining activity cards with computer menus seems the best way to offer choices. Data bases and menus array not only options among activities but also suggest further options routing learners from one activity to another. However, when one is actually carrying out an activity of any length or complexity, a computer may quickly become a nuisance since students do not want to be continually going back and forth between a screen and the activity. Fortunately, this problem can be solved quite simply; with desktop publishing equipment and a laminating machine, schools can make activity cards from their own menus. This makes available both electronic and physical sets of directions.

Students should play a large part in making activity cards or menus and indeed in creating activities themselves. A major purpose of activity directions is to help learners outgrow them, to conceive their own activities. This works in a couple of ways. Starting with others' directions for doing something shows how to conceive and carry out something you want yourself. This accustoms learners to choosing what they will do and acquaints them with some ways of realizing their choices. At the same time, these activities serve as modules that learners can put together in their own ways to carry out more extended or complicated projects of their own devising.

Suppose, for example, a student has routed herself through the reading, discussing, writing, and printing up of some fables. Alone or with partners, she gets the idea of going through a similar cycle with another type of discourse such as parables or true case histories, it too culminating in a booklet. Or she may want to mix fables, parables, and case histories because they all seem to give examples of how to live more wisely. Or she may decide to use these forms to wage a campaign for some cause. Partners would create booklets of fables, parables, and case histories, both original and compiled, and print and distribute these for some audiences and adapt and perform them as Readers Theater for some others.

An original project like this would treat smaller previous activities as modules to combine and would benefit from the student's experience of having parlayed one activity at a time into another that led to still another. Thus students would learn for themselves how to concatenate activities into meaningful projects. In other words, we can envision a progressive transition from learning stations to activity cards and computer menus to original projects, which would then remain the major learning unit.

Projects

Contrast the self-contained, prescheduled course given as a class with the story James Watkins tells in *The Double Helix* of how, in pressing forward to discover the DNA molecule, he turned aside temporarily to get tutored by a colleague in some math he had never had but required for the next stage of his problem solving, to which he returned provided with just what he needed when he needed it.[5] *That's* how it has to happen—as part of a project, the natural unit for individualized, interactive, interdisciplinary learning.

Watson's framework was a project. Organizing around projects rather than around subjects will better teach the subjects, which need each other and a purposeful framework to realize themselves. This way of organizing education, furthermore, accommodates student-centered learning, because students conceive their own projects for some real-life purpose—to make something, investigate something, or improve something. As distinguished from a drill or exercise, which is done only in school, a project is an authentic act or series of acts complete for the purpose of the participants.

Many projects are based on the arts, avocations, and vocations, which can provide media and materials, settings and conditions. In fact, playing a musical instrument or gardening or repairing cars amounts to an ongoing project. Arts, avocations, and vocations are by their nature never drills but authentic activities that people do for personal motives. Action-oriented, realistically motivated, they can act as a natural base or framework for projects. Collectively, they constitute a roughly developmental progression and so can serve to launch and foster projects from one age to another. That is, the arts are accessible to everybody, even the youngest. Hobbies, crafts, and the other favorite, optional activities that make up avocations come into their own during the middle years, when children gain familiarity with what there is to do, competence in how to do things, and some independence in setting up and getting around. Since vocations often depend on safe mobility into the community and the maturity to communicate and work with adults, vocations become important during adolescence. As suggested earlier, these three form another sort of progression to the extent that arts generate avocations, which inspire and prepare for vocations.

Doing and making things of real importance must be a main feature of future education. This connects directly with community service and with the consolidation of social programs advocated in Chapter Twelve. The mixed-age members of a given project have access to the knowledge and expertise of the whole communitywide network. Everyone can at any age be involved in competent projects that implement actual needs or visions, both pragmatic and artistic. The real-life problems of poverty, homelessness, hunger, addiction, crime, pollution, health care, channeling of sex, and so on can be seriously dealt with through student projects coordinated with agencies charged with these problems. This allows students to take a proactive approach to social ills early in their lives.

While learning from all this, the individual is also constantly logging the positive experience of producing and succeeding. Projects may flounder or go completely awry, but the individual doesn't bear alone the onus of failure for a group venture, and besides, any failed or unfinished project simply becomes the basis of another project benefiting from that experience. The flexibility of a self-generated, community-supported curriculum makes it unnecessary for there to ever be any losers.

The central point is for students to teach themselves, to engage their inner world with external realities and resources, to discover ways to find out what they want to know or know how to do. This learning system depends basically on two things—personal choice and responsive counselors who play to an individual's patterns of choice. At first the system staff arrays a limited number of subjects and activities until students get the idea and can seek or invent them on their own and farther afield. One can start with easy choices and let the difficulty of the decision making increase with experience and sureness. Learners unused to choice or unsure of interests can be advised to start exploring some universal subject.

Everybody is interested in the body, for example. The human organism itself provides an excellent learning framework. Practical matters such as the effects on the mind and body of certain foods or activities lead easily to physiology and then to biology, chemistry, and physics. Curiosity about health, sex, or mental and physical prowess could thus begin sequences that would take learners from their here-and-now preoccupations through the organic disciplines to the remoter sciences. Concerns about feelings and personal relationships could lead to observations and readings about other people's behavior and hence to psychology, sociology, and anthropology. Such activity suggestions for projects to learn about the human organism can surround children during the years when their mobility is limited and they look more to elders to help them get going.

From the individual organism and interpersonal relations interest may naturally shift to human-made environments—dwellings, workplaces, and cities. This leads into architecture, city planning, and the ecological interplay of society with nature. Designing and building things people need or want

brings students to learn arithmetic, geometry, algebra, trigonometry, calculus, statistics, and probability.

The role of learners in projects evolves as learners grow. That
is, inexperienced students might choose among a variety of
purposeful activities arrayed in the immediate environment—make a maze or interview an elder, for example. As
they gain confidence and competence, they can conceive activities for themselves, partly by combining activities already familiar into more complicated, longer-range projects. At first, they
may also participate in a project designed by other, perhaps
more mature students, or co-conceive a project with colleagues.
These approaches prepare learners both to lead group projects
and to plan and execute projects alone.

As a learner advances, he or she takes on more and more the
responsibility for leading group projects and for the learning of
others. This makes for very strong and moral individuals, both
self-reliant and sharing. At all stages, however, individual
projects would be mixed with group projects. The very fact of
being able to draw on many powerful resources encourages
people to solo, as do the competence and confidence acquired
participating in group projects.

Growth and Mobility

Project now onto any scale you like the process of choosing
activities and building them into projects. It can exist in any
of the concentric arenas—self-contained classroom, school enclave, school, set of schools, whole district or community, or
even across nations and the globe. The size of the arena depends
first on the scope of the organizing entity and second on the
maturity of the learners. Self-contained sites better suit young
children, who need much adult supervision and cannot get

around much on their own. A communitywide network accommodates the more mature students who are ready to work farther afield and more on their own. It can also facilitate mixing ages, which can liberate younger children by providing them with a mobile base in the form of adolescent or adult project partners.

Growth corresponds in some measure to increasingly broader time-space arenas in which people carry out activities as they venture beyond the home and the neighborhood into more extended social groups and more distant recreations and workplaces. How long in time a project can last depends to some degree on how far in space the learner can move. Small children's need for more protection and direction keeps them closer to home and therefore more in need of a local site. Such a building and grounds need not revert to a school in the traditional sense of a preprogrammed common curriculum, segregation by age, classrooms, textbooks, tests, subjects, and so on. Rather, even if the building should be a former school, it should become as much as possible a microcosm of the total community learning network.

An old elementary school building would be divided not into self-contained classrooms but into activity areas, and children would have the run of the whole building and grounds. Appropriately staffed and equipped, areas for the graphic arts, the lively arts, physical activities, nature experiments, group discussion, group reading, group writing, and meditation would be open the whole time that the building is open, given some practical exceptions. Adults can share these same areas and activities, and many of the staff for them might be volunteers or paraprofessionals. With counseling, learners would make up their own daily and weekly programs for using these areas. Part of each day they would spend in staple shared activities of their choice, and part of each day they would pursue other activities chosen alone or with partners. These activities go on in daily group sessions that individuals can join or in special areas where they can do them alone and practice concentration.

Community centers for preschool children would be merged with public day-care centers, as recommended farther on. Children there would experience the arts as a natural habitat— singing, instrumental music, dance, drawing and painting, and constructing of all sorts. The arts foster sensorimotor acuity and coordination and generally develop the whole nervous system, including the brain. They tie in easily with crafts and sports and other such avocations that harmonize mind and body and that teach the most central learning activity of all—concentration. Part of this matrix or initial learning ambiance that educators can prepare for younger children should include play and work with the body, which is indeed in several senses the measure of all things. People of all ages metaphorize from the body to emotional, mental, and spiritual realms. Learning to do something new with the body can exhilarate and enfranchise a person well beyond the physical accomplishment, just as understanding something new about the body seems to reverberate elsewhere in one's being, as if we transfer or translate experience from realm to realm.

While doing projects with older learners, small children can go out very early into the larger community. Or older people can simply take them out individually or in small groups to visit places related to current projects or interests. This is a good role for volunteer adults or for mature adolescents whose project or community service entails being with younger children. Also, outsiders can come to the children to coach, tutor, entertain, do demonstrations, or help with projects. These neighborhood centers should thus provide many outside relationships that not only instill early in children a feeling of membership in the larger world but also actually begin to teach how to get around in and draw on that world.

How soon learners can range farther afield depends on their individual maturity, their family's sense of what is safe, and the type and size of the community. What could help is to employ some former school buildings as a combination of shelters and resource and counseling centers where older students can stop off, check in, get help, utilize such facilities as computers or labs, or perhaps avail themselves of certain specialized resources located only there. This provides students at once with bases to touch when navigating around in a large community and more resources than one site could afford. To this add libraries, museums, community centers for crafts, sports, and other activities, and the myriad public and private enterprises where learners will be visiting, taking lessons, apprenticing, or doing community service.

Adults and mobile youngsters would be crossing paths and working together quite frequently as they choose, say, the same gardening or computer-programming course, visit or apprentice at the same business, carry out a project to put on a musical, or do such community service as feeding the homeless or running a teenage advice center. Adults in our society will continue to change jobs or vocations as technology and the world economy evolve and, especially, as capital and other resources are diverted from harmful old industries (like production of certain chemicals) and reinvested in positive new businesses in maintaining healthy bodies and a sound environment.

Mobile youngsters need to be scouting the sites of science, the arts, business, and government so that they know early what's going on and can even take part. During or before their teen years, many people show astonishing entrepreneurship or technological capacity or artistic talent—if afforded opportunity to manifest them. Some teachers have shown their middle-school students how to lobby so successfully that they have gotten certain bills or resolutions passed in state legislatures. Specialized magnet schools have allowed students to discover and develop abilities that would otherwise have lain latent. But *every* person has to have this opportunity, not just those in a certain school. And you shouldn't have to buy a specialty by sacrificing other opportunities and experiences that only the whole community can supply.

It's clear that adults have chronically underestimated children's capacities. More accurately, we have unconsciously held the young back in fear of their creative forces, which we have not known how to handle. And keeping youngsters out of adult affairs has headed off competition in the job market between them and adults. But making public education a compulsory holding tank has helped to create some of the major societal crises like addiction and street gangs and unwanted pregnancy that adults cannot control. If the innate life energy, the creative capacity, of people of any age does not find expression, it becomes destructive.

Initial Literacy

My experience tells me that no efforts to transform education will get far if the obsessive problem of initial literacy is not dispatched, to the reassurance of everyone involved. Whereas students today spend an enormous portion of school time attempting to learn to read and write, most with limited success and many with none, learners of the future can through this integrated, individualized approach make reading and writing a way of life in the spontaneous manner that many children have acquired literacy at home without being aware of how it happened. So before pursuing the broader elements of the universal schoolhouse, let's focus for a while on the one sort of learning by which schools of the present stand or fall and on which any reform will founder if not successfully handled.

To blow the minds of elementary school principals, I have

sometimes asked them to consider a requirement that children should be able to read and write *before* they enter school. Though this would not be just or feasible for all families, I can almost see the crowd of thoughts that this idea brings to the minds of educators whose whole professional life would be changed if literacy no longer dominated schooling. Such a prospect, in fact, can be terrifying. What would we do with those children for twelve or more years if schools were not preoccupied in one form or another with literacy? After all, most of school science, math, and social studies concerns the understanding of texts as much as does literature. It is not so much out of cynicism as sympathy that I wonder, indeed, if the massive resistance to teaching literacy realistically stems from just this terror of confronting the void resulting from success.

An effective literacy program requires only a reorganization of human resources so that any people already literate can pass it on.[6] *All* children, "at-risk" or not, can learn to read and write within a learning field featuring projects and other personalized activities. There are three methods for teaching literacy that are known to work but that schools have not accommodated sufficiently, relying instead on commercial materials that fill the curriculum and force out the interpersonal relations that really work.

When done in school these practices are called "read-along," "language-experience," and "invented spelling." That is, older children or adults read to beginners as the beginners follow the text (read-along). Concurrently, beginners dictate to older children or adults things they want to put on paper and watch as their speech is written down (language-experience). Also concurrently, beginners write independently, guessing at spellings on the basis of whatever phonetic understanding they have picked up from the alphabet or the other two methods (invented spelling).

Although these alone would teach literacy very well if schools were totally committed to them, computer technology is affording other means as well whereby beginners can see and hear spellings in synchrony. One can now type words and hear them sounded as well as see them appear on a screen or—better but not yet readily available—speak words and see them typed. Seeing and hearing words simultaneously teaches literacy, whether the learner, another person, or a machine supplies the spoken language and whether the learner, another person, or a machine supplies the written text. The more this audiovisual experience occurs in a personal, meaningful context with whole continuities of text, the better.

Rarely have any but certain special schools ever thrown out the impersonal instructional systems and pulled out all the stops on these methods that have worked at home as well as in school. Schools of education have not prepared teachers to work without commercial materials, so that even though the "whole-language" or "emergent literacy" approach, as such natural means are now called, have recently dominated the *discussion* of literacy education, most teachers are thrown into consternation when threatened with actual removal of the old crutches and asked to make a total committment to using only children's literature and children's own language as texts and to using only human resources for the methods. This is a school problem I'm personally familiar with. Since my books and workshops have for years sought to help teachers initiate literacy in this natural way, I have often been asked in recent years to work with teachers specifically on how to get children reading and writing without textbooks or systems instruction, in the way that many parents have done.

This approach raises of itself the whole matter of restructuring classrooms and schools, because to afford beginners the constant and copious experience of reading along and dictating, they need to be paired off almost daily with literate helpers who have to be made available from beyond the self-contained classroom, which has to be thoroughly decentralized at the same time. Much research in "emergent literacy" reports promising experiments in how to mobilize family and community so as to foster these activities in and out of school, along with oral language practice and other concomitants of literacy.[7] Proven by research with preschoolers to improve ultimate reading ability, invented spelling is, by its nature as independent writing, an activity that also flourishes only in an individualized setting—in the past usually at home. In fact, none of the three methods requires a school or professional teachers, and all suffer, in fact, from the familiar school conditions.

One might assume from the nation's terrible record in literacy that how to teach it remains an enigma. This is not so. We simply do not do what we know works, for the reasons treated in Part Two. These three practices work but require throwing out other ineffectual ones and dropping textbooks and tests. They also should not be singled out as reading instruction but should be woven into an individual's total learning program. This depends, in turn, on a reorganization permitting learners to choose activities and participate in projects while also affording them plentiful access to literate helpers and to counselors. Part of a counselor's job is to keep an eye on how well opportunities to become literate are occurring in learners' choices. But being read to, giving dictation, and writing independently are all activities that preschool children have so frequently chosen to do for pleasure at home that, like the arts, they can very nearly be regarded as universally desired.

What we know includes not just how to initiate literacy via the three practices cited above but also how to make reading and writing a way of life for life, that is, how to help children see why they might *want* to read and write. It is essential for teachers to array samples of all the various types and purposes of writing, from fables to drama to journalism. Let students find out for themselves from experience why one might want to pick up a book or a pen—or go to a screen and keyboard. This can be done first while reading to them and taking down their speech, but as they gain independence from helpers they need to choose their own texts to read and their own topics to write on.

This is where schools' obsession with control has spoiled the whole process. Good elementary teachers have, when allowed, individualized some of the reading, but even so they have usually had to force certain other reading on students because it was required. More than any other single factor, giving ownership to the state and not to the reader has made literacy fail in this country. In authoritarian societies, you can still force students to learn literacy without regard for their will and motivation. Our children, however, are growing up in a society so committed to personal liberty that they don't understand why they should do something out of sheer compliance. Literacy, and education in general, must be made consonant with the human rights codes by which students are being raised (or at least bombarded in the media).

It is neither necessary nor feasible to rely on conformity to teach literacy, which remains a huge stumbling block to educational reform precisely because we have not made the learning of literacy accord with our present culture and consciousness. As soon as we arrange for literacy to ripple down through the populace according to practices that from both school and home experience we know work, we will liberate public education from a great burden, and it will then be possible to carry learning much farther forward than ever imagined before. Despite making schooling overly bookish, literacy has been so stalled that twelve years of it have amounted to appallingly little. Once we trust that literacy will thrive through interactive individualization, and can relax about it, we will more readily believe in and work for the radical proposals made in this book and elsewhere.

Besides freedom of choice and sociality, the other main way to make reading and writing a way of life is to integrate them with other subjects and activities. The International Reading Association publicly proclaims that reading comprehension should not be taught separately but rather by means of other subjects, that is, through the varieties of content usually placed under social studies, science, or literature. To discover reasons to read and write, children have to do projects that *entail* literacy—put on a play, build or operate something according to written instructions, take notes on an interview-visit, do consumer research on some commodity, and so on. Greater involvement with projects, apprenticing, and community service will all draw young people into literacy because of the role it plays in all sorts of practical and public affairs that they become interested in.

But that first marriage with reading and writing comes from the delights of being read to, of finding out what goodies are in books, and from the satisfaction of putting one's own speech and thought out there in visual form. For beginners, making texts and making out texts are a form of play. It is not just the content of texts but the sorcery of literacy that attracts children. Later reading and writing activities should just extend these associations of pleasure.

If we consider literacy holistically, then, we realize that it grows out of nonverbal contexts—out of play, out of sociality, and out of physical activities that include the arts. The graphic and lively arts especially prepare for and support the language arts, because they express and symbolize thought and feeling. They are competing and complementary media in which people pattern experience. So strong, in fact, are the affinities between the language arts and the other arts that any literacy program not embedded in them is seriously crippled.

All of us educators carry on about student involvement and motivation, but the best learning takes place in a virtual trance.

The primal function of participating in music, dance, drama, literature, and visual arts, I believe, is precisely trance induction. For the real learning that takes and counts, one must *undergo* something in order to understand it. The arts are not mere things to learn but ways to learn.

Just as the arts originated together as a sacred matrix from which they later singled themselves out, the infant starts at one with the cosmos and the mother and then gradually separates itself. Within, it differentiates its global self into diverse abilities according to what the new environment exacts of it. As the limbs and senses specialize into their different destinies, they inaugurate the arts. Nose and mouth, then hands and feet, then ears and eyes edit and compose the environment into some sort of creation. In the crib the infant of several months pulls itself up on its feet, hanging on to the side, and rocks rhythmically in a facsimile of dance. It vocalizes its own songs as it practices and plays with its expanding repertory of sounds, some of which will become the speech of its parents. Language is only one of many special abilities the child develops that together utter it and join it to life on the new plane. Eventually secularized as poetry, the mantric incantation of language formed part of the trance induction for which the arts were first used.

Like moving and sensing, talking is so much a body activity, so inner, so much also a social activity, so behavioral—and learned so early—that it's practically unconscious, unobjectified. Though an obvious outgrowth of talking, reading and writing require children to objectify speech as never before, to externalize and instrumentalize it. As a second-order stage of verbal communication, literacy breaks further out of the sacred matrix of original unity. Reading and writing are "out there" in the form of texts produced by the external instrumentation of pencils or keyboards and existing independently as books or video displays. As moving and sensing grow also in their specialized ways of composing reality, they continue thus together to make sense of the outer world while expressing the inner. In doing so they found the arts, which are ways of knowing through creating.

Children can best parlay talking into reading and writing if they can make the transition within the context of the other arts, so that becoming literate benefits from the rich kinship with these other activities derived from the same sacred matrix. Let's consider some of these connections. Like literacy, drawing and painting and creating three-dimensional things also make use of external instruments and materials to express and symbolize. Preliterate civilizations relied heavily on graphic and architectural arts to store knowledge of biology, astronomy, agriculture, mathematics, and history. Visual and physical models of reality remain important today to complement verbal symbols. Drawing, in particular, evolved from representational pictures to stylized pictures or ideograms to an alphabet for symbolizing word sounds.

In contrast to these spatial or graphic arts, the temporal or lively arts like music and dance resemble literacy by moving in time, by making use of the dynamics of flow and succession—accumulation and entailment, reversal and repetition, rhythm and proportion. While remaining body activities like speech, the performing arts also develop a repertory of dynamics, as texts do, by sustaining a more deliberately composed and usually longer continuity than speech. Music and dance also employ instruments and specialize body movement for expressive and symbolic purposes, like writing. Language too moves in time. The oral traditions of preliterate cultures not only stored and transmitted knowledge but created the first literature. Story telling remains a lively art, comprising a past sequence of events and a present flow of performance.

At once verbal and nonverbal, singing constitutes a special case. Its language is metered, cadenced, or otherwise rhythmized, like poetry and music, both of which it resembles also in its sound play and tonality. Though both singing and speaking involve vocalizing, song lyrics are usually scripted, like theater, composed in advance. The very artfulness of art prefigures writing, which is more planned than speech. In fact, the concept of *composition* best captures what the nonverbal arts share most with the language arts.

As these examples are meant to suggest, in somewhat different ways the nonverbal arts help prepare for literacy and should accompany its emergence. While practicing the arts for their own sake, children can learn literacy through the arts. Sometimes this works out in practice as activities that naturally merge texts with graphics, music, or movement, like illustrating stories, captioning pictures, writing about pictures, acting out texts, singing texts, writing songs, and so on.

Beyond the overlays, lead-ins, and follow-ups that the arts provide reading and writing, they teach literacy even when practiced separately from it for their own sake. Certain fundamentals of composition, for instance, are shared by all the arts, verbal and nonverbal. Thus we can speak of rhythm, leitmotifs, and tonality in painting, sculpture, and literature as well as in music and dance. Proportion, contrast, repetition, reversal, development, and unity are common issues of making something, including texts.

Likewise, comprehending such creations requires and develops certain faculties common to the arts and to literacy. The beholder, audience, or reader must put together all the cues to best understand and undergo the creations. The recipient creates too, as implied in the concept of *construing*. *Compose* means 'place together', and *comprehend* means 'take together'—about the same difference as between construct and construe. In other words, interpreting the arts calls for the same kinds of learning as practicing the arts. These activities of both literacy and art resemble in turn the constructivist way in which people create knowledge.

If it seems extravagant to recommend that children be totally immersed in the arts as a first priority, consider the fundamental role the arts play in making things, whether objects or knowledge. Writing is making texts, and reading is making out texts. As Frank Smith has documented and eloquently argued,[8] literacy emerges from such personal construction. Creativity is not a sentimental or romantic concept; it is the most practical fact of human learning. Until we honor it, we will never make reading and writing a way of life so natural that education can assume literacy and go on to other things. The spiritual way is the practical way as much in learning to read and write as elsewhere. The language arts and the other arts engage the inner life with the physical and social worlds. They partake of both mind and matter. In this sense, as incarnation, they are all soulful and best learned soulfully.

10

▲

Global Thinking

The more we expand the scope of the educational arena, the more we should appreciate and renovate two key means by which schools came to deal with the swelling student populations of the twentieth century—homerooms and counselors. Homerooms came into existence to provide a social and emotional haven within larger, anonymous schools. Counselors undertook not only to deal with the social and emotional problems of individual students but also to guide students through the bewildering, depersonalized system of choices, requirements, and procedures.

Expanding the learning arena from classroom to community or beyond creates needs very similar to those that caused schools to come up with homerooms and counselors. How do you give individuals choice in an ever-expanding learning field and still anchor them emotionally and socially so that they feel secure and well supported? Many alternative schools do not have to deal with this question, either because they limit projects mostly to their campus, which they make a rich environment, or because they are small enough and well enough staffed to send learners out into the community and still provide the needed base.

A Transitional Model

Let's look now at an experiment that faces this problem inasmuch as it assumes public schooling expanding out across the community. In association with Project 2061 of the American Association for the Advancement of Science, a school team in McFarland, Wisconsin, has been working out a model for a totally individualized project approach to learning and has considered unusually well some of the practical matters that this entails.[1] The McFarland Model, as it is named, is organized around what I call projects and McFarland calls *vistas*, "open-ended, cross-disciplinary experiences which a student designs." Although in this case the projects are framed within a few broad themes, they do indeed seem open, and the experiment is very close to what I would urge schools to work toward as part of the transition to a community learning network.

The individualization of the vistas is offset by *clusters*, which are communal units. Each cluster consists of twelve students and a teacher who meet daily and stay together several years. The ages in a cluster span about four years. "A portion of cluster time is used for acquiring beginning skills within a meaningful context, initiated from the desire or need to know from the vista experience." Some of each cluster period is also devoted to sharing music together, to discussion, and to physical activity. These wisely chosen three staple activities foster not only communal feeling but personal development as well. "Clusters also provide time for in-depth pursuit of a personal interest, either alone or in a group."

Cluster groups are the basic unit for practicing democracy. "Five clusters, spanning all the ages (K-12) join together to form a *house*," which has approximately 60 students. Five houses form a *community* of 300 students and 25 teachers, which acts as "a mini United Nations." Any large facility would comprise several communities. Besides self-government, these communities also facilitate cross-age and peer tutoring and community service and apprenticing.

"For each learner there is a conference group consisting of the learner, two educators (one the current cluster teacher), and two other adults (parents, when possible)." This group helps a student plan vistas and monitor progress over the years. When a student's planning conference team decides it is time to move into the next cluster—at around ages eight, eleven, and fourteen—a *Passage* occurs, an occasion for summation, demonstration, and celebration.

"A vista is staffed by a small team of teachers with a variety of experience as well as community resources, older citizens, and others who would lend experience to the learning environment." This staff works with university students and staff and the business community. Flow charts are kept on each learner's coverage of organizing concepts over the years.

Each day's 7:30 to 3:30 schedule provides one and a half to two hours of cluster time, three and a half hours of vista time, an hour and a half of group performance time at the end of the day, two hours of common teacher planning time at the beginning of each morning while school care is provided for children arriving early, and another four and a half hours of teacher time during the latter part of each Wednesday.

Although some of us other reformers might want to dispense with themes and modify this model in minor ways—and that is part of the point of it—its architects are definitely on the right track. The communitywide learning network for all ages and all subjects, occurring at all sorts of sites, can evolve from something like the McFarland Model, which still assumes "schools" and "students." Before the learning system has reached much beyond self-contained classrooms, it could rely on learning stations, activity cards, and localized projects to individualize learning across whole schools. Then something like the McFarland Model could take over as a transition between self-contained schools and the broader arenas. Schools experimenting with it will find out what they need to know to make themselves the vehicles for ultimately transforming the whole community into the universal schoolhouse.

Precedents and Predictions

It is important to realize that similar experimental schools have been created in the past and their work documented in ways that can benefit today's reform efforts. John Dewey's University of Chicago lab school in the early 1900s was one, followed by another at Ohio State, both of which inspired a number of other schools, public and private. In 1932 the Progressive Education Association (PEA) organized thirty such schools into a project called the Eight-Year Study, the purpose of which was "to find out whether the traditional college entrance requirements and examinations made any difference in success in college, and what secondary schools would do if these requirements and examinations were abandoned."[2] Though limited to secondary schools, the project sought evidence that might remove one of the major determinants of schooling of the sort that I delineated in Chapter Five as dictating curriculum from without. A summary of results followed this statement of purpose in the introduction to the last of the five volumes in PEA's *Adventure in American Education* series:

> To this end about three hundred colleges and universities agreed to accept or reject the graduates of thirty secondary schools on the basis of records of their development submitted by the schools, without reference to the usual requirements and examinations. A study of their success in college,

broadly defined, was made by a staff of college personnel officers. In twenty-five representative colleges which enrolled the majority of the graduates of these Thirty Schools, each graduate was matched with an equally good student of the same age, sex, and race, who came from the same type of home and community, who was pursuing the same field of studies in college, and who had met the customary entrance requirements. Graduates of the Thirty Schools did as well as the comparison group in every measure of scholastic competence, and in many aspects of development which are more important than marks, they did better. The further a school departed from the traditional college preparatory program, the better was the record of its graduates. Thus it was proved that the traditional college entrance requirements and examinations are no longer necessary to insure adequate preparation for college.

The second major hypothesis of the Eight-Year Study was that the abandonment of these requirements and examinations would stimulate secondary schools to develop new programs which would be better for young people, for success in college, for success in life, and for the future of our society than the traditional college preparatory program. Volume II, *Exploring the Curriculum*, reports the developments in this direction which the staff of curriculum consultants regarded as most significant.[3]

Besides the obvious failure of this evidence to overcome a critical establishment barrier to change, we should note that (1) the colleges accepted the schools' assessments of graduates'

development, (2) college personnel officers judged college success, and especially (3) the external requirements and assessments were proved not merely unnecessary but a formidable
stumbling block to educating for higher personal and social
goals, which were being sacrificed to college admission. Paul
Diederich, author of the introduction and one of the associates
on the project's evaluation staff (which was directed by Ralph
Tyler and included the likes of Hilda Tabler and Bruno
Bettelheim), put the research question as "what secondary
schools would do if colleges let them."[4]

Both the second and fifth volumes of the PEA series give
accounts of what the thirty schools did. Their practices were
not uniform, because the project itself stipulated nothing, but
all the schools generally implemented progressive principles of
active, individualized learning in ways common to most of today's alternative schools. What the thirty schools shared was
a college-bound kind of student and a tradition of superior
education, as most still do today. Besides the lab schools referred to earlier at the University of Chicago and Ohio State
University, and another one at Teachers College, the experimental group included, among the public schools, New Trier
Township High School, Bronxville High School, Horace Mann
School, Shaker High School in Shaker Heights, and the Denver,
Tulsa, and Des Moines Junior and Senior High Schools; and
among the private schools, Beaver Country Day, Dalton
Schools, Francis W. Parker, Germantown Friends, Milton
Academy, and North Shore Country Day.

Among the curricular innovations that these leading schools
and the leading educators behind them tried to get across were
many proposed in this book and elsewhere as part of a school
reform facing the same old impediments. It's often said that
America tried that old Dewey progressivist stuff and it didn't
work, it just died out, a flash in the pan. It died out for reasons
that this Eight-Year Study makes clear—not because it did not

work, but because it was simply dismissed by the colleges. They have continued to band together through the College Entrance Examination Board and other agreements to restrict education in a way comparable to restraint of trade by the collusion of profit corporations, as demonstrated in a court ruling of 1991 that colleges may not agree on scholarship stipends. Though colleges don't see themselves as trying to dictate school curriculum, they have to take responsibility for the consequences of their collective action, which places their concerns about admissions problems over the commonweal. Avoiding the holistic view ends by hurting oneself. The graduates that colleges do admit are getting an education far inferior to what they might, and this in turn stalls the more sophisticated kind of curriculum that universities could and should develop.[5] If most colleges are just high schools with ashtrays, as one wit said, then what distinguishes them now that the ashtrays are gone?

Though colleges influence most the best schools, private even more than public, their admissions policies amount to only one of the many external determinants of schooling, as we saw in Part Two. Universities themselves, after all, conform to the societal values and conditions that ultimately account for past failures to change education but that may now be themselves changing enough under stress to encourage finally what seemed impossible as recently as 1977. That was the year when an experiment ended that probably made the best attempt, before the current reform initiative, to create a model like the one in McFarland that might serve as transition into a total community learning system. It took place at another lab school, the Wilson Campus School at Mankato State University in Wisconsin, directed by Don Glines, who is still quite active in reform today.

In the fall of 1968 the Wilson Campus School was abruptly converted into an all-year, all-day learning complex, open to all ages and offering continuous personalized learning that could be partly carried out in the community and even in certain faraway places. Bells, grades, requirements, and conventional classes all disappeared at once. Students chose facilitators and advisers, who helped them individually make up a program from day to day, week to week. Not even themes of the McFarland type were preconceived. Seminars or small classes were arranged ad hoc as needed. Nursery children mixed with adolescents, Mankato State graduate students, and town seniors. Any testing was used only to help individuals assess with their advisers how they stood in relation to the goals they had set for themselves. In conferences with students and parents, advisers said what they thought their charges were missing or ought to work on.

This experiment ran from 1968 to 1977, when it had to end because the state closed down all of its lab schools. In its July 28, 1969, issue, the *National Observer* said, "Wilson is probably the most innovative publicly supported school in the country."[6] The processes and the problems, the circumstances and the consequences were well researched and documented and can help current innovators.[7] The many educators who valued this milestone venture had to put their faith in the readiness of regular public schools to take over and develop the model, but that faith was to remain misplaced until further crises whipped up a public outcry for reform.

By 1992 the New American Schools Development Corporation (NASDC, referred to earlier as part of America 2000) had funded eleven projects to develop radically new learning models (just getting under way as of this writing). Many of these emphasize practices recommended in this book, but none puts all of them in play at once, partly perhaps because they feel obliged to skew their design in order to stand out as unique, partly too because the scope of the thinking is still not holistic enough. Thus different projects feature technology, math and science, E. D. Hirsch's cultural literacy, Outward Bound, specific themes, reorganization of resources, relevance and authenticity, or community projects.

The project titled The Co-nect School combines student-initiated projects and teacher-initiated seminars, both leading to products. "Each student has a personal growth plan regarding his/her curriculum, focusing on long-range goals and what it will take to accomplish them. . . . A re-structured school community will be created—featuring self-managing 'clusters' of students, teachers, administrators, and community members."[8] This project starts only in elementary school and heavily emphasizes technology.

In the Los Angeles Learning Centers, "each child will be linked to an individualized learning network through a 'Moving Diamond' matrix, which matches a younger student at the base of the diamond with an older student at the top, a teacher at right; and at the left, the student's parent(s) and a community volunteer," all of whom remain together for several years. The site-managed learning centers will be open from early morning through evening, fifty weeks of the year, and will integrate health and social services of some thirty agencies, from prenatal care to job readiness.

The plan of the Bensenville [Illinois] Community Design is "to create an environment where the entire community serves as campus. At the heart of the community will be a Lifelong Learning Center. Non-traditional learning sites, such as government offices and industrial complexes will become classrooms, as well." From sampling some of these more promising designs one can see that while some of the projects include important elements of what I am calling a total community learning system, these plans would have to be synthesized with each other to fully realize themselves. No one of them alone puts together lifelong learning, year-long and day-long use of facilities, full individualization, learning families or clusters, full use of private and public community sites and resources, and integration of education with other social services (dealt with in Part Four). Such a synthesis of designs may very well occur at some point in the evolution of these projects themselves or in the efforts of other communities to adapt them. But in order to create an ideal combination of these promising elements, some other elements that merely reflect current trends in policy-making circles or the conditions of the NASDC awards would have to be eliminated or downplayed. To qualify for funding, for example, all these experiments must still take part in a national examination system.

While I have serious reservations about the government-business framework in which these experiments are being carried out, it is encouraging that innovative models are receiving official sponsorship, since the public and local school districts will take them more seriously than they did earlier projects like that at Mankato. My hope is that by the time the NASDC projects reach full implementation and begin to be seriously compromised by the commitments to universal core curriculum and universal assessment, the self-contradiction between these commitments and the professed goal of "a new generation of American schools" will become so apparent through tension and conflict that this unnecessary insistence on state ownership of education will be dropped.

For a universal learning network making a whole community a school while turning over the programming and assessing of learning to the users, we have no model that has ever been implemented. In 1971 Ivan Illich proposed "deschooling society," by which he meant replacing compulsory schooling and teacher certification with public facilities that would enable people of all ages to come together with the teachers, partners, facilities, and resources they needed for learning whatever they wanted to know or know how to do.[9] No one took up Illich's proposal to abolish existing public educational systems and establish such a totally different role for government. Restructuring the entire learning processes of society seemed beyond possibility then. Indeed it does entail far more than merely restructuring schools.

In the same year that Illich's iconoclastic book appeared, the Minnesota legislature formed the Minnesota Experimental City (MXC) Project, which set about designing a model future city to serve as a laboratory for working out all the physical, social, economic, and ecological problems that urban planning had so far not solved. As described by its Director of Educational Planning, Ronald Barnes, the learning component of the city would have implemented something very close to Illich's vision.

> In the Learning System the community is the primary learning laboratory and every person in the community is a potential learner and a resource person for other learners. . . . There are no schools and no fulltime teachers; therefore learning, not teaching, is the central theme. . . . "Seekers" and "teachers" are matched by a sophisticated computer information storage and retrieval network that reaches throughout the community.[10]

Can transforming local government from an imposer of state-set education to a facilitator of personal learning occur without starting a new community from scratch? The future of education can't depend on such rare projects—and MXC was dropped, we note. It is more likely that changes occurring in all the concentric arenas will coalesce with each other and with other social changes to transform old communities.

Concentric Communities

However public education proceeds to make the community itself one big school, it must maintain strong bonds at the two extremes of expanding arenas—at the most personal, among individuals, and at the most inclusive, among communities, including nations. Social groups are learning fields, and every social group limits as well as facilitates knowledge. For the sake of full education, any community or region needs to be supplemented and complemented by others. It is essential that any educational experiment join a far-flung network of other schools or communities also striving to convert conventional schooling into a total learning environment for everyone.

This measure is to ensure against local limitations in traditions, ethnicity, atmosphere, and other conditions. Experiments move faster, moreover, if they borrow from each other, troubleshoot together, and support each other practically and spiritually. Electronic communication and transmission make this especially feasible. Exchanging actual visits creates particularly strong and useful bonds, but exchanging videotapes of student activities or audiotapes of staff discussions will help considerably also. Electronic networks already exist for students to exchange their writing with pen pals far away while their teachers too exchange ideas. Such relationships forged for mutual aid will set up practical contacts enabling older students to carry out projects either by actually going to other communities or by otherwise availing themselves of distant people and facilities.

A small college that my older daughter went through exemplifies how a project approach might work worldwide for mature young people. At the same time, it suggests one way in which colleges generally might start to reform themselves to accommodate personal choice and integration of learning. No school reform will go far without massive overhauling of higher education, which not only has set models for schools but also trained the teachers who staffed them. If spoon-feeding is inappropriate even for elementary and secondary education, it becomes scandalous in the college and university. Students who had put together their own programs in earlier years as I'm proposing would force institutions of higher learning to reorganize for educational self-determination.

Friends World College (now incorporated into the State University of New York system) consisted of neither a campus nor a curriculum but of a network of counselors situated in foreign countries who facilitated student projects by putting them in touch with people and resources that they could work with and otherwise learn through. During orientation by staff at the headquarters in Huntington, Long Island, students began to formulate a project that they would then work out further abroad after establishing a relationship with a counselor in their chosen area. Students kept copious notebooks, registered the ongoing experience in other appropriate media such as films or collections, and periodically reviewed progress with the counselor. Projects often evolved unpredictably as students learned more about both the subject and themselves. In this situation, students certainly learn how to learn, but part of becoming very resourceful is finding out how to get help.

Something that even many good alternative schools do not allow for enough is sustained personal quest, the effort to realize some inner impulse that carries the learner across different sorts of activities, subjects, means, media, and so on until some sort of resolution or clarification begins to emerge—or until she delves so deep into some specialty that she becomes an expert. My daughter apprenticed to various archaeologists around the United Kingdom, some of whose projects took her to the Balearic Islands and to Syria. Starting with a curiosity about hunter-gatherers and the changes that took place in people as they became herder-farmers, she developed a strong interest in ancient plants and learned to identify plant remains, often charred, in archaeological digs. This required studying botany along the way and reading a lot in anthropology. On the basis of this experience and these contacts, she was hired after graduation as an archaeobotanist at a British university, even though a foreigner, because few people had yet been trained in this field.

Most of the projects done by undergraduates at Friends World College were more important and original than those done in standard Ph.D. programs. One young woman in my daughter's class got herself adopted into a Bedouin tribe of the Sinai peninsula and spent most of her four years of college living as the Bedouin women did. By the time she left, she probably knew more about these people than any outsider in the world, partly because former anthropologists who had studied them (and whom she had studied) were male. Another student worked with a theater group in the Philippines that was teaching peasants in the provinces how to put on plays as a way to raise consciousness against the despotic regime of Ferdinand Marcos. Such a project combined a foreign language and culture with politics and art.

Yet this unorthodox college could not at that time get itself officially accredited. Like the certifying of who is to teach, the accrediting of institutions limits severely the capacity of education to move in sorely needed directions. Both of these validations (and the certifying of students as well) are based on old notions of exclusion that we must reconsider and perhaps abandon. Friends World College not only embodied the individualized, project approach to learning but also fostered global consciousness. It represented one school's effort to set up internationally the sort of learning environment that we have been considering as extending throughout only a rural or urban community. Imagine how well the individual projects of older learners could fare if they had access not just to the counseling resources of one small college like Friends World stretched thinly around the world, or to one exchange arrangement between a couple of schools in a couple of countries, but to a worldwide network of educational resources allowing endless permutations of possibilities. The idea of the community as school can be expanded, for learners who are ready, to the idea of the world as school. It's all a matter of seeing ourselves as living at once in concentric communities of varying magnitudes, all of which are learning environments.

A Broader Notion of Teachers

Practically, this vision of expanding learning fields has to translate into a network's human and material resources, which are both public and private. A new covenant has to be agreed on between not only the community and the education profession but between the public and private sectors. Though school districts should not merely, as the privatizers wish, issue vouchers that allow students to enroll in some all-purpose private school, some kind of disbursing of public funds for private resources will indeed be necessary to enable learners to utilize as teachers many people not regularly hired by the educational system. Public education money going to the private sector would go to individuals or very small businesses, like studios, whose main function is to teach a specialty such as ballet or martial arts when no volunteer teachers or public facilities of equal worth are available.

Devising a way to incorporate private enterprise into the community network poses an important practical problem that I don't pretend to have a solution for but that I feel sure the various parties in a community can work out, once convinced of the necessity of pooling all local resources into a total learning network. The problem should be considered within the framework of reinvestment dealt with in Part Four, since these individuals or small companies represent just the sort of enterprises that would warrant investment capitalization when reinvesting societal resources.

A huge number of people in recent decades have begun to teach privately a wide array of skills and subjects that schools don't include. Biofeedback, aikido, or herbalology don't fit readily into traditional subjects and teacher training, but many such "alternative" subjects deserve to be taught more than some things enshrined in traditional schooling or at any rate ought to be made available as schooling turns from standardization to individualization. The principle of maximum accessibility requires widening the faculty to include many more teachers than just those certified in the very limited set of traditional subjects. Many people qualify as teachers who never try to get certified, and some who are certified are not good teachers.

Public education has not always attracted the best people because it is too restrictive, not to say downright demeaning, in which case certification standards mean nothing. It does no good to hoist standards for teachers if most people who can pass them refuse to work in such poor conditions. The fact is that public schools have never been able to let certification stand in the way of recruiting the number it takes to staff schools. State certification has not protected the public against massive bad education, because the institutions that train and certify teachers perpetuate some of the very practices and conditions that have to be reformed. But many people would like to work with human growth, which is far more exciting than the stuff of many other vocations.

We must reconceive certification in a comprehensive way that embraces all the many people who are qualified to teach something and deserve compensation for it. Typically, state control of any professional certification protects certain established practitioners and excludes others. In the name of the citizenry, it thus decides for the citizens, with the force of law, which courses of action they may or may not take. As the example of medicine painfully illustrates, government agencies and professional organizations not only cannot protect the public this way but themselves often become accessories to abuse and block needed advances. As much as possible, the learners would collectively determine who is qualified by using the community network itself as a consumer service. Nothing will better protect the public against charlatans and incompetents than an educational system where people learn to think for themselves.

The fact that many people besides trained educators will be tutoring or coaching does not devalue professional educators, who will be needed as much as ever to run a community learning system. It is they who will be matching up learners with the right resources at the right time, routing them around within the learning network, and tutoring and coaching within their own specialties. Understanding how growth occurs and knowing something about a particular subject or two are the essential qualifications. Professional educators will have to learn in addition how to run a community learning network that has never existed before. Schools of education will have to reconceive self-contained subject areas so as to facilitate the integration of knowledge and to foster the total personal growth of individuals. Professional educators will differ from the other teachers, coaches, and mentors in the community network in that they will not only know a specialty but also be trained to run the network itself.

Counseling

These future educators will have to be good epistemologists, experts in the nature of knowledge and in how people construct knowledge integratively by all means at once. Maximizing access for everybody to all resources at any time requires a new and fine art of playing to individuals on the one hand and, on the other, keeping in touch with a far-flung, multifarious complex of potential teachers, learning sites, and other educational resources. Many if not most learners will not know what there is to be learned, what might interest them, what places, people, and materials they might want to utilize. Unless these educational counselors constantly make them aware of the possibilities, freedom of choice will have little meaning. Whereas past education required students to react to what teachers did, future education will make students proactive and educators reactive. Playing to personal patterns of need, interest, learning style, and background is essentially what will transform public education.

This exciting new art crosses epistemology with counseling. These educators will also have to know one or two disciplines well so that when an individual or group needs advice about which way to go next in pursuit of a subject or activity, they can recommend specific people, places, materials, sources and other resources in that field as well as work directly themselves with these learning parties. Obviously much depends on wise cross-referral so that when counselors run out of their expertise, they can shunt learners to other people better versed in what is needed. Each learner will at any given time be in the charge of some counselors who know her or him well (like the learner's adult committee in the McFarland Model or the Moving Diamond matrix in the Los Angeles Learning Centers) and of some who may not know the learner but can advise well on current plans or activities. While following all of these recommendations, learners are also getting familiar with the network itself and becoming able to help each other get around in it.

Each learner of whatever age should benefit from the advice

of several parties all the time, some of whom may be expert general counselors, some peers in various groups, some members of a "family" that stays together for several years, and some temporary specialists for a certain project. As in the rest of the system, this pluralism is essential for balancing biases, filling in gaps, and approaching impartiality in the overall effect. Advising may concern physical and mental health or practical matters like employment and human relationships, as well as more traditional learning aims and means. Combined with the very pluralism of the whole network, which constantly mixes people together as they share resources, counseling can help overcome racial and religious intolerance by honoring all equally and by helping individuals to see how crossing boundaries can further their own aims. Intolerance or bias is simply one part of the overly narrow conditioning that everyone needs to escape by joining a larger community.

All matters have to be considered in relation to each other, as only a thoroughgoing "client-centered" approach makes possible. Advising must be well coordinated so that the individual can assimilate and truly utilize the recomendations from various advisers. Thus a learner has to see how health and state of mind are influencing or being influenced by various current activities and relationships and then to make plans that will correct, fill out, or balance these circumstances. All parties must understand that counselors will say what they think is best for their client but that the client will make the final decision, often in consultation with family or others close and trusted. Some counseling, for example, may be to read such and such a text, talk with so and so, join a certain group or project, take a course, take a certain medical test, follow a certain diet, or pursue some old interest in a new medium or facility. Through referrals from one counselor to another, an individual's total well-being, including emotional and physical health, may be continually attended to within a single system.

Assessing

Whereas assessment looms as a formidable issue when done as a special activity for outsiders, it takes its proper place as part and parcel of the learning activity itself when done by and for the learner. Anyone who wants to do something she or he cares about wants to know the outcome. Even if no product results, we want to know the personal value of the experience. Assessment, in other words, is built into the original motivation. Did I accomplish what I intended? If not, what might I have done differently? What can I now do that I could not do before? What do I now know that I did not before? Did our community project make a difference? Did my audience get the point of my story? Everybody wants to find out the consequences of their actions—if they *chose* to do them. More generally, people want to know where they are headed and how they are doing. Am I growing into the kind of person I want to be?

Like the learning activities themselves, assessment does not interrupt real-life pursuits, because both *are* real life. However, one does not assume that people know from the outset how best to determine results, any more than one assumes that people grow up naturally knowing how to make good decisions. Like creating a curriculum for yourself, assessing the results of it for yourself is precisely what the system of individualized learning aims to teach. Again, colleagues and counselors play an indispensable role here. It is by heeding feedback of some sort that we learn the consequences of our actions. Partners and recipients feed back to us simply as part of their involvement in what we are doing; coaches and counselors reflect results as they play to their clients' patterns of action. Members of a workshop join together in the first place to exchange helpful and sensitive responses to one another's work. Wherever reciprocity is strong and goodwill high, as it should be throughout the whole learning network, people do this for each other. Assessment is built into the very nature of interaction as it is into motivation.

But sometimes we don't know how to heed or read feedback and consequences. We need sensitizing so that we can detect results. A coach may have to help us hear the false note or the rushing of tempo as we practice a musical instrument. Not all effects are social, but through other people we can learn to pick up on what we were deaf to at first. Techniques may be involved, like operating instruments that detect results, or making calculations. Audio- and videotapes reflect oneself back in very useful ways without judgment by other people. Even small children make observations about their behavior from witnessing playback. Looking back over portfolios and other products helps discern traits and trends indicating growth or problems. This sort of periodic review should be standard preparation for conferences with advisers. Sometimes "objective" tests of one's skill or knowledge may be useful if the learner sees their value for the aim in mind (presumably to compare oneself with others). Assessment is as various as enterprises themselves. Choosing the means of assessing equals the learning task of finding the best means of fulfilling the goal in the first place.

Part of what one learns is the relationship between setting and meeting goals. As people mature, their goals sometimes need to be changed. Counselors should be alert to disparities between old goals and new growth, or between conscious goals and actual patterns of choice or behavior. But not all learning is by any means goal-oriented in a specific or predetermined sense. What happened when I just fooled around or experimented or played for fun? What is going on in this job or relationship? In its broadest sense, assessment is a matter of staying aware of what is going on in all aspects of one's life.

Ultimately, both counseling and assessing should be guided

by the question, "What purpose or meaning does my life have?" Much groping and discontent pertain to this issue of feeling significance in what one does. Counselors need to be always alert for this question, to recognize it under various guises, and to help their charges make their life mean something. They should not impose a meaning but patiently counsel within a spiritual framework allowing meaning to grow as people grow.

11

▲

A Spiritual View
of Growth

How counselors advise their charges and how learners use the community learning network will obviously depend considerably on some aspects of general child development and human growth. It can be helpful to know how psychologists conceptualize this on the basis of scientific research, but I urge two qualifications.

First, customizing education automatically accommodates each learner's particular manifestation of general child development without the risks of applying generic concepts of growth to individuals. Much harm has been done trying to fit all children into a sequence of stages necessarily rendered even cruder as practiced in a mass institution than as distilled from research. The beauty of truly individualizing is that educators don't necessarily have to have in mind in advance a clear sequence of stages and can even let individuals show *them* what the stages are. When students respond to prearranged stimuli, what we learn mainly is the presumptions of those who programmed the curriculum. When educators allow students each to establish a pattern of choice to which the *educators* respond, then the learning environment itself becomes a natural laboratory in which to refine any notions of human development.

Still, educators will always have some asssumptions about growth that will influence the decision making of the students they counsel. So in one way or another we do have to allow for theories of growth. My second qualification about them concerns their parameters, to use a research term for what I have been calling a frame of reference. What may be true enough in one framework may mislead in the next larger or smaller context. Thus descriptions of child development made by scientists may be valid and even acute *as far as they go* (that is, for the given material framework) but may seem limited or blunted from a metaphysical or spiritual perspective. They might be deemed not so much wrong as incomplete—but still misleading.

Comparing Scientific and Spiritual Views of Child Development

Comparing Rudolf Steiner's teachings about child development with psychologists' concepts of it demonstrates the issue. Founder in the 1920s of the Waldorf schools, now playing an important role in the alternative school movement, Steiner split off from the Theosophists to establish his own spiritual organization, Anthroposophy. He combined a scholarly education in traditional science and philosophy with clairvoyance and spiritual discipline, which he considered a science also. Whether or not one believes in clairvoyance and can accept his sometimes astounding utterances, his ability to see at once from both spiritual and material perspectives makes it worthwhile to at least entertain his ideas of child development, especially if one wishes to supplement scientific concepts with a spiritual perspective.

Interestingly, Steiner's notions confirm far more than contra-

▲

dict these concepts, but he embeds our commonly held ideas of growth in a context, very strange to most of us, that would explain our ideas in far greater depth and would sometimes indicate different ways of proceeding in education if we accepted it. Even a Freudian-based theory such as Erik Erikson's eight stages between infancy and mature age would not belie what Steiner says. The crises of trust, autonomy, initiative, industry, and identity (Erikson's first five stages into adolescence) derive, like many other scientific descriptions of growth, from physical, social, and cultural phenomena as interpreted by a sensitive therapist reflecting on rich clinical experience.[1]

The work of cognitive psychologists fits Steiner's perspective better, up to a point. Typically, as in Jerome Bruner's enactive, iconic, and symbolic stages—cognizing through the body, then images, then abstract symbols—children grow from concrete to abstract.[2] These correspond roughly to stages of biological, social, and ideational maturation, as developed also by other theorists. Children internalize exchanges with material objects and people into thought and language, creating an inner speech and inner life, according to social psychologists Lev Vygotsky[3] and George Herbert Mead[4] and also to "genetic epistemologist" Jean Piaget. Piaget's five stages consist of a sensorimotor stage (birth to age two), a preconceptual stage (ages two to four), an intuitive stage (ages four to seven), concrete mental operations (ages seven to eleven), and formal logical operations (ages eleven to fifteen).[5]

These and virtually all other scientific theories of development share a movement toward complexity that is resolved by continuous integration of stages with one another. As perhaps best decribed by Heinz Werner, the human organism gradually breaks down its initial global perception through a process of differentiating itself from the environment and then differentiating outer and inner things from each other.[6] This analysis is countered by a constant effort to synthesize, to reassemble reality by abstract, hierarchical organization of the mental life. Globalism corresponds to what Piaget and Vygotsky call egocentricity, self-centeredness not as mere selfishness but as an orientation of perception, emotion, and thought that fails to distinguish self from other, inner from outer. Werner "finds the same structural principles to hold in the mental life of 'primitive' men, children, and of certain psychotics. In all these groups he discovers essentially the same utilitarian concreteness of mental life, characterized by syncretism, synesthesia, animism, conservatism, and magic."[7] Through cultural anthropology Werner does expand the perspective on human growth, but for him these traits indicate an earlier stage in mental development, whereas Claude Lévi-Strauss regards them as alternative, not necessarily prior or inferior, modes of knowing.[8] This more positive view of syncretic, animistic, or magical thinking brings us closer to the attitude of Rudolf Steiner.

With a peremptory authority that is disconcerting for those of us not endowed with clairvoyance, Steiner founds education on the process by which an individual spirit incarnates into the material plane. According to him, the stages of child development derive from the gradual nature of incarnation, which is phased in over the years of youth by the fact that human beings comprise multiple bodies or vehicles, each of which has its own time to incarnate. As mentioned in Chapter One, these bodies constitute together what may be thought of as a vibrational spectrum of multiple realities making up both nature and human nature.

Steiner treats four of these bodies, the other three of the traditional seven being too inconceivable for practical exposition except as developments of the first four. Two of the four are the familiar physical body, whose incarnation we call birth, and the etheric or subtle body (double or doppelgänger), also physical but detectable only as an aura and only by some people. The third is the astral body, nonmaterial and associated with emotion and intuition, clairvoyantly detected as a luminous ovoid aura of shifting colors. The highest is the egoic body, vehicle of the soul, the spiritual *I* that remains across incarnations.

Each body or vehicle works on the ones below, first while still withheld from the material world and only loosely connected to the physical person, then it becomes increasingly active on the material plane as it gradually incarnates. Steiner recognizes three main stages of child development of seven years each. During the first stage, the physical body outgrows, under the governance of the slowly incarnating etheric body, the original physical inheritance begun in the womb. By the time the second teeth are in, around age seven, the individual is creating a new body more or less its own, and the now fully incarnated etheric body is developing under the governance of the still hovering astral body. The awakening of the reproductive organs accompanies the incarnating of the astral body during puberty, and both are completed around age fourteen, after which the egoic body is incarnating, up to around twenty-one, the traditional age of "majority."

This process determines the traits of each stage, which depend on the particular work being accomplished by each vehicle as it incarnates or governs another's incarnation. Before the second teeth, says Steiner, the individual is one large sense organ that barely distinguishes self from world, inner life from outer. This hypersensitive organism is directly and indelibly imprinted by the environment, to a degree never later repeated except perhaps in some extraordinary state of consciousness. The child does not merely receive sensations but "incarnates" them so that they are almost literally absorbed into the soul and into the body, causing permanent casts of mind and, when negative, specific illnesses much later. According to all this, *imitation and example* constitute the characteristic learning mode of these first seven years, especially the first half.

This is exactly how Maria Montessori describes this age in *The Absorbent Mind,*[9] and it accounts for her insisting on a prepared learning environment for the preschool years. The people and the objects surrounding the child have such a life-long impact, both she and Steiner feel, that they should be carefully selected, the people so as to establish warm and loving social bonds and to set the best example by their nature and behavior, the objects so as to exercise and stimulate senses and muscles. The children should be licensed to explore and manipulate the environment. Steiner recommends lots of singing and dancing, and both educators emphasize the arts to develop movement and to educate the senses. This is the stage Bruner designates as "enactive," and it covers Piaget's "sensorimotor," "preconceptual," and "intuitive" phases.

Like Burton White (*The First Three Years of Life),*[10] most developmentalists and pediatricians now believe what these spiritual educators—along with that soul scientist, Freud—understood at the beginning of the century, when childhood was generally regarded as indifferent: that the most important formation occurs soon after birth and that preschool learning conditions influence later life more than schooling because they affect more the inner being, the life core. Though Montessori enormously influenced American nursery schools and kindergartens, which now feature sensorimotor learning, a stimulating environment, and healthy self-expression, the pressures of ambitious parents and institutional accountability work constantly to push verbalism, testing, and high-priority subjects downward into these play years. Now governments sponsor early childhood programs that too often address more the letter than the spirit of these innovative insights.

The animism, syncretism, synesthesia, and magical thinking that even a later researcher like Heinz Werner is still apt to treat as *only* primitive, immature, and pathological accord with Steiner's characterization of early childhood. For Steiner, however, this global perception makes for a natural *homo religiosus,* as he terms it, precisely because the child experiences body and spirit, self and world, as one. The educator's task is to "give over to earthly life what in the child has come to us out of the divine-spirit world."[11] This notion that the child comes "trailing clouds of glory" was rendered definitively in poetic form by Wordsworth and taken seriously by the Transcendentalist Bronson Alcott, who transcribed in *Conversations with Children on the Gospels* how his students at the Temple School in Boston interpreted scripture.[12] Similarly today, psychologist Robert Coles has recorded the religious observations that his child subjects have made.[13]

Entertaining this spiritual interpretation of well-accepted childhood phenomena may prove useful to educators in considering the now also widely shared idea that preschool children command an extraordinary creativity that shortly disappears, as expressed in the titles *The Magical Child* and *The Radiant Child* of psychologists Joseph Chilton Pearce and Thomas Armstrong,[14] both of whom count so-called psychic abilities among these talents. A second-grade teacher reported in the professional magazine *Learning* that his pupils often said they saw "lights" and auras in or around the bodies of people and other living things and colored forms floating in the air.[15] Drawings they made of these were included in the article, and one appeared on the cover. This teacher had done six years of investigation with such children in school and summer camp and combined this with theoretical research to produce a master's thesis on this subject. When a four-year-old boy walked into my living room and looked at my yoga teacher (an Indian swami), he paused, pointed, and exclaimed, "He must be a king—he's got stars all over him!" One can get an idea from a diary that a clairvoyant Victorian boy kept[16] of how such an ability might be real and also of how it might be lost if adults put it down to wild imagination, as in his case.

The point is not that educators should necessarily believe in clairvoyance, telepathy, and other extrasensory powers but that any frame of reference for educational planning should allow for, not rule out, such possibilities, which, if real, would be extremely important not so much for the powers themselves as for what they would imply about human nature and capacity, including the understanding of other childhood creativity. After all, even Freud, who tried poignantly hard to be a good materialist, reluctantly came to believe in telepathy because of experience with his patients and came up with the speculation—far-reaching for developmental theory—that telepathy may have been humankind's medium of communication until supplanted by speech.

Just as the human embryo passes from a single cell through the evolutionary scale of animal orders, the child tends to recapitulate the psychological development of the human species, as Werner and other anthropologically oriented developmentalists indicate. But the subconscious nature of our earliest experience renders adults amnesiac toward this stage when, because of the very diffusion between inner and outer, we are at once most egocentric and most attuned to other people, creatures, and perhaps frequencies.

According to Steiner, after the replacement of teeth, which begins the child's assertion of its individuality against its inheritance, the outside environment can influence the now fully incarnated etheric body, which has an affinity with the plastic arts. As part of neural development, the rhythms of breathing and blood circulation now need to be harmonized, which calls for music and poetry. These children are natural artists. They also become more self-aware and distinguish themselves from the outer world, which they are eager to learn about. With selfhood comes a great memory capacity, which is bound up with the molding of the etheric body. Combined, these trends mean that the time is right for study of nature and society, but through artistic not intellectual modes, especially soul-satisfying pictures and parables, imagistic stories that *symbolize* knowledge.

As I interpret Steiner, animism is transmuted into an identification with other creatures and the earth; syncretic or global perception into a holistic ecological perspective; synesthesia into integrated arts; and magical thinking into creative imagination. Note that these aspects of "primitive" thinking are there to begin with but become more "cognitive" and "artistic" as the child becomes self-conscious and socialized. All this jibes well with Bruner's "iconic" stage and Piaget's "concrete operations," which are mental but not formally logical, that is, internalizations of physical and social operations strongly based still on imagery.

Steiner repeatedly warns educators not to rush literacy and discursive learning. Subject matter and ideas that have been assimilated through the senses and arts, and through human interaction, will be worked over by the intellect when the time is right. Students should learn to write from drawing and painting and do so before learning to read, because interpreting text requires more abstractive development than transcribing your thoughts, which will naturally stay within your own range of reasoning.

During the second stage, "discipleship and authority" replace "imitation and example" (Steiner's terms) as the principal learning interaction. The spirituality of still being attuned to the cosmos turns into a reverential attitude toward key adults, who may exert enormous influence for good or ill. Most educators, including myself, would feel prostrate with inadequacy before the high spiritual criteria that Steiner sets for teachers. Clearly, a major problem is how to muster from our adult world and set before youth something worthy of its reverence, on pain otherwise of losing a major growth force. Only an assumption of remarkably evolved personnel could justify entrusting children to the same main teacher for eight or so years running, as Steiner recommended for his Waldorf schools. But the same problem obtains in fact in stage one: how many parents can serve well enough as examples for such impressionable creatures to imitate?

With oncoming puberty the astral body is incarnating and hence open in its turn to influences from the earthly environment. Since it is the emotional or feeling vehicle, its association with adolescence makes sense, as anyone who knows the volatility of the thirteen-year-old can testify. It also has a special affinity for music and rhythm, which play a formative role in the body, especially in coordinating the nervous system, breathing, and blood circulation. "The astral body with its musical activity beats in time with the etheric body which works plasticly."[17] During puberty and the establishing of sexual identity, the intellect comes into its own, says Steiner, in consonance with Bruner's "symbolic" or discursive stage and Piaget's "formal logical operations."

Between puberty and adulthood, the third seven-year period, the egoic body is incarnating. It works through words and ideation. Intellect, logic, and independent judgment come fully into their own. Twenty-one represents adulthood because we then belong fully to ourselves in the sense that all our vehicles are now in place, congruent, and the one that bears our *I* from one incarnation to another is now installed in the physical body. Of course this whole development is cumulative, so that no earlier traits or capacities are lost, though they may be transformed or covered over.

Utilizing the Spiritual View

Educators lose nothing of scientific understanding by considering this spiritual view of growth, which does not contradict it but goes beyond it. To take only my own case, it has helped me to think about some important learning issues that material psychology does not seem to deal with, even though some involve common practical problems.

Females, for example, generally mature sooner than males and so are often regarded as adults at eighteen rather than at twenty-one. Boys commonly lag behind girls during most of the school years. Steiner says that this is true because males incarnate more deeply into the physical plane and therefore take longer to mature. Because it is metaphysically founded, Steiner's description of development is consistent across his explanations of apparently disparate phenomena. Thus one gender difference he sees is that the imagination is more developed in females; in males, the will. This is a difference between inner and outer orientation and therefore helps explain why males should incarnate more deeply into matter. Without exaggerating such traits into gender stereotypes, we can see for ourselves this difference in children's behavior, most boys being from birth notoriously more difficult to control as they manipulate the environment and most girls attending more to feelings and the inner life. Of course, we have to understand this contrast as between male and female *tendencies*, which are differently blended in a given individual, each sex bearing, in Jungian fashion, the potential of the other. Only individualizing learning will accommodate sexual differences—mostly ignored in modern schooling.

Steiner says that small children are boisterous and clumsy and scream a lot because they experience tremendous difficulty adjusting to physical embodiment. Used to the unconditioned freedom of the spirit world, they unconsciously expect to live here as there and so undergo enormous frustration. What adults regard as restless, hyperkinetic, and inattentive behavior derives considerably from the trauma of transition, birth being only a more obvious dramatization of the long invisible process of incarnating. All while suspending belief, we may test out the explanatory power of incarnational development by trying to apply it to realities like these that we may know all too well.

For years I have pondered a universal learning problem that observant teachers and parents of elementary-school children never fail to notice. A big learning slump occurs around the end of third grade, at or after age eight. Formerly enthusiastic children become listless and don't like school. They seem to forget what they knew, and their scores go down. Bright turns dull. What's happened to my child? But it happens in at least some measure to virtually every child at this time—at least in this culture.

Not only is the problem important for practical reasons, it also raises significant issues about the interaction of biology with culture. How much does some inevitable, inborn schedule produce this slump, and how much does acculturation in general or some acculturation in particular account for it? It is scientifically difficult to factor out these variables. You can compare growth in different cultures, but everyone grows up in some culture that cannot be filtered out from biological determinants. Perhaps partly for this reason, research has very little to say about the problem. It is possible that the very holistic complexity of the slump makes it hard both to frame as a problem and to investigate by traditional science.

Several things occur simultaneously at that age that may each play a part. The two hemispheres of the brain, which have been functioning alike, as in other mammals, differentiate into the specialization described in the well-known and ongoing literature on split-brain research. Like any such big change, this unsettles the organism. Also, the thrill and challenge of getting out of the home among other people has worn off. The socializing and acculturating process has started to suppress the originality and creativity of the preschool and primary school child, who now becomes conflicted between self-expression and conformity. This is the age, after all, when self-awareness replaces the fusion of self with world.

For its part, school begins to drop play and the few art activities and focus on discursive subjects like social studies, science, and literacy in isolation. The specialization that begins within the self-contained classroom culminates in middle school or junior high with the traumatic fragmenting of education into separate classes with separate subjects, teachers, rooms, and hours, from which few students fully recover. The physical dropping out of many students at this time consummates their inward dropping out at the dispirited stage foreshadowing it.

Suppose for a moment that the child does incarnate from the spirit world but that this radiant infant, this creative dynamo, this natural *homo religiosus*, eats of the tree of knowledge by becoming accommodated to matter, acculturated, and self-conscious, and is then barred from the tree of life, cast out of Eden. The third-grade slump would then be a stage in the Fall, the descent into matter, in which case Wordsworth's ode "Intimations of Immortality from Recollections of Childhood" may be the best treatise ever written on child development.

> Our birth is but a sleep and a forgetting:
> The Soul that rises from us, our life's Star,
>   Hath had elsewhere its setting,
>   And cometh from afar:
>   Not in entire forgetfulness,
>   And not in utter nakedness,
> But trailing clouds of glory do we come:
> Heaven lies about us in our infancy!
> Shades of the prison-house begin to close
>   Upon the growing Boy,
> But he beholds the light, and whence it flows,
>   He sees it in his joy;

> The Youth, who daily farther from the East
> Must travel, still is Nature's priest,
> And by the vision splendid
> Is on his way attended;
> At length the Man perceives it die away,
> And fade into the light of common day.

The whole ode is encapsulated in this stanza, the opening lines of which clearly refer to serial incarnations, as do an astonishing number of passages in Western literature and philosopy.[18]

Too often we prefer to read these references as flowery speech and poetic fancy than to take them seriously. "Shades of the prison-house" catches our child's feeling by the time of the slump, and "beholds the light" may well refer to clairvoyance, since in the first stanza Wordsworth says there was a time when everything "To me did seem / Apparelled in celestial light." The "vision splendid" of Youth aptly renders adolescent idealism, a resurgence of the child's natural spirituality after the revitalization of puberty accompanying the incarnation of the astral vehicle. The Man later falls into disillusionment as this vision is obscured by "the light of common day." I invite the reader to revisit this poem in the inner light from which it was written, forget it as an example of Romanticism, and pay close attention to what Wordsworth is saying in each of the lines as they build across the stanzas this picture of the human cycle as spiritually viewed.

Do things have to happen this way? How much do all efforts to describe growth, including spiritual ones, reflect merely things as we know them, growth as deformed by materialistic culture and not necessarily as it might occur under changed conditions? Must the individual be "haunted forever by the Eternal Mind" without regaining access to it, always rattling the locked gates of Eden but never finding the lost paradise before death? These questions rephrase the question of how much human development is unalterably programmed by our biology and how much merely determined by culture, which humankind can change. Maybe, for example, the slump does not have to occur if communities create a learning environment that avoids or offsets those cultural factors that dispirit the child.

Premature verbalism surely counts among these—the pushing for early literacy to meet a state standard or to allay parental anxiety, both unnecessary. The question is not whether small children *can* learn to read and write but whether they *should*. Literacy should enter each individual's program at a time that best befits that person's total growth and learning pattern. Excessive early verbalism is a factor of our culture's tendency to overvalue naming and stating things, as if ticketing and talking up reality necessarily increases understanding and utility. Einstein did not talk till he was three, Buckminster Fuller stopped speaking for a year before inventing the geodesic dome, and much practical evidence suggests—including the effects of wordless meditation—that language can seriously interfere with intuition and creativity. It may in fact kill extrasensory capacity, in keeping with Freud's speculation that speech supplanted telepathy. Adults usually talk children out of "seeing things" so that if indeed clairvoyance exists, children lose it.

One theoretical explanation for the specialization of brain hemispheres around eight or so is that language comes to so dominate consciousness that the only way our spatial, kinesthetic, rhythmic, and intuitive intelligences can save themselves is to claim a part of the brain for themselves at the cost of separation. Hence the so-called nonverbal, artistic, creative hemisphere connected to the left hand in right-handed people. Imagine what happened to left-handed children when teachers used to make them write with their right hand. This practice, we trust, has now disappeared, but it stands for the much broader sacrificing of the nonverbal, intuitive part of our human being to discursive learning.

Along with forced literacy and excessive verbalism, our culture violates the very development from concrete to abstract that constitutes the most widely agreed upon feature of mental growth. The whole point of delineating stages as Piaget or Steiner has done is to indicate how necessary these are and how educators must allow for them. Under various social pressures, however, our schools have rushed too soon to higher abstractions and spoiled the abstracting process that is central to discursive learning itself. This error takes the form of teaching too much nomenclature and taxonomy, as in the sciences, given the little concrete knowledge that students yet have of the things in nature referred to. As Montessori emphasized for small children and Caleb Gattegno demonstrated even for adolescents, arithmetic and math can be learned through manipulable materials that embody abstract relations and principles.[19] Gattegno uses color-coded Cuisenaire rods of different lengths, which he introduced into America, to teach even algebra. Though such things as geoboards, blocks, rods, and other manipulables have become familiar in U.S. schools, now blessed as "hands-on" learning, they are still eclipsed by the ponderous math textbooks, which increase rather than diminish the abstractness of math that poses the main problem for learners.

The concept of hierarchical levels of abstraction has been a central one for me in working with educators in the language arts. In an early work I proposed correspondence between stages of mental growth and levels of abstraction.[20] Though very well received, this proposal has always been hard for schools to implement because allowing children to dwell as long as needed in the concreter realms of thought and discourse makes their work look less "advanced" than teachers and parents think it should. Adults feel better if students are reading

▲

certain classics, even if they don't understand them well yet and the experience turns them off from literature. It looks better if students are writing exposition and argumentation, even though they may do these mechanically, plagiaristically, and ineptly just because they have not been allowed to work their way up to this level of abstraction through concreter kinds of discourse like letters and journals, personal narratives and reportage, informal essays and reviews. In trying to cover too much material too fast, history textbooks synopsize the human story to the point of devitalizing the narrative and of stereotyping the experience. Literature is historicized and scientized with conceptual handles that format it to courses and exams.

This conversion from right to left hemisphere, from the imagistic and intuitive mode to the taxonomic and conceptual mode, typifies the way schooling hustles children up the abstraction ladder to comply with society's misguided, overly male notion of progress. Not honoring equally all stages of the concrete-to-abstract development actually short-circuits intellectual advancement and thereby shortchanges the learners.

Finally, a spiritual perspective like Steiner's introduces ideas for which scientists offer no parallel, mainly those clustering around incarnation. Here we have a circular problem. If we don't believe in clairvoyance, because we feel we haven't experienced it, then we may react to Steiner's description of development with great skepticism, if not alarm. If people like him who say children are incarnating from the spirit world are not themselves clairvoyant, then why should we believe children are? If, on the other hand, we think at least some children have extrasensory powers, then Steiner could be clairvoyant and therefore seeing true. That's one circle.

Another is that we may not believe in clairvoyance and incarnation precisely for the reason that the very process of incarnating induces amnesia as materialization and acculturation—"the light of common day"—obscure spirit. To put it the spiritual way, as higher vehicles enter matter, they become temporarily subjugated by it, and the *I*, fully centered after adulthood in the physical vehicle, cannot know its real nature and origin unless, through some gift, it retains consciousness of its higher vehicles or, through special education, regains such consciousness.

Whether regarded as incarnation or not, the notion of passing from a relatively unconditioned state to a highly conditioned state seems to me very valuable for educators to contemplate. Never will people be as open-minded again as in infancy, when we are so absorptive and receptive, unprogrammed yet, that we will believe anything. Life does seem to be a process of gradually committing ourselves to people, circumstances, behaviors, views, and ideas that progressively narrow what we are able to see, think, and do. Much education, in fact, consists of trying to offset this by finding out things and having thoughts that go beyond these commitments ("travel is so broadening"). Since spirit may be defined as an absence of conditions, and incarnation as the acquiring of conditions, it could be useful to think of education as deconditioning, as undoing the epistemological effects of cumulative material commitments without undoing the commitments themselves. In other words, we should be able to materialize, join the human race, become a member of a certain family and other social groups, spend time certain ways, choose a profession and mate, live in a particular locality, and let ourselves undergo all sorts of other experiences and conditions but not let our inner life shrink to fit these external limits. For this double process of simultaneously committing ourselves externally while liberating ourselves inwardly the model of incarnation and reawakening does justice to the practical realities of everyday life.

The notion of multiple bodies or vehicles corresponding to plural realities might illuminate some commonly recognized psychological phenomena. A major issue in this cosmology concerns the interrelationships among physical, etheric, astral, and egoic bodies. The relative solidity and stability of most adults, for better or worse, owes to the "settling down" of bodies after complete incarnation. This state would be very different from earlier stages when the vehicles are "at sixes and sevens," as growth is often described. The fact that a young person's bodies are loosely related to one another, not all "in their place," and becoming congruent with varying degrees of difficulty may help explain how "getting it together" works or fails to happen.

So-called hyperkinetic behavior might indicate a looser connection than with some other children between the physical body and the others, which, remember, each govern the one below even while "hovering" before their own incarnation. Autism may represent some recalcitrance on the part of one or more of the higher bodies to enter the material plane, leaving the child uncommitted to the physical world except to repeat mechanical behavior such as bumping the head, sticking obsessively to routines, or reciting set litanies. Often bright and creative, autistic people may be "old souls," highly evolved individuals who are reluctant to leave the spirit realm for earth. Thus disconnected from the astral (emotional) body, say, the autistic earthling feels little and does not relate to others.

Schizophrenia may consist of an invasion, on the other hand, of the mind by another realm of reality such as the astral world, to which the astral body gives access. Though some schizophrenic "hallucinations" may indeed be fantasies projected as real, owing to a confusion of inner and outer, others may be sights truly coming from outside the person but not from the material plane. Much clairvoyance is said to be uncontrolled and unconscious. Balance and interplay among vehicles would be critical, and imbalance and disconnection might account for much.

The very looseness obtaining among the bodies as they successively incarnate would produce a state conducive to unusual experiences such as are often attributed to childhood. The lack of consolidation plus the late arrival of the egoic body itself postpone the formation of the spiritual *I*'s material counterpart, the human self or "ego structure." Since it is the incarnated *I* that filters and structures experience, this labile state would make the child more sensitive to earthly influences and at the same time more open to the extrasensory channels by which telepathy and clairvoyance would operate.

In speaking today of experiences of near-death, of anesthetic or certain other neurochemical effects, and of childhood trauma such as severe physical and mental abuse, we resort increasingly to some notion of "going out of the body." Both the early psychoanalytic concept of dissociation and the more recent concept of multiple personality assume some splitting of the individual, but what splits off from what? It is no more scientific to speak of mind and body separating during trauma than it is to say the astral or egoic vehicle withdraws from the physical vehicle and hovers nearby, as in the classic near-death or operating-room account of looking down on one's body from above. For one thing, we have little idea of what we mean by "mind" in these cases, and secondly, some of the mind obviously remains present and conscious during such traumatic moments even though amnesia may set in afterwords. In a multiple personality, different minds or personages succeed one another in ignorance of each other.

At any rate, the mobility of the vehicles during youth might help explain, in a unified way, some phenomena now accounted for in piecemeal fashion or just shunted aside. That emergent adolescence is turbulent we take as commonplace and joke about on sitcoms, and grades seven and eight are the Siberia of the school years, the "terrible twos" returned with a vengeance. Is that thirteen-year-old "elementary" or "*junior* high"? All right, that's just the stormy transition into puberty. We leave so-called poltergeist phenomena to sensational movies. But why are those flying objects and electrical high jinks, which have been witnessed for a long time by many sorts of people, reported to occur in the presence of youngsters going through puberty—the stage when, according to this spiritual view, the astral or emotional body is penetrating into the physical? The creation of a disturbing energy field as a special temporary aura around the person might be one effect of the astral vehicle penetrating the physical in cases where the particular conditioning of the person makes the onslaught of sexuality more emotionally turbulent than usual.

I do not intend by these examples of my own tentative thoughts within such a framework to persuade the reader either of these explanations or of the incarnational theory that prompted them. I mean merely to suggest how such a theory might apply in useful ways to some old problems and might introduce into our deliberations some concepts new in education that have previously been taboo in our society, partly because our scientific paradigm could not account for them. The subject of human development needs some master concepts that can apply beyond artificial splits into "cognitive" and "affective" and beyond specialties like learning psychology or psychotherapy. Humanistic and transpersonal psychologists like Charles Tart[21] have drawn from beyond traditional science, including from spiritual traditions and parapsychology, in efforts to deepen the understanding of ourselves. Steiner's account of child development and human evolution, though personally perceived in its details, accords profoundly with the universalist cosmology I sketched in Chapter One, which is older than the Vedantic literature that transcribed it.

Unfortunately, ideas that mature thinkers entertain seriously elsewhere in our society are excluded from education, no doubt because of both its pragmatic orientation and its political sensitivity. Ironically, public education has failed pragmatically and politically as well as spiritually. It needs ways of thinking about growth that speak at once to *all* human phenomena, that apply equally to physical, emotional, intellectual, moral, and spiritual levels, and that can deal in one framework with disparate problems at different ages.

Cultural Bias

Some current cultural biases underlying our notions of child and human development need questioning. Literacy and discourse, verbalization and conceptualization, for example, are always considered desirable, whereas it is entirely possible, even likely, that in the growth of both civilization and the child these are bought at a price we don't reckon. In a more sophisticated and practical perspective, we would acknowledge that trade-offs occur—intuition for intellection, perhaps telepathy for speech, certainly socialization and acculturation for originality and openness.

Another bias is that a later civilization or an older person represents a higher value. Isn't growth always toward a desideratum? Doesn't nature know what it's doing? But human nature is variable because we have more freedom than other creatures and can develop toward good *or* evil. If to mature is to harden in thought and feeling as well as in arteries, to lose idealism in favor of materialism, and to become like everyone else, what sort of growth is that? Concepts of development involve plural possibilities and values.

Descriptions of child development can mirror quite accurately what has happened and what is happening but not necessarily what may happen. After admitting that growth as we know it may include priceless losses, we then become free to ask if tragic trade-offs can be avoided. Is there some way we can socialize and remain unique, learn to talk and read and think but stay intuitive, develop muscles and senses along with "extrasensory" or "paranormal" capacities, become a realist and stay an idealist, keep spirit right on into matter? Whatever we believe or disbelieve, educators have to keep the meaning and the possibilities of growth open for the young. How good was our own education that we should know what the limits of reality are?

Finally, among these possibilities is that the *I* is an individual spirit, represented by the egoic body and incarnated as a soul, and that it does indeed exist independently of a physical body and can not only be born again in the original sense of reawakened while in the flesh but also literally born again and again. Imagine that looking out of those fresh children's faces gathered in school are individuals who have long histories, unique to each, of which we, and they too, know nothing. Should this be true, it would give a new, not to say harrowing, meaning to the idea of individualizing education; far from being similar neonates awaiting impressions, differing only in genes and environs—already quite enough, God knows—these children would differ also in having patterns of experience accumulated across plural lifetimes comprising a larger destiny with its own meaning and requirements for fulfillment. If nothing else, this point of view would accord children the respect that is due them. We cannot continue treating children as nonpersons until *we* make something of them.

Suppose, in other words, that each lifetime is itself a stage of growth. In this case, one incarnation unfolding across such stages of growth as we have been examining would in turn partake of another growth continuity taking place across plural lifetimes. Furthermore, since neither student nor teacher ordinarily knows what an individual's unique cosmic history has been, no one can plot a curriculum for it in advance. Educational needs have to manifest themselves through the decisions learners make as they go about trying to fulfill their present promptings, which in the system I am proposing will evolve under the influence of interaction with others in the system. So the completely customized learning system that aims at traditional goals would serve perfectly for the possibility of soul growth as well. By its very nature as self-realization, spirituality inherently calls for the same thoroughgoing individualization that most efficiently accomplishes worldly learning.

In order to make this system work, to neutralize biases and keep alternatives open, advisers need to be both individually various and plentiful. I have carried these reflections on growth to some length to indicate the range of considerations that advisers should keep in mind when working with their charges and to suggest the nature of any training that might prepare them for such counseling. If training is too conventional or narrow, advisers will simply not be capable of presenting enough avenues of thought and enough choices for students to be able to realize all aspects of themselves, whatever these may be.

▲

PART FOUR

▲

Social and
Personal
Rebirth

The spiritual perspective is naturally allied with a holistic approach to problem solving because both are all-inclusive. What our framework comprises is what we comprehend. Admittedly, unifying does risk boggling the mind with intricacy, but simplistic, small-minded action has proven catastrophic, and if people collaborate instead of compete they can deal effectively with the intricacy, as we know from complicated scientific and technological accomplishments by teams.

Unifying must not occur by destroying or swallowing up the lesser wholes that it embraces—the cultures, subcultures, and individuals, all of which are entitled to their own integrity. Within the unification, there needs to take place decentralization. An embryo grows from the original unity of a single cell by differentiating itself into specialized parts like limbs, organs, and networks that at the same time it keeps reintegrating into each other as a coherent organism. Since this organism must have the benefits of both unity and specialty, the great principle of biology—and the model for personal and cultural development—is this simultaneous movement toward both integration and differentiation. We will see how this paradox characterizes spiritual evolution also, as the One becomes the All and the

▲

All the One again. Things or people unify at one level across differences at another level.

For education to be transformative it must permeate the society, not remain a professional enclave within it. In the last section of this book we look beyond educational organization as something unto itself and consider other agencies and governments, because they will have to change to realize the universal schoolhouse. As the concept of social transformation is extended further into the political arena, the concept of personal transformation is translated deeper into metaphysical terms. So the proposals and observations that follow here finish universalizing the schoolhouse, going beyond the pooling of community learning resources to the merging of education with other public services and to the (re)unification of the individual with the cosmos.

12

▲

Integrating
Public Services

The idea of educational reform as cultural transformation follows the principle that problems are best solved when pooled together. Sometimes one problem can even solve another problem. Thus some teenage mothers need someone else to take care of their children while they attend school, whereas other teenagers need some children they can tend to learn child care. Some high schools give courses in child care that use as subjects the children of their student mothers, who are thus enabled to stay in school. Other schools looking for a solution to dropouts have arranged for students several grades apart to buddy up so that the younger can work with someone older and so the older will develop a relationship that keeps him or her in school. These are small examples, drawn from today's familiar school world, of the multiple-purpose way we have to think in the future about even the very largest problems of the whole society.

Some elementary schools are calling on senior citizens to come in and read, write, and talk with their pupils. Such literacy programs can be combined with programs sponsored by senior centers to help people otherwise sidelined in unwanted idleness to find meaningful and gratifying things to do. Some nursing homes import children to cheer up seniors unable to travel. These visits too could become occasions for tutoring literacy and other things. Older students could individually visit seniors expert in some profession or interest that they too want to pursue.

Going a bit beyond schools now, some parents need to be around children less, while other adults would like to be around them more. Some mothers and fathers may work and need care for their children or simply be overstrained by the role of parent. Large numbers of children are spending the most influential period of their life with relatives or commercial caretakers who cannot afford to give them the attention or stimulation or learning opportunities that this age especially demands. The problem of day care for those who cannot afford private centers could be partially solved by the problem of lonely retirees or those childless adults who want children in their lives.

Good child care always goes beyond baby-sitting to include activities that further the growth of the child. Public day-care centers could become preschool learning centers staffed mostly by volunteers but led by professionals in child development. What they do with their charges could be coordinated with the rest of the learning network, which might enable this merged day-care nursery school to be free to all. Day care should become a standard part of a cradle-to-grave public learning network that draws on total community resources and in turn serves the total community.

Similarly, some problems of adolescents and employers could benefit each other. Teenagers feel barred from mainstream public life both by the confinement of traditional school itself and by adult distrust of their inexperience and immaturity. They need to move about in the marketplace before being thrust out into it on their own, when they can't simply examine it because they're too intent on making a living from it. Teenagers need situations where they can try themselves out in that world without making big commitments and taking big risks. Employers waste a lot of resources training people to work for them who are not very valuable until later and who often leave after they have become valuable.

On a mutually beneficial basis, businesses can be a part of the learning network, so that students can observe or apprentice on site and employers can give special sessions for students who choose to attend. Depending on who's benefiting more, students might or might not be paid. While aiding students' career education, this would also settle down sooner the employment process by shortening on-the-job training and lengthening the period of valuable employment. Generally, closer contact with public life brings students' knowledge abreast of what's going on at the same time that it helps shift the certification for job eligibility to employers, where it belongs. Actually, the learning network could serve all parties quite usefully as an employment network simply by setting up contacts for educational purposes but without any obligation to test students or otherwise take over from employers their responsibility to screen job applicants. Individuals learning out in the world and also programming their own destiny with the aid of ongoing counseling will be able to respond much more swiftly to changes in the economy and in the nature of jobs than when a bureaucracy is mediating between them and the workplace.

If adult and youth education were merged, then any funding for job training could be applied more efficiently to an overall educational system that included, say, apprenticing and re-training, whereby learners of any age visit, observe, and take part in certain on-site work activities and talk with veterans in any sort of trade or profession. The system would keep data banks on all opportunities for apprenticing, interning, service training, or employment itself. By making career experiences available as part of public education for those who choose to include them in their personal programs, it becomes unnecessary to identify so-called at-risk or disadvantaged or minority populations as targets of special (welfare) programs. Nor would one assume that any sort of population will or should end up in particular sorts of jobs.

Broadly construing the nature of the learning field not only permits a more efficient use of resources but reduces conflict about some parties benefiting more while others are paying more, since education for the workplace is universal. Singled out and targeted at poor minorities, job training constitutes part of a welfare system or at best workfare system. Being taxed for such a service feels fairer when it is merged in a total system of public education whose resources are used by all populations and ages.

Education as Master Social Service

The most creative solutions treat several problems simultaneously. The crisis of schooling interlocks so closely with other societal problems like unwanted pregnancy, overpopulation, drug abuse, crime, ill health, selfishness, poverty, unemployment, debtor economics, deteriorating families, crumbling infrastructure, and environmental pollution that to deal with it and them in isolation only invites failure. Working on all problems in concert makes most likely the best solution of each. Sometimes one even holds the key to another. Especially might the problem of public education hold a key to the others.

Simultaneous problem solving seems the only way both to think about and pay for answers. We have to view all societal problems as functions of each other, as a single, multifaceted problem. This will make it easier to see how they feed each other and how we may more readily solve all by a concerted campaign. Instead of legislating for crime here and health care there and environmental protection somewhere else, we should begin to incorporate most public services into a master education service.

For a moment let's construe some examples of common problems as essentially educational. People need to feel needed, useful, purposeful. We want to know that what we do is significant, that our life has meaning. Street gangs, addiction, crime, and teenage pregnancy make something happen, whip up a drama, that promises to fill this need. Immature or desperate people don't know that other activities will also make them feel good—better than these—without wounding themselves and others. The educational system has to show them this. In doing so it will alleviate considerably some major social problems. People who learn to feel good and find meaning through the community-as-school will not only stop being problems themselves but also learn to help those who remain charges on the society, much as former convicts or addicts work with ones following their troubled route.

Public education must offer alternatives to street gangs, addiction, crime, and unwanted pregnancy, all of which are based at least partly on a need to bond. Youth bond into street gangs because they can't find any other kind of group to belong to, just as they turn to crime because they can't see any other way to make money. Both gangs and crime provide a subculture to belong to. Sexual union is an effort of course to bond with the world by means of the other gender. Through pregnancy, moreover, girls can create, in fantasy, their own loving companion or the beloved child they wish they had been. In this sense, as some have admitted, pregnancy is not always unwanted. (And of course poor women sometimes have babies to get child-support money—the only way they know to earn money.) The highs of drugs and alcohol also dissolve isolation in a temporary merger with the world. Bonding to other people and to the universe represent a primal spiritual need to feel part of the All.

Traditional schools have been unable to fill this need, and families fail to satisfy it in the measure that parents have broken their bond with their own offspring or are too distressed by destitution to answer their children's emotional needs. By doing no more than what a community learning network requires, society can almost automatically furnish alternatives to street gangs, addiction, crime, and unwanted pregnancy, because the best public education of the future will consist of good opportunities to bond with other people and the rest of creation.

A personalized, warmly communal, realistic learning environment that enables everyone to build competence and confidence, raise self-esteem, bond with others, and find gratifying things to do will naturally put sex in place, head off addiction, and render street gangs and crime unnecessary. People who learn early how to take care of their health, each other, and the environment will not only better think of solutions but quit causing problems. Used to collaborating for mutual success and to identifying with each other, they will be less selfish and work better together to eliminate poverty and unemployment, which involve, after all, sharing the available resources across social and ethnic boundaries to make sure there are no losers.

Practically, this curative educational culture mitigates social ills in three main ways. First, it places learners in concentric "families" of mixed ages, as exemplified in the McFarland Model. Second, the partner arrangements, rippling, counseling, collaborative projects, apprenticeships, community service, and many other interpersonal relations make up the very functioning of the highly social learning network. Third, the incorporation of most public services into public education provides a master problem-solving process.

As regards the last point, one of the inherent connections between self-education and community service is that learning projects can be about the problems that various social agencies exist to eliminate. Of the three purposes of projects noted earlier—to make things, investigate things, and improve things—the last especially lends itself to doing what government agencies themselves attempt. Urban self-help projects such as renovating run-down neighborhoods, planting gardens, running off drug dealers, mounting health campaigns, securing financing for small businesses, and lobbying officials for other changes show how spirited collaborative organizations can work wonders in depressed areas. Public education can boost such neighborhood efforts by incorporating them into its more extended community learning network.

Most public services should coalesce into their natural matrix—public education—reconceived as ongoing learning for everybody in all aspects of their lives. Imagine that this consolidation of resources at the community level incorporated not only Head Start and other educational entitlements but job training and placement, prenatal clinics and day-care nurseries, adult education and senior facilities, and public health education. Imagine that its network overlapped with youth correction, penal rehabilitation, and parole operations and included agencies for foster children, abused children, and battered wives; counseling centers for rape, suicide, and legal aid; and other publicly supported sorts of specialized aid.

Imagine that it also included in its network the many functions for which individuals have organized privately in the form of women's or men's groups, meditation and discussion groups, self-help addiction treatment groups like Alcoholics Anonymous, and other therapeutic or self-development activities such as classes in arts, crafts, martial arts, and other avocations. People of all ages could participate together in such activities as part of individual programs worked out with their counselors.

Imagine, finally, that public education takes over the state and federal wars against (and funds for) poverty, crime, drugs, hunger, and homelessness and recasts these crusades within the possibilities of the community educational network. This would make education so proactive and preemptive that young people would be already working on social problems while learning, alongside professionals and other adults—as a *way* to learn. The ideal interplay of action and knowledge can occur through well-orchestrated personal learning programs made up of projects, apprenticing, and community service. Pooling problems and resources will certainly cost less money in the long run and quite possibly in the short run as well.

Health expenditures alone are undermining the whole economy, as President Bill Clinton rightly insisted. Employee medical programs cost so much as to endanger many companies' solvency, and private medical coverage frequently costs more than a family's food or housing. People are so ignorant about the body and how to care for it that they place themselves at the mercy of hospitals, medical practitioners, and manufacturers of pharmaceutical drugs and medical hardware, many of whom cannot resist the temptation to exploit this vulnerability in an area so important as well-being and life itself. Through fore-knowledge about good habits of diet, exercise, and stress management, the vast majority of health problems can be avoided entirely and most genetic problems can at least be mitigated. Good understanding about the body and some instruction in emergency treatment can even reduce considerably the consequences of accidents.

Our medical establishment is still oriented, like the whole society, toward remediation, not prevention. Part of the reason for this is that we have become accustomed to depend on negative conditions to maintain the economy. Really learning to take care of ourselves would throw huge numbers of us out of work and wind down an industry grown so large that its very expense to consumers, on the other hand, also threatens the economy. This crisis orientation—the after-the-fact treatment of ills already allowed to happen—nourishes the medical industry, especially in an era of privatization of hospitals and increasing selfishness of physicians.

Amid their involvement in malpractice suits and fraudulent claims by some medical officials, insurance companies certainly have a motive to prevent medical problems. Right now they focus on protecting themselves by denying claims payments and by raising premiums or refusing coverage itself to people with health problems, but they have sometimes invested in efforts to inform the public and could perhaps become an important ally in preventive medicine and self-healing. Potentially promising too is some of the new scanning, monitoring, and diagnosing machinery. Whereas the medical-industrial complex has oversold much of this glamorous high-tech hardware and the medical profession has overused it, partly to protect itself from malpractice suits, equipment for scanning and imaging could be utilized to reinforce preventive health care by teaching people how to look into the body and see how to head off problems. Now, however, it is usually brought into play only after trouble has started. Moreover, its considerable diagnostic capacities outmatch the scanty treatment repertory, which is based far too much on surgery and chemotherapy, which in turn support heavy industries in hardware, pharmacy, and services.

Looked at from the viewpoint of business, such positive things as good nutrition, exercise, personal knowledge of the body, and self-healing are uninteresting if not downright alarming—unless one can see a way to make new businesses out of them, as is starting to happen, though not always in a desirable way. But all that is required is to shift focus from remediation to prevention, from a childish dependence on specialists to self-care. This means viewing health services as essentially a form of education and finding ways to diffuse specialty knowledge throughout a community.

Like education, health and medical care have been too dominated by the private sector to serve well the public itself. National health insurance, on the other hand, could merely perpetuate the huge costs, bureaucratic morass, and greedy abuses
of the medical-industrial complex by continuing to sponsor the
old emphasis on crisis intervention and authoritarian specialization. Proponents of national health insurance focus mostly
on how to reduce and how to pay for the costs of current
medical practices and very little on how the medical profession
might teach people to lead healthy lives and treat themselves,
as some honorable and caring doctors have always tried to do
within the limits of private practice and as some special clinics
and agencies now try to do to stall epidemics or to counter the
many health risks of poverty. So great are the costs to families,
to businesses, and to governments of the nation's current poor
health and misdirected medical practices that a universal education in physiology, health, and healing, employing all sorts of
professional medical resources, could effortlessly pay not only
for itself but for other reinvestments proposed in this book,
should any new money be required.

Learning how to take good care of one's own body could
alone transform the nation. Not only would its citizens feel
better, think better, work better, behave better, and treat each
other better, they would break through to a new sense of self-
reliance, of power, of being able to control their lives that
would in itself elevate the quality of personal and social life.
The body is not only the necessary vehicle for the mental and
spiritual life on this plane, it is a fundamental metaphor for
nonphysical life of any sort, so that what people can learn to
do with their own body tends to symbolize their other personal
possibilities and the potentialities of life itself.

Health education is needed at all ages and by all social
classes. Mixing it with science education and making it available to both children and adult learners would permit combin-

ing the resources of regular education with those of special health education programs in and out of school, some of which currently deal with chemical dependency, pregnancy prevention, protection against AIDS, prenatal care, child care, and consumer education about nutrition.

Let's take now the much more difficult example of crime. Since well over half of prison inmates can't read or dropped out of school, it is obvious that crime offers an alternative to education as a way to make money and get ahead. If education reformed itself so that it could reach *everyone*, regardless of his or her family background or personal makeup, then no one need turn to drug dealing and crime as an alternative. No one would want to drop out of a warm human community comprising an attractive array of choices and places regarding what and how to learn, where testing and grading didn't exist, no one ever failed, and you could always find things to do and ways to build a life.

Education's role in *preventing* crime is easy to see. But what about the need to maintain enormously expensive law enforcement operations and incarceration facilities for those who do commit crimes? Everybody knows that convicts could be sent to college for the cost of imprisoning them, that recidivism rates are appallingly high because little regeneration occurs during imprisonment, and that prisons are so dangerously overcrowded that judges and parole boards are shortening sentences despite public outcries to be tougher on criminals. Many dangerous criminals are now being given short, plea-bargained sentences to save court costs or released early to save prison costs. Like the wars on drugs and poverty, the war on crime has cost fortunes for decades but is failing. The reason for such staggering inefficiency is that no such problem can be successfully solved when considered alone. An educational system that acted as a lifelong support system and never, in any sense, failed anyone, could so reduce crime through prevention that the treatment afforded those who do commit crime could focus on rehabilitation, which is itself a form of education.

It's necessary to incarcerate many criminals to protect the rest of the citizenry from them, but it's a colossal waste of public funds to create a pure convict culture in which inmates can only degenerate and from which they usually issue only to commit new crimes. Prisons are crime schools and the scenes of crimes. It is perverse to spend public money to subsidize further crime. Rehabilitation would be far more cost-effective, because to the costs of incarceration you have to add the costs of repeatedly detecting, trying, and paroling the same people. Convicts need another environment than the criminal one they know. Most are not destined to stay long in prison and must start new lives but will, without help, return to the milieus that influenced them toward crime. When I did some volunteer teaching at San Quentin Prison, I learned that the prospect of returning to society terrifies most inmates, because they don't see how they can behave differently than they did before. They came voluntarily to these all-day workshops, which I was giving with a counselor there, in hopes of relearning about themselves in relation to the frightening outside world.

Electronic surveillance may allow some convicts to be restricted to quarters outside of prison, in circumstances permitting some community education. By judicious sorting, convicts could be assigned varying sorts of restriction and afforded whatever educational opportunities their sort permits. Most prisons do offer some job training, some academic courses, and some counseling. As with public schools, however, the culture in which these occur undoes most of the learning. As much as is consistent with the protection of the public, education for convicts must include a curative environment. This means arranging for some to participate in the regular community learning network and finding ways to extend the network to those other convicts, presumably a minority, who really must be incarcerated under strong security. Creating a rehabilitative correctional system will depend in any case on regular public education preventing crime well enough to reduce the number of convicts for whom special education has to be arranged.

I have focused on crime for a moment because it poses an especially tough challenge to my own proposal to pool resources for related social problems. The more the schoolhouse becomes the community, and the more the whole community takes on the responsibility for crime, the more possible it becomes to eradicate crime through both prevention and rehabilitation occurring in many different sites and circumstances. So long as we don't yet regard law enforcement, judicial proceedings, the parole process, and incarceration as special programs that will self-destruct in time, these may have to remain distinct entities with their own budgets. Agencies in all four areas already make some effort to prevent crime or to reeducate criminals, sometimes in collaboration with schools, and will reduce crime far more effectively if we begin to think of them more as learning services.

Other programs with targets that may more readily be thought of as temporary could, however, start merging their functions and their funding with public education. Different agencies cannot always be collapsed together, as we presently conceive them, but when allotting resources to the totality of its agencies, society needs to rely much more than it now does on catching problems at early stages. We tend to be crisis-oriented because it is easier to target the undesirable ends than it is the desirable means. Hence the ineffectual wars on crime, poverty, drugs, disease, and illiteracy. Most of the exorbitant costs of treating illness and crime can be avoided. Remediation is the least cost-effective approach to problems possible, but it is the one that dominates present thinking.

Replacing Welfare

Such an epic educational initiative could also resolve a major conflict today between those who resentfully pay for welfare and those who resentfully take it. As the middle class itself undergoes new hardships, it increasingly rebels against taxation to support others, especially those who reproduce far faster than itself and threaten to engulf it, if not by sheer numbers then by the problems of poverty that these numbers multiply in turn. Crime, addiction, unemployment, disease, hunger, and unwanted pregnancy will swamp any taxpayer class of whatever wealth so long as these problems are dealt with remedially and separately. The various wars on social problems cannot be won in this way and will only exhaust what resources remain. By contrast, if we construe the eradication of these ills as an educational goal, all at once we take social services off a welfare basis, direct efforts at the roots rather than the symptoms of problems, and create an efficiently concerted program of social reconstruction.

Most political controversy centers on one faction trying to enforce sharing by legislating social programs while another faction fights to avoid sharing by reducing its taxes, which in a democracy tend to equalize wealth. Good education would submerge this fratricidal conflict into a common effort to spread resources so effectively as to eliminate the poverty that causes most overpopulation, crime, addiction, ignorance, and much bad health. Up to now democratic governments have tried to solve these problems as if they were unrelated, by funding separate social programs for each problem. These sum up to costs so crushing that they endanger the economy and make the sturdier taxpayers resent the recipients, who comprise a large number of minority people and of women trying to raise children born outside of marriage or left to them from a broken marriage. Once large enough to get out of hand and become subject to fraud and inefficiency, these programs become fair targets for criticism and reduction, especially during financially hard times.

Sharing must occur *before* the sheer enormity of poverty overwhelms the middle and upper classes that are capable of financing the kind of welfare now relied on to offset inequalities. That is, the critical fact about population explosion is that it is the poorest part of the world's populace that is exploding—generating problems of health, crime, addiction, poverty, and violence that will break the banks of the wealthiest nations along with the earth's bank of natural resources. In the past, the number of poor people was regulated by sending them into war and by letting the very conditions of poverty itself—like violence, famine, and disease—kill them off. But as ideals of human rights increasingly rule such brutal measures out of both official and unofficial public policy, and as technology keeps more people alive, from newborns to seniors, the world faces a new problem created by its own social and scientific progress. At work here is the deadly ratio that as the wealth of the rich increases, so does the population of the poor. In current terms, more equalization is needed, but a point will be reached where even forcibly distributing the wealth would not avail.

The dilemma comes down to this: huge outlays seem required very soon to reverse this exponentially accelerating mega-problem before it truly becomes impossible to control, but these costs seem already to have created so much economic and social turmoil that government will become locked in political conflict until it is too late. It is very unlikely that the well-to-do will become enlightened enough, especially given traditional education, to realize this and share sufficiently to solve the problem in time, even though it will destroy them and democracy along with the poor. We can't count solely on the middle class to lead, especially as the increasing concentration of wealth over its head is threatening more of its own members with impoverishment. Through public education, the potential recipients of social services must learn how not to perpetuate the problems of poverty that are breaking the bank and the good will of the well-off. "Too late" means either that people will drown in the sea of their own numbers and environmental wreckage, or that only the desperate dictatorial measures of a permanent martial law—that is, *enforced* sharing at the sacrifice of personal liberty—will stave off societal collapse. While the well-off will be learning to share wealth voluntarily, encouraged by the far greater efficiency of pooling public services under education, the poor will be learning how to earn their fair share of the wealth and to share leadership for solving social problems.

This proposal, then, is to construe education so broadly as to (1) encompass provisional social programs designed to eradicate certain ills and (2) coordinate much more closely with education those social agencies regarded as permanent societal functions. One purpose is to shift problem solving to a more perceptive and more effective level. A second is to pool functions and resources for greater efficiency, coordination, and economy by eliminating shortsighted thinking, compartmentalization, and duplication of effort.

Another purpose of bringing together all societal functions within the matrix of education is to reform public education, which desperately needs just these practical realities to enliven the academic subjects, to prepare students for the world, and to engage their whole being in their own learning. Adults need ongoing learning, and youth needs to become involved much earlier than it is now in the actual workings of the society it will take over. Combining personal development, social bonding, and practical problems with substantive knowledge and intellectual growth allows societal and environmental problems to become the wherewithal by means of which to learn academic subjects. Integrated learning matches the way real life mixes up the ingredients of problems. Such proactive education will then become really relevant and will engage the next generation with the problems that have to be solved in their lifetime. Seeing school as the community and the community as a school is the best way to realize all the aims of education, whether these are practical and intellectual or moral and spiritual.

13

▲

Reinvesting and Reapportioning

A final purpose of integrating social services under education is to prevent psychological and material investments in programs targeting ills, since participants in such programs are motivated, if only unconsciously, to prolong the very ills they are attempting to eradicate. The current fashion of atomizing social reconstruction so that problems can be separately dealt with and accounted for actually squanders resources, though it is done in the hope that specific allocation of funds will ensure cost-effective accountability. Actually, it provides incentive to prolong the problems so targeted, since jobs funded for such aims end if the problem does. Targeting symptoms creates agencies and programs that become long-term, if not permanent, and hence causes people to invest in the perpetuation of the problems themselves. Many private industries like those providing security systems and guards also depend on a problem *not* disappearing. Truly eradicating crime, addiction, poverty, illiteracy, or unnecessary bad health would throw huge numbers of people out of jobs in both public and private sectors and devastate major areas of the economy. We have to start shifting resources and investments from symptoms, which look unrelated, to causes, which more easily manifest connections.

While shifting our minds from negative to positive, this avoids investing in something we really want to end. It is essential not to become married to the problems.

Much of the inefficiency we attribute to bureaucracy in general owes specifically to fear of working oneself out of a job. Even parents and teachers tend to hold children back for this very reason, because the faster the child matures or learns what the adult knows, the sooner the jobs of parents and teachers are over. To keep our roles we tend to rationalize infantilizing. This is unnecessary, since new children are always coming along who still need us, not to mention other adults who need us to parent them and teach them. Program and agency employees, however, can literally end their employment by succeeding in their mission.

Public education construed as all learning of all sorts for all ages and all purposes will never end. It constitutes not only the most fundamental social program but the one that is surely indispensable. Most others exist to eradicate something—poverty, crime, poor health, addiction, pollution, unwanted pregnancy, racial inequality—and would self-destruct if they succeeded. Programs of which this is not true—like job training, child care for working parents, or health education—are ones that can be rather directly incorporated into a community learning network anyway, being by nature educational.

These and other positive, permanent social functions are those to which the private and public sectors should shift investments for the sake of both the economy and the general welfare. Education will always remain necessary and positive and worthy of permanent allocation of human and material resources. As suggested earlier, furthermore, the incorporation into a community learning system of all the many private kinds of coaching and teaching would encourage shifting capital into education. In keeping with the already well-noted shift in America from manufacturing to information, a central industry of teaching one another would ensure permanent markets, at home, and steady employment for large numbers of people, all relatively independent of the usual product trends and foreign competition.

Aside from survival industries themselves, what other enterprise deserves investment of capital and labor more than human growth? The reason that the medical, defense, agricultural, and energy businesses have acted so arrogantly, and been so favored by government, is that they control goods and services necessary for life itself. No one dares challenge or refuse them much. Education too is of the order of these survival industries, as recognized in the large percentage of public funds allocated for it, but unlike health, food, and energy, significantly, education belongs almost wholly to the public domain, like defense.

Interplay of Public and Private Sectors

Casting some life-essential enterprises into the private sector and some into the public makes little sense today, if it ever did. For one thing, a handful of private contractors make most of the weapons for the Defense Department, which collaborates so closely with this monopoly that free enterprise and open competition hardly exist in defense procurement, and the relationship differs little from the one that was obtained between the Kremlin and its arms manufacturers. As indicated in Chapter Five, a few large private corporations make the materials that constitute the curriculum of most public schools. Corporate agribusiness and the medical and energy industries, on the other hand, though private, enjoy enormous public subsidies and patronage because of their essential nature. Like transportation and communication, they are also regulated in varying degrees by government agencies—as in food inspection, hospital standards, and utility rates—but in fact the regulatory bodies are no match for these private corporations, which overwhelm them with everything from superior expertise and inside information to seductive lobbies and greater lawyer power.

Part of what we have to rethink, in other words, concerns the status of enterprises, including education, that are indispensable to life and society. In some free-enterprise countries, industries such as energy, transportation, and communication have been socialized, like education and defense (that is, run directly by government), then sometimes privatized again by being thrown back onto the market. U.S. counterparts of these industries have been regarded as semi-public, permitted a monopoly but under heavy government regulation. In this sense, our gas and electric companies are called public utilities although operated for profits shared by private stockholders. A monopoly may exist in either the public sector, as for municipal transportation, or the private sector, as for electrical power. Sometimes government runs enterprises directly, as Washington does the postal system and Amtrak, but most often it goes to the private sector to purchase many of the goods and to contract out services, because it cannot maintain personnel and facilities for all the specialties these functions require. There is no way for education and other essential industries not to be both public and private, because everyone needs them and because no government commands all the resources except a totalitarian apparat.

Societal transformation does not depend on one economic or political system supplanting another, since in reality a mongrel system has evolved that expediently interplays public and private sectors for the sake of both collective and individual wills. But important changes could be made in this evolution, which has occurred haphazardly and needs deliberate direction based on consciousness of this very confusion of public and private arenas. Many minds must bend toward this end, but

as one example, I suggest a change that relates to the matter
at hand, reinvestment, since future investments in education
will continue to come from both public taxes and private
capital.

Rechartering Corporations

This suggestion harks back to an issue raised in Chapter Two,
namely, that the incorporated now overpower the unincorporated. Incorporations can of course be either private, like commercial companies, or public, like municipalities. Some private
incorporations are run not for profit but for some other end.
In any of these cases, individuals are outmatched when interests
conflict, whether one is pitted against a commercial company
or fighting city hall or a lobby. Hence the frequent need for
class-action suits to offset this inequality. Most generally, the
overwhelming of the unincorporated by the incorporated occurs as unorganized citizens are taken advantage of, either individually or collectively, by for-profit corporations.

In today's era of weakened labor unions and legal evasions
like chapter eleven bankruptcy, most employees stand among
the vulnerable unincorporated who can be fired for whistle-
blowing or for getting old enough to reach higher salary brack-
ets or retirement benefits. Consumers have to devise costly
ways at personal expense to fight against shoddy products and
breaches of contract, whereas large companies avail themselves
of legal counsel that is part of the overhead and mount lobbying
campaigns against consumer protection for which costs can be
passed on to the consumer in the form of industrywide price
hikes—all as tax-deductible expenses under for-profit incorporation.

Collectively, the unincorporated suffer as that public whose
"common wealth" includes natural resources and the environ-

ment that corporations have for generations raided and polluted with desperately inadequate control by the one incorporation that the public should be able to count on to champion
it, the government. In considering, then, how private and public
sectors might more equitably interact as we envision reinvestment, perhaps we should scrutinize the very nature of incorporation.

My suggestion aims to deal at once with the confusion between private and public sectors, the inequality between the
incorporated and the unincorporated, and the investment in
education from both tax funds and capital outlays. It is partly
prompted by trends within some for-profit corporations themselves to (1) make employees stockholders represented on the
board of directors, (2) expend great efforts in market research
to ascertain what consumers want and how they feel, and (3)
do right by the natural and social environment both out of self-
interest and to temper the profit motive by some real social
conscience. It is only a step from these trends—but a big one
that would surely galvanize many corporate lobbies—to what
I propose, which is to alter the terms of commercial incorporation so that companies large enough to sell shares would build
into their board such effective representation of employees,
consumers, and the commonweal that labor unions, consumer
groups, and government regulatory agencies would be rendered
obsolete.

Commercial companies would thus incorporate into themselves those normally unincorporated individuals with whom
they already have a relationship and would at the same time
internalize the perspective of the public sector. As some compensation for not opposing this sharing of power, some of the
funds these parties normally spend to contend with these companies in collective bargaining, consumer lobbying, and governmental regulation might be made available for a time to
protect profits during transition. In the long run, of course,

companies have to allow anyway for the needs of employees, consumers, and common resources for the simple holistic reason that nothing will profit them otherwise.

Decisions about investments made by such rechartered corporations would harmonize profit-making with those social functions that define the public sector but that need to be implemented through the private sector. If all those who have a stake in what a company does take part in making decisions, then reinvesting private capital for societal transformation becomes a more likely possibility. This would make a big difference, for example, in how many products and services of commercial corporations might be utilized within community learning networks.

But what about companies too small to sell stock, like the many studios offering private classes in ballet or computer graphics or glass-working or tai chi that would have to figure among the options open to learners in the universal schoolhouse? Their very smallness makes for more personal relations with employees and consumers and helps keep the enterprise sensitive to local conditions and needs. Someone running their own little operation with only a helper or so can't afford to feel apart from the community. But the main check on educational businesses too small to be affected by the new articles of incorporation involves consumer education itself.

Real Free-Market Education

When the data banks and electronic bulletin boards of the community learning network start listing private classes or studios as options for customized learning programs, this will strengthen such small businesses and encourage many people to make a living by teaching some specialty they know. Besides boosting small business, this can help shift capital and employ-

ment away from unhealthful or unnecessary products and services that need to be phased out and into the positive enterprises
that transformation requires. It will also surely tempt the un-
scrupulous or the incompetent to set up shop and get a hand
in the public till. How do we screen these out of the system to
avoid undesirable investment?

Following the principle that you give while you get, learners
and counselors feed back into the data banks and electronic
bulletin boards what they learn about the various private offerings and thus make the learning system a consumer network
as well. Also, following the principle that good action serves
more than one purpose, learners can avail themselves of a sort
of project already popular among students today—creating
consumer guides for items or services they value. Motivation
runs high for a group to try out and compare commodities,
survey customers, interview purveyors, do background research, and put together text and graphics synopsizing results.
Such a project teaches a lot in that it usually involves some
science, math, and social studies as well as techniques of investigation and composition. Part of what the network does anyway
is disseminate the results of projects of all sorts, so that the
welcoming use of these products by others constantly inspires
further projects. Consumer guides will be a major and constant
product.

Instead of relying on a local government agency to screen
and certify entrepreneurs for the learning network, the system
builds self-protection into itself as part of the very learning
process, which must include how to find out for yourself and
report to others what products and services are worthwhile.
Official certification by either a profession or a government
may be no more reliable than this network, could never keep
so up to date with all the offerings, costs consumers through
either taxes or raised prices, and risks favoritism or even pay-
offs. A citizenry of toughly trained consumers thinking for

themselves will of itself play a role in discouraging business abuse and encouraging socially sound investments.

This is all by way of saying that much thought must be given to how a communal network may avail itself of private enterprise to extend the learning spectrum beyond what public employees can offer and how it may at the same time influence the reinvestment of private capital as well as public funds into broader social transformation. Paying some private teachers from public funds is very different from putting all public and private schools into competition with one another. A voucher system seems to create a free market in education, but as explained in Chapter Six, users still have only a gross choice among schools all complying with the same government policy, none of which can possibly offer what a community learning network can arrange. It is fine to let the *vendors* compete to serve the network—the private teachers or manufacturers—but the public resources themselves should not be parceled out into little capitalist schools to compete among themselves. A free marketplace would allow the real consumers to choose from anything available anywhere and not force them to settle for being *proxy* consumers for whom others are selecting and canning an education. This point obtains for all forms of institutional prepackaging, most emphatically including textbook adoption and other purchasing of curriculum.

The problem at hand is to find out how best to arrange this truly open market so that users can choose from it on public funds, regardless of whether the goods and services are private or public. The educational equivalent of food stamps (without of course the welfare stigma) is a possibility but one that would be open to corruption because of the bureaucratic anonymity of the method. Personally signed chits are better, but the exact form of the exchange between public and private sectors may have to be worked out locally and perhaps in relation to other practical arrangements made within the community system.

Generally the very personal nature of relationships among learners, counselors, project partners, and "family" members will act as a safeguard against a practice such as signing up for an outside class without attending, just to get a kickback. Illegally tapping into public funds is a chronic problem, but state and federal funds present more nefarious possibilities because they are harder to monitor than local monies. Also, this sort of abuse of public funds most often entails the cooperation of the authentic recipients, who in the case of learners using the network will be influenced by the whole atmosphere of respect and responsibility toward both oneself and others.

Reallocating Governmental Functions

Tax money disappears in governmental mazes, and the higher up the governmental hierarchy the money goes, the more the increasing concentration of wealth invites misuse and defies accountability. It is very inefficient for agencies at a higher governmental level to devise strategy for people to follow somewhere else—to take taxpayers' money, attach directives to it, then return the remainder of it (minus a huge slice for operating expenses) on condition of complying with the strategy. It is far more effective to treat problems not only *together* but *locally.*

Sending huge funds to Washington for them to become nationally politicized and then trickled back down not only wastes a large fraction of the money but distorts strategic thinking. Since education promises the best solution, prevention, and since education is primarily a local function, it makes no sense to run wars on poverty, crime, addiction, and so on out of the federal government, which legislates and funds problems one at a time, remedially, as national attention flickers back and forth among them. It is better to decentralize taxation so that more of it can be kept in the urban and rural communities to set up the comprehensive educational networks that can get at social ills right on site. Since property taxes in poor areas cannot adequately fund education, it may often have to be supported by regional sales and income taxes as well.

Social action initiated and funded by the federal government lacks understanding and practical direction, which its remoteness from the sites of action precludes. In giving money from afar, it has to set policies and conditions that are often inappropriate or ineffectual but that assert its will and give it the illusion of accountability. For its part, conventional schooling alienates the young because it lacks action and clear, compelling connections to what is going on in the rest of the world. Both schools and governments, in other words, divorce knowledge from action, whereas for effective policy they should fuse the two.

Federal government can best serve the public by concentrating on truly *national* functions that do affect these social problems such as the regulation of economic forces and corporations, environmental protection, and international relations. Any societal reform today, educational or other, must presuppose some reapportioning of governmental functions, even if this entails creating new entities larger or smaller than the old ones. Since the federation of the United States already comprises four levels of government stretching from federal to state, county, and municipal, some reforms require only shifts of function among these according to which level, at this point in our cultural evolution, can most effectively carry out each function. For some functions relating to global economy and resources, the United States may have to join a larger governmental entity, while it should relegate to local governments most social programs, including education. But either tax collection must be relegated there along with them or state and federal governments should generously share revenues with municipalities to establish equity among them.

Only after World War II, against great resistance, did the federal government begin appropriating funds for education. This occurred as part of a general self-aggrandizement of federal government that took advantage of the Depression and the mobilization of World War II to extend emergency powers into periods of prosperity and peace. Just as the temporary War Department became a permanent Defense Department, Depression welfare programs for jobs and doles became accepted as part of Washington's role. Even those measures like deposit insurance for banks and savings-and-loan companies that the crash of 1929 may have warranted temporarily making a federal function should be reconsidered in the light of the abuses resulting in the biggest financial debacle of our history, the savings-and-loan collapse. If lending institutions organized their own deposit insurance, they could surely prevent the recurrence of such fraudulent and careless handling of other people's money. It stands as a catastrophic example of how private interests can tap off public funds when collected into huge federal pools.

Welfare merely palliates today's long-range problems of poverty and unemployment. As a massive permanent federal program, it invites fraud. As the population of the poor increases disproportionately, the enormous costs of welfare make recipients out of contributors. It has disenchanted most of its former proponents. Some critics are pointing out that the federal government is not the best one to tackle crime or drug abuse or bad education, because there is little inherently *national* about these problems. The fact that they occur all over the country does not justify sending money to Washington to fund federal programs that for the most part have to be implemented, in the end, locally—like education.

Generally, governance in the United States is top-heavy, meaning that federal and state government take too much money and authority to do too many things in the counties and cities. Aside from sensible coordination and sharing of information across levels of government, problems like crime, addiction, and disease mostly have to be dealt with where they occur. Ideally, the higher the level of government, the more it would merely (1) play an informing role as a central exchange to help localities know what is going on elsewhere and what their full range of options is, (2) watchdog improprieties in municipal or county functioning so as to prevent some individuals or factions from abusing others and (3) spread taxes over disparate localities to equalize community resources, as for education. A major value of higher government is precisely to provide balance and equity, to spread information and resources, and to offset local partialities in any sense, whether poverty or prejudice. Sharing and broadening are, after all, what confederation exists to do.

The self-aggrandizement of the federal government did not occur so much in education after World War II as it did in other social arenas, because the tradition of public schooling as a function of local government was partly maintained by some old political fights about federally funding private and religious schools. The rationalization for bucking this tradition was that the Soviet Union was winning the space race and hence the Cold War through a technological superiority that only some reform of American schools could counter. Nationalism, in other words, justified making education a function of national government.

Once in place, this federal funding from the National Defense Education Acts found a more positive justification inasmuch as the later civil rights legislation withheld this money from schools that did not integrate. Given the unwillingness of many local governments to give an equal education to all citizens, federal intervention had a moral warrant. Indeed, only Congressional legislation and Supreme Court adjudication could have championed equal educational and employment opportunity so successfully in some localities. But this federal intervention still cannot enforce educational equality where racism permeates the consciousness and where the economic inequality is so great that the different socioeconomic classes or ethnic groups live too far apart to integrate. Moreover, if the ideology of the presidency shifts against equality, as has happened, the federal government may undo its own good work and act as a negative rather than a positive social force.

President Reagan tried to get Washington back out of education by actually abolishing the Department of Education. Both he and his protege Bush tried to roll back desegregation along with other civil rights advances and to reduce federal funding for schools. But neither returned to taxpayers the money they cut, so that it could be spent locally. In general, the policy of "getting government off our backs" simply relegated more responsibility for social programs to the states and cities without releasing to them the tax revenues to fund them. Federal government can seize control of education through universal testing, in the name of mobilizing national human resources, as with America 2000, but, in the name of honoring the tradition of local autonomy, leave to the school districts the means and costs of accomplishing these lofty goals.

One popular federal program for education that Congress and the presidency dared not cut was Head Start. It deserved continued support, but there is no inherent reason why the federal government should run it. Not only is it far less qualified to do so than lower levels of government, but it has to keep part of the money for its own bureaucracy, to pay the cost of channeling the funds back down to the schools via all sorts of regulations designed to assure accountability. Furthermore, even its supporters now acknowledge that by second or third grade Head Start children score no better than other pupils, and one of its founders, Professor Zigler of Yale, said on television news in 1993 that nearly two-thirds of the schools involved were continuing it in merely token fashion.

For one thing, Head Start's specific aim of preparing at-risk children for the regular curriculum still limited their education to the very schooling that needed reform. There was no follow-up. Also, to realize its deeper purpose, Head Start has needed more scope. Those educators who realize this have made it some sort of a model for innovation by extending its involvement with health and family life. Head Start has always vaccinated about 98 percent of its charges. But organizations such as Parents and Children Incorporated were founded to give Head Start more scope by, for example, monitoring the health of all family members and by teaching illiterate parents how to read.

In a master service, such health management and parent education become a routine part of cradle-to-grave education construed as growth and care of the whole person. When each individual is being attended to personally by many people for all aspects of her or his development, special initiatives for at-risk people like Head Start—a vestige of welfare—become unnecessary. It is supplanted by a permanent solution having in its very conception the scope that Head Start always needed. When you have a comprehensive plan, you don't need *compensatory* projects. But federal programs almost have to be patchwork, because national politics and national funding prevent the pooling and scope that a local community can achieve.

Distinguishing different functions for different levels of government is essential for the future. The argument that states and cities can't deal as well as the national government with many societal problems becomes true only because the federal government holds too much of the nation's tax money, most of which should go to the sites of action. Distinctions can be made for aspects of these problems that centralization can best deal with, such as research about AIDS or other diseases for which special facilities or personnel are needed. But even these cases don't necessarily require a federal agency. Americans are still taking all their problems to a big daddy, the president, instead of to their less emotionally symbolic but certainly more appropriate local governments.

Many of the social functions that are inappropriate for federal government to commandeer are also inappropriate for state government, though, again, a higher level of government can sometimes play a helpful role without building up a large agency and siphoning up large tax revenue. Much of the argument made for shifting power and money down from Washington applies to state capitals as well. Governors and state legislatures have aggrandized themselves in parallel with federal centralization. State income tax imitated federal income tax. Both levels of government have gained far more control over the unincorporated than over the incorporated, over individual citizens than over businesses or special-interest lobbies. State social services purport to help individuals, but the farther a program is run from the sites where such help may really occur and the more the state unnecessarily regulates and taxes these individuals, the more wealth and power concentrate in the agencies and the more temptation and opportunity exist for the incorporated to exploit the unincorporated. Agglomeration, in other words, increases all the risks as governments and corporations interact over the heads of the unorganized citizenry.

Various Ways to Band Together

Agglomeration will occur also, it's true, in shifting more social functions down to the community level and in consolidating them under education. Still, this represents a far better risk, generally, because the citizenry has a better chance to get in on decision making about taxes and how they are spent. Specifically, the incorporation of most social services into a community educational network will make them much more responsive to local needs and local evaluation. The very populist, decentralized nature of such a system allows individuals to see better what is going on in it and to adjust it. Individuals within it go for what they want and are constantly helped to find the means, wherever it may be, without being shuffled from pillar to post in a compartmentalized bureacracy. Such a communal network operates laterally, not hierarchically. Because it is organized for flexibility and mobility, for access and personal choice, individuals control it in the sense that they can get out of their community whatever can possibly be made available. More than is otherwise possible, a self-programming, self-assessing learning system approximates a situation in which everybody and everything is self-regulating.

Social functions are by definition based on agglomeration of some sort. Thus the risk of abuse arises for any effort to band together to help each other. The ideal for safety and efficiency requires an agglomeration to become no larger than necessary and not large in the wrong way. If expanding the demographic arena, the geography and population, serves little purpose, don't do it, because operating over broad expanses of time and space and across greater numbers is riskier and more expensive. Consolidating both the problems and the resources of a local community, on the other hand, best ensures that people can bring the resources to bear on each other to solve the problems.

If something outside a community is still needed, then the definition of it might be expanded—from a suburb or inner city or rural town, for example, to a metropolitan area or county. If some community has too little facilities, variety of opportunities, pooled knowledge, or just money, there may be ways of consolidating with other social entities. If some localities are simply too poor in one thing or another, they may have to connect with a contiguous area so as to equalize tax money or other human and material resources across a broader social spectrum. After all, if certain professions are not practiced there, or if few kinds of commercial or scientific or artistic enterprises go on there, many kinds of projects or apprenticing or rippling cannot occur. Indeed, any community of whatever size will lack some resources and thereby limit local educational possibilities.

We must keep in mind that community learning networks consolidated with social services will create markets and job opportunities that will draw talents and resources into an area. Some localities will always have less industry than others, but every locality generates its own educational enterprise. The larger it is, the more self-sustaining becomes the community, because most money spent on education will circulate locally. This consequence of reinvestment would foster real urban renewal. But poor communities will need higher governments to equalize revenue until the learning system has enabled them to climb out of poverty and generate enough tax monies for themselves.

Banding together for mutual benefit need not take a political form but rather a selective consolidation for a certain purpose. A county government or multi-county confederation might levy educational taxes, for example, in order to equalize financial resources across urban and suburban areas but leave the actual governance of a community's education to the community. Nor does affiliation have to be physically contiguous. In the era of the global village, people do not have to band together only into geographic units but have options to connect up through telecommunication. Defining a community geographically and demographically, and then as an extended educational network, will always constitute a major task in balancing the gains and losses of aggregation. How big should the community get? Big in what sense?

Between these large and small living units we must find ourselves, appreciate what both unity and specialty have to contribute. Today the whole nation sometimes looks, through
journalistic feature stories, at how one particular community
has undertaken to improve its health services or waste disposal
or unemployment. This healthy trend points up the value of
diversity, especially when mass media can immediately pass
good ideas from one locality to another. The pluralistic differences that seem to create problems for unity also pay off for
all parties. When individuals and communities identify with
each other across these differences, they can make use of variety
to thrive in their individuality. Spiritual traditions teach
that we live in multiple realities, comparable to the concentric
arenas of learning or the concentric communities of society
and nature. If, likewise, each of us comprises multiple levels
of reality within, then our similarity and individuality are per-
ceptual options that we may play at will, and the paradox of
being both one and many dissolves.

14

▲

Soul School

Spiritual education centers on personal growth, which will solve more social ills and material problems than any other sort of educational orientation. Unless the raising of consciousness and culture is the primary goal of education, people eventually betray their practical goals such as material improvement and social amelioration. Americans are losing both prosperity and democracy because they are too undeveloped to make freedom work. But aside from any worldly payoff, personal development may also be the main purpose of life.

The Earthly Schoolhouse

Suppose it is true, as spiritual traditions maintain, that people are here on earth to grow, not primarily to achieve or acquire except as doing so enhances inner growth. Since what we achieve and acquire mean little in the end, this inner cultivation seems a more likely purpose for life. Suppose we do not learn merely in order to be able to get by, get along, get around, and get ahead. These are all essential, but they fare better when education aims beyond them on the assumption that *they* are

the means and *education* the end. Suppose we don't so much
learn to live as live to learn. Once understood this way, knowing becomes a different matter—and a much more important
one. Making a living and making a life become part of making
sense of life, so that everything in it has meaning.

Notoriously, people fall apart when they reach their goals.
Someone struggles fanatically to become rich and famous and
then, when successful, takes to alcohol or other drugs. Success
breeds despair as much as does failure. Husband and wife work
zestfully to build their dream house and then get divorced. Or
plan and strive to make it big in the middle class—white-collar
jobs, a house and cars and friends that show their status, children with straight teeth who go on to good colleges. Then in
middle age they don't have a basis for action any more, no
motive or meaning. What do you do after you reach your goals,
especially now that life expectancy is longer?

Some find new goals in time to regain meaning, but the problem is that the goals are usually too small. It's wrenching to
see people constantly turning over jobs, hobbies, houses, mates,
friends looking for new stimuli, gratifications, reasons to live.
Actually, such people are not as shallow as they seem. They
want meaning, but they are fixated on small goals—to win this
person, to make their bedroom look as stylish as those in *Better
Homes and Gardens*, to fit an image of a sporty businessman,
to impress professional peers with an article in the right journal.
If you're trying to reduce suffering or explore the mysteries of
life, you'll never run out of goals. The big aims are rarely
reached in a lifetime—and even those that are, like making a
scientific discovery that has taken many years, can be parlayed
into another long-range goal. Indeed, there's nothing wrong
with small goals if they are integrated into bigger ones. So goes
holistic thinking.

Living to learn makes whatever happens useful and meaningful, but it takes a spiritual framework to keep the "learning

experiences" that are painful from becoming a mockery. Such lifelong learning is not idle, for its own sake, or even for the sake of curiosity. After all, native curiosity itself most likely represents an innate feeling that we are here to learn. Suppose growth is the master goal. Then the focus of public education and the purpose of life would be one and the same—inner growth for meaning. If so, one's talents and traits, predispositions and predilections, would develop not merely for their own sake but as part of an individual's evolving toward spiritual fulfillment.

What would this super-goal be if not the full realization, at all levels of being, that one is a spirit, a part of Spirit, temporarily incarnated, exiled, and therefore in a state of amnesia? Fairy tales of urchins discovering they are princesses or princes may be taken as the wish fulfillments of peasants longing for ease and opulence, but all literature is at bottom a secularization of holy lore.[1] Underneath the stories of rags to riches, of unknown inheritances, of mistaken identity, of high estate disguised as low, lie ancient gnostic myths of self-realization in its true meaning of Self-realization. The protagonist overcomes the amnesia, the forgetfulness of the River Styx separating the spirit world from the physical world.

Perhaps we develop ourselves not only because it is the most practical way to live on earth but because it is how we find out who we really are, which might be more than we think. According to this view, personal development is transpersonal development. Traditionally, enlightenment or awakening transforms one's life. Since one then actually recognizes (re-cognizes) one's true nature as Spirit, it would be more accurate to regard this transformation as a transfiguration. One's nature has not changed, had never changed, but now one sees through the material plane to the radiance within, as the three Disciples of Christ and Arjuna were permitted to behold.

To realize oneself means to fulfill oneself, to bring all potentialities to realization. The army recruiting slogan, "Be all that you can be" typifies popular understanding, which unwittingly caricatures the spiritual truth it intuits by casting it in material terms. *Realize* means both 'become aware of' and 'make real'. That is exactly what happens, it's said, when enlightenment or self-realization occurs. One comes to know Spirit with the same sense of reality as we feel about the objects and events of daily life. In realizing the hidden nature of one's self as Self, one at once realizes also the hidden nature of the universe, the two being both Spirit, consubstantial. Thus realized also is the basic meaning of *religion* as 'rebonding'.

The religious mysteries of antiquity provide the model for this experience of realizing in the double sense. The hierophant placed the initiate in a deep trance underground for three days, during which time the spirit could disengage itself to go out of the body and be conducted on a sort of tour of higher planes. As disembodied consciousness, the initiate then saw spiritual reality so directly and convincingly that henceforth no teaching or scripture was necessary, and the reality of the experience remained forever. Christ's and Lazarus's three-day burials and resurrections represent this original born-again, out-of-body "witnessing," so debased in later exoteric misunderstanding. A vast, gradually secularizing literature has constantly attested to or reworked this breaking through to other planes of reality—from myths of being abducted underground like Persephone through the entranced, spirit-guided revelations of other worlds in Vergil and Dante to modern night journeys, underground heroes, and doppelgänger stories, to which may be added many science fiction stories voyaging to alternative realities as well as the recent clinical literature of near-death experiences and shamanistic alterations of consciousness.

It has become commonplace to point out that *educate* means to 'lead out', but lead out *what*? What is there in us to draw out and develop besides the garbage of conditioning and the private wealth of narcissism? What seeds grow into what fruit? What of this inner world is to be made real in the outer? What is so great about fulfilling myself if I'm a rotten person? Or innately depraved? In the spiritual view, no one is rotten *to the core*, because at the core is the soul, the seed of Spirit planted in an incarnated individual that if fulfilled will decontaminate the garbage and transmute the narcissism from self-cultivation to Self-realization. What is led out—awakened—is this soul. Earth would be only the growing medium.

Continuing Higher Education

If earth is a soul school, why does it have so short a session—a mere blip in time for any one spirit, which is, after all, immortal? What in blazes is this spirit doing all the rest of the time, before and after its four score years or so on the physical plane? And if it never incarnated, it would never become amnesiac in the first place and would never need redemption through awakening. The answer from esoteric literature is that the spirit is getting schooled on one or another of the planes of reality engendered by the successive emanations. More evolved spirits (the oldest of "old souls") never need return to the physical plane once they have learned all they have to learn here. Even as earthlings, it's said, we travel astrally out of the body at night (in a sort of mini-initiation), and this is the chief purpose of sleep, still puzzling to scientists. (Asleep, we are "dead to the world," *this* world.) So earth is only one school, and through sleep, ecstasy, or other experiences that temporarily release our higher vehicles from the physical body, the soul divides its learning time between different planes during even its assignment to this terrestrial classroom.

Most religions assert or assume, as early Christianity did, and as esoteric teaching makes most explicit, that individuals incarnate many times on the physical plane before they no longer need to return. If earth is a soul school driven by spiritual evolution, then reincarnation is inseparable from personal spiritual growth. Unfortunately, the idea of reincarnation is repugnant to modern sensibility, mostly because its early repression in Western culture caused it to be misunderstood and debased. Outside the whole spiritual framework in which it makes sense, it can seem bizarre and even ghoulish, but whether one believes in it or not, it stands as an excellent model of individualized learning.

One reason reincarnation is hard to believe—the fact that we don't usually remember past lives—is explained in the very concept of it, which includes amnesia. Compare the plural lives of reincarnation to the plural selves in a psychiatric case of a multiple personality. If the multiple selves knew of each other, that would thwart the very function of the multiplicity, which is to permit conflicting aspects of the person to exist by keeping them from confronting each other. If an incarnated individual knew of its former lives, it would, for one thing, have to have access to a plane of consciousness higher than the physical one, since knowledge of those lives cannot reside within the memories acquired in the present life but only in some vehicle of the person meta to the physical. Accessing higher planes from this one would mean that the person could also know the long-range spiritual reason for this incarnation and might try to avoid doing what is needed, likewise thwarting the whole point.

In other words, just as the healing of the multiple personality has to be conducted from a perspective meta to that of the patient, through some collaboration between the psychiatrist and the most inclusive self of the patient, soul growth is plotted between lives by the spirit while enjoying the higher consciousness of the discarnate state and the help of more evolved individuals present on that plane. Were the patient to know all selves at once, she or he would already be cured. Were the soul in one life to know of other lives, it would already have raised its consciousness beyond the physical plane. But the patient *begins* to learn of other selves, and the soul of other lives, while still in the restricted state, eventually integrating them into a new state.

Now compare both of these to a student. Reincarnation makes no sense without karma, which corresponds remarkably to the process of self-determining or individualized education. Karma refers to the experience an individual is logging inasmuch as it indicates patterns of the past and needs for the future. Commentators often define it by the biblical quotation, "As you sow, so shall ye reap," which is indeed pertinent but too compact and figurative to convey the whole concept unless you understand it already. It's not a statement about justice like "an eye for an eye" or "you get what you deserve." It means that each individual creates a history or pattern of action all its own that must ultimately be filled in, offset, balanced, and otherwise amended until the soul has completed its experience on this plane and learned all it can. It is basic trial-and-error learning enabling the soul to live out or live through the physical plane, to outgrow materiality. Before reincarnating, the soul takes stock of past and future in its higher state of consciousness and in consultation with those more evolved, just as, between projects or phases of activity in an individualized learning environment, secular students periodically review and preview their work from the longer-range perspective of their total growth in order to decide with counselors their next action.

The main thing that the patient, soul, and student have in common is that what they do at each step depends on awareness of what they *have* done and on its meaning. This process is holistic and individual. It cannot be standardized, because current decisions depend on unique personal patterns of the

past requiring unique future steps. Everyone's karma is different. Trying to save souls by general rules, formulas, and programs does not work any better than trying to heal emotions
or educate minds by uniform procedures. Eventually churches,
hospitals, and schools all have to learn this. Though I believe
it's helpful to reflect on these parallel learning experiences, reason alone should tell us that, by the very nature of growth,
learning will always require individualizing. To grow is to
change, and change has to proceed from wherever a person
has fetched up at the time learning begins. The end may be
generalizable as a common goal or desideratum, but each person starts toward it from unique circumstances and conditions
in which he or she is enmeshed, like the spirit fallen into and
involved in matter so idiosyncratically that only certain paths
or means will work. Education consists of finding for oneself
what these are.

One by One

If life on earth is one big soul school, it surely runs on an
individualized curriculum. If there is anything to the spiritual
view besides superstition and wish fulfillment, each exiled spirit
has to wend its own way, because deconditioning oneself is
different for each person. If we are all too involuted in matter
to see straight, surely we have different labyrinths to unwind.
We're not born with the same inheritances or into the same
circumstances. Each life weaves its own web. Out of one, many.
To rejoin the One, we must travel back by different paths. But
who knows the path for oneself let alone for another? Does
the state know which course each must pursue? If it cannot
know how to select and order experiences even for material
learning, as I would assert, but must allow for individuals to

work out their own ways, how can it possibly know how for spiritual revelation?

This is not a negative situation unless you insist on the supremacy of the state. What the state *can* know is that learning of any sort, material or spiritual, occurs as part of some individual unfolding that efforts to standardize impair immeasurably. The same self-determining learning fields that it can set up to prepare people most effectively for employment in the workplace will foster mystical ecstasy if that is what an individual feels impelled toward. It's not the state's business to decide whether I'm to have *either* a secular *or* a spiritual education. Separation of church and state is not an issue, because in customized education the state does not set the curriculum and because spiritual development has no necessary connection with a church anyway. As public schooling has been, the state has excluded the spiritual on grounds that jobs, not religion, are its business. In other words, spiritualize on your own time.

But in requiring me to attend school all my youth, the state leaves me little time on my own and subjects me to conditions that work against my spiritual development. Most of my daily life is programmed not only from the outside but by people who take their marching orders from a policy that is far from impartial. On the contrary, it imposes a fixed curriculum standardized for the lowest common denominator and based on a political notion of majority rule that should not apply to learning. Are we to understand, as is argued for the military, that public education constitutes a special exemption from democratic ideals such that you must check your civil rights at the door?

If there is any chance at all that the spiritual reality and purpose I have tried to describe exist, then absolutely nothing should be allowed to interfere with the self-realization that would align individuals with it. Nothing. The state does not have to decide whether it believes in it or not. It has only to organize resources so that people can find out that or anything else for themselves. It is much harder to determine who you are and what you may do even in the worldliest matters when others are constantly forcing things on you and planning everything for you—that is, when you are reactive. It's essential to assert feeling and will and thought proactively enough to establish your *own patterns of action*. Then you manifest something of yourself out there for you and others to respond to so that with their help you can chart past and future.

We have to enact our conditioned being as we are now and at the same time draw on the unconditioned being that sleeps within. Then we command the personal and transpersonal material we need to work with for growth. This self-realizing sort of acting out replaces the self-destructive acting out occurring now from the rage and impotence of being manipulated and robbed of one's life. So long as we are only reacting to a predetermined curriculum, we are forced to construct our knowledge and to pattern our action according to public decision making and group consciousness. This interferes with each person's process of growing up, healing, and finding the best work, personal bonds, and social roles. It interferes with the flow of energy and intuition that the surface self should be able to tap from its central inner source. And, if spiritual teaching is true, it interferes with the growth of the soul toward real redemption, which would be "making good on" the Spirit it incarnates.

State-set standardized learning programs also resist the evolution of individual consciousness, which transformation of the culture awaits. Self-consciousness and self-determination have surely not evolved as far as they have only to self-destruct and ruin the culture in which they have grown. If this evolution is destined from without, then we should go with it, not fight it. If we ourselves can determine the course it takes, then we should see that it consummates individualism in a way best fitting all purposes. This would be the spiritual way. It alone allows for all needs, all possibilities, and all realities, because it embraces all.

The esoteric teaching says that Spirit ensouls animals collectively, each species having a group soul that beams to individual members of it their considerable knowledge, which we call instinct because they do not have to learn it personally. Human beings also partake of a group soul into which they are bonded genetically or culturally, in addition to being individually ensouled. In keeping with both Richard Bucke's "simple consciousness" and Julian Jaynes's "bicameral mind," early human beings abided essentially within the group soul and only gradually developed a personal soul. People today scatter across a wide range of such development and so are at odds about how much to adhere to or depart from a common ethos, the cultural embodiment of a group soul. It may be useful to regard this conflict as the tug-of-war everyone feels between the group soul and the personal soul or, in secular terms, one's collective and individual natures.

Individual souls must differentiate themselves from the group soul of the race or culture and identify, beyond these, with the All or One itself. With rare exceptions, we are still balking desperately at doing this. Most of the strife in the world today is occurring between religions and ethnic groups, that is, between group souls that ferociously refuse to accept each other because each takes itself for Spirit instead of for one localized manifestation of Spirit. The vicious intensity of the slaughter and rapine by religious people who are quite civilized and moral among their own kind is difficult to explain by ordinary psychology. Why such intransigeant refusal to tolerate differences that are spiritually superficial? Why not live and prosper together rather than laying each other waste in "ethnic cleansing" one generation after another? Such consuming hatred of outsiders can hardly be explained except by the malingering of individuals in group souls, by the great difficulty of breaking away.

Like a clutching parent who fears self-elimination if truly successful in bringing children to maturity, the culture does not really want its members to grow up, although it exists to benefit them. So the culture and individuals have to co-evolve. The reason that history shows a pattern of consciousness evolving from collective to individual may be that this direction does indeed fulfill a cosmic purpose. In any case it seems sensible for a culture to undertake today to wean individuals from itself if only to halt the slaughter and strife. This means deliberately educating for self-direction and self-realization. A new cosmopolitan kind of citizen will result who feels psychologically and spiritually self-sufficient enough to transcend ethnic and religious boundaries and put union over difference, cosmos over country or culture. Only then will the wars end.

Regarding religious, ethnic, and other groups as group souls in an evolutionary context should help us think about conflicts even if one regards the spiritual account of it all as merely mythical or metaphorical. In any case, people who fulfill themselves tend to stop making trouble. One can stop at this thought and still arrive at the need for a spiritual education. What I'm suggesting in addition is that considering the esoteric account seriously, with or without believing it, may improve the quality of our problem solving and also allow for whatever may prove true. Instead of keeping its members dependent, a culture must, like a good parent, ready them and release them to go forth as free souls. In the words of a popular song, "God bless the child that's got its own."

Homeward Bound

Why the evolution of consciousness in the first place? It's as if Spirit wishes to parcel itself into manifold manifestations (out of One, many), a sort of self-realization or self-expression of its own in the direction from energy to matter while also remaining as it was. This would proceed by global ensoulments such as the Solar Logos, Spiritus Mundi, Plato's Soul of the World, and the various group souls as of animal species and human races. This precipitation would culminate in individual incarnations and the materializing of all aspects or potentialities of Spirit. Whereas Spirit realizes itself by manifesting itself through a spectrum of successively denser emanations, its incarnations realize themselves by becoming conscious of Spirit as their true nature and of the incarnating process itself. What we feel as grace is the homeward pull of Spirit; what we do in prayer is call home.

In this sense that the Creator needs its creation, God is said to depend on us, divinity on humanity. Thus the real humanism is not secular. *Anthropos* was always considered in spiritual traditions as God on earth, by the very nature of incarnation. This is why Christ is referred to as both Son of God and Son of Man. Only by denying our inner divinity can we regard humanism as secular. Using our faculties to the fullest to create the arts and sciences and civilization is manifesting Spirit through our own incarnation. In fulfilling ourselves we are playing our part in the self-fulfillment of Spirit itself.

The mission is to respiritualize oneself *while matter* and thus to spiritualize matter, transform the world. It's as if the cosmic goal is for Spirit to enjoy the best of all worlds at once. Simply being part of Spirit like a foetus in the womb contrasts with being individually *conscious* of being part of Spirit. Consciousness makes all the difference, and the purpose of evolution seems to be to bring about on the lowest plane total consciousness of the highest plane. Apotheosis, becoming God, models this process, exemplified in the lives of avatars like Moses, Buddha, Jesus, and Mohammed who achieved cosmic consciousness while incarnated in mortal form.

Consummating individuals means bringing them home

again. As they return to their common origin, they rejoin each other but in a new union beyond the old group souls. For the individual to evolve from self-consciousness into cosmic consciousness, it must paradoxically lose itself, in keeping with the biblical idea that the seed must die in order to fruit. In shamanistic mythology, the initiate is dismembered and reassembled into a new being, like Orpheus and Osiris. The individual cannot remain merely self-conscious and self-serving but, rather, must be reborn through an expansion of consciousness and identity that comprehends all other people on its way to comprising the cosmos. Being torn apart represents the deconditioning from heredity and environment that must precede the unconditioned state of pure, free being. It resembles the process of being wounded and healed, as is to be expected, since some therapy will always have to prepare for spirituality. To be here is to be wounded, and recovering will hurt. But losing oneself leads to ecstasy, which means literally being *outside* oneself, transported, as in the expression "She was beside herself with joy."

Of course the paradox, the 'dual teaching,' of finding oneself by losing oneself refers us to the very nature of incarnation. The highest frequency is stepped down, via the successive emanations, to the lowest frequency—or heaviest "vibe"—in the form of some physical body. A human being partakes of all emanations or planes of reality at once without knowing it until he or she achieves cosmic consciousness, which is in fact defined by this realization or awakening. This is the esoteric meaning of "know thyself," which post-Freudian people are apt to understand as merely making the unconscious conscious, as psychological awareness. This is indeed important and, like therapy, a prerequisite or concomitant of this spiritual consummation. But the ultimate meaning of "know thyself" seems to be "know thy Self," thy origin in Spirit, which is tantamount to comprehending the cosmos itself, since the interplay of these plural realities makes up both it and oneself.

The notion of *correspondences* between an individual and the universe explains much of spiritual thinking. It is the counterpart of some scientists' holographic conception of the universe, in which each part reflects the whole.[2] It underlies teachings such as "Man is the measure of all things," which means "Understand how you are made, and you will know the nature of creation." From antiquity different cultures have transmitted the adages "Thou art That" and "As above, so below." You are a microcosm of the cosmos. It is in this sense that God is said to have made the world and humankind in its own image. If you know how you are composed, you know what the world is like.

This correspondence changes utterly how one interprets the idea that self-knowledge is the gateway to knowledge of other things. Otherwise, "Know thyself" may seem like a pious effort to make a case for the inner life or to justify self-cultivation for its own sake. Without understanding this relationship between identifying and learning—sympathy in its basic sense—it is also difficult to see why forms of meditation and trance-state attunement are primal learning methods. You don't have to subscribe to the esoteric view to see how much we learn of something outside by concentrating on it so raptly that counterparts within us give rise to thoughts, feelings, and images that inform us about it. This is the heart of intuition. Resonance overcomes the boundaries between inner and outer. Raptness expands consciousness, which brings on rapture.[3]

Regarded as secular, soul school provides an education full of soul—spirited and loving. It is powered by the life force, like the African-American radio station I once heard identify itself as "broadcasting with 50,000 watts of soul." It is soulful also in that it works through deep feeling. It honors the experiencer, and the range and depth of experience is the key to growth. Regarded as sacred, soul school provides the material experience that, spiritualized, enables the exile to return, awake now to *all* worlds. In every sense of finding and fulfilling oneself, going to soul school is coming home.

NOTES

▲

Preface

1. Since not everything about a subject as intricate as this one can be effectively said in a single work, some ideas underlying this book are more fully developed in a companion volume, *Harmonic Learning: Keynoting School Reform* and in other of my books, to which I will occasionally refer for those readers who might want certain points further analyzed or situated. These titles are cited in a separate section of the bibliography following these notes.

Chapter One

1. Alfred North Whitehead, *The Aims of Education* (New York: Dutton, 1949), p. 51. Originally published in 1929.
2. Ivan Illich, *Deschooling Society* (New York: Harper and Row, 1971).

3. Richard Bucke, *Cosmic Consciousness: A Study in the Evolution of the Human Mind* (New York: Viking Penguin, 1991). Originally published in 1901.

4. A fascinatingly comparable effort to evoke spiritual experience through the lives of avatars appeared in 1889 in France—Édouard Schuré's *The Great Initiates: A Study of the Secret History of Religions* (Blauvelt, N.Y.: Rudolf Steiner Publications, 1961).

5. Julian Jaynes, *The Origins of Consciousness in the Breakdown of the Bicameral Mind* (Boston: Houghton Mifflin, 1976).

6. In *Points of View: An Anthology of Short Stories*, Kenneth R. McElheny and I arrayed stories in a spectrum illustrating this point.

7. Clive Beck, "Education for Spirituality," *Interchange*, Summer 1986, pp. 148–156; and David Purpel, *Moral and Spiritual Crisis in Education: A Curriculum for Justice and Compassion* (Westport, Conn.: Bergin and Garvey, 1988).

8. In the account of universal esoteric spirituality that follows here and in the last chapter, I will rely on, without citing in the text, a body of literature represented by the special bibliography for Universal Spiritual Traditions that begins on p. 362.

9. See physicist Fred Alan Wolf's *The Eagle's Quest* (New York: Simon & Schuster, 1991).

10. In the aftermath of a fundamentalist rebellion against some schoolbooks that included a progam I had directed (referred to in Chapter Five), I wrote in *Storm in the Mountains* about this relationship between ethnocentricity and a materialistic understanding of spirituality.

11. See Bernard Fayë's *Revolution and Freemasonry, 1680–1800* (Boston: Little, Brown, 1935).

Chapter Two

1. Richard J. Barnet, "Reflections: Defining the Moment," *New Yorker,* July 16, 1990, p. 58.

Chapter Three

1. Norman Maclean, *A River Runs Through It and Other Stories* (New York: Simon & Schuster, 1976).

Chapter Four

1. Erich Fromm, *Escape from Freedom* (Troy, Mo.: Holt, Rinehart & Winston, 1941).
2. In the afterword to *Points of View: An Anthology of Short Stories,* I discussed the expansion of consciousness through multiple viewpoints, which are illustrated by the stories arrayed as a spectrum of increasingly broader narrative perspectives.
3. Maria Montessori, *The Advanced Montessori Method* (New York: Random House, 1989).
4. Rudolf Steiner, *The Arts and Their Mission* (Spring Valley, N.Y.: Anthroposophic Press, 1964), pp. 25 and 17. Originally delivered as lectures in 1923.
5. John Dewey, *Art as Experience* (New York: Minton Balch, 1934), p. 195.
6. Herbert Read, *Education Through Art* (London: Faber and Faber, 1943, 1958), p. 110.
7. Suzanne Langer, *Mind: An Essay on Human Feeling* (Baltimore, Md.: Johns Hopkins University Press, 1967), pp. xviii and xix.

▲

8. Read, *Education Through Art*, p. 11.
9. Howard Gardner, *Frames of Mind: The Theory of Multiple Intelligences* (New York: Basic Books, 1983).
10. Read, *Education Through Art*, p. 8.
11. Ibid., p. 196.

Chapter Five

1. Respectively Herbert Muller, *The Uses of English* (New York: Holt, Rinehart & Winston, 1967), and John Dixon, *Growth Through English* (London: Oxford University Press for the National Association of Teachers of English, 1967, revised 1975).
2. David Krathwohl, coauthor with Benjamin Bloom of *Taxonomy of Educational Objectives: the Classification of Educational Goals, Vol. 2: The Affective Domain* (White Plains, N.Y.: Longman, revised 1984), and Robert Mager, *Preparing Instructional Objectives* (Palo Alto, Calif.: Fearon Publishers, 1962).
3. "Misbehavioral Subjectives," *Coming on Center: Essays in English Education*, p. 13. The long headnote there gives a more detailed account of this Tri-University Project. This essay was originally published under the title of "Misbehaviorist English: A Position Paper" in *On Writing Behavioral Objectives for English*, ed. Anthony Tovatt and John Maxwell (Urbana, Ill.: National Council of Teachers of English, 1970), which includes a rebuttal by one of the project directors as well as various other views.
4. B. F. Skinner, *Verbal Behavior* (New York: Prentice-Hall, 1957), and Noam Chomsky, "A Review of B. F. Skinner's *Verbal Behavior*," *Languages*, 35:26–58, reprinted in *The Structure of Language: Readings in the Philosophy of Lan-*

guage, ed. J. A. Fodor and J. J. Katz (New York: Prentice-Hall, 1964).

5. Richard Lloyd-Jones and Andrea A. Lunsford, eds., *The English Coalition Conference: Democracy Through Language* (Urbana, Ill.: National Council of Teachers of English, 1989); and Peter Elbow, *What Is English?* (New York: Modern Language Association, 1990).

6. *The Emerging Requirements for Effective Leadership,* an unpublished report prepared for the California State Board of Education, 1964; quotes taken from pp. 16 and 17.

7. Edward M. Gramlich and Patricia P. Koshel, *Educational Performance Contracting: An Evaluation of an Experiment* (Washington, D.C.: The Brookings Institute, 1975), pp. 50 and 62. The authors were on the staff of the U.S. Office of Education during the era of performance contracting, and this report confirmed the conclusions of the USOE itself.

Chapter Six

1. Quoted in "Curricular Standards: Federal or National?," *Reading Today,* June/July 1993, p. 40.

2. *Designs for a New Generation of American Schools* (Arlington, Va.: New American Schools Development Corporation, 1991), pp. 50–52.

3. Evans Clinchy, "America 2000: Reform, Revolution, or Just More Smoke and Mirrors?" and Harold Howe, "America 2000: A Bumpy Ride on Four Trains," *Phi Delta Kappan,* November 1991, pp. 210 and 192.

4. Milbrey W. McLaughlin, "Test-Based Accountability as a Reform Strategy," *Phi Delta Kappan,* November 1991, p. 248.

5. "Go Slow on National Curriculum, Tests, ASCD Warned," *ASCD Update*, May 1991, pp. 1, 6–7.

6. Ibid., p. 6.

7. Lauren B. Resnick and Daniel P. Resnick, "Assessing the New Curriculum," in *Changing Assessments: Alternative Views of Aptitude, Achievement, and Instruction*, ed. B. R. Gifford and M. C. Connors (Boston: Kluwer, 1991). This chapter was prepared for the National Commission on Testing and Public Policy. Lauren Resnick sat on the National Council on Educational Standards and Testing, set up by the governors' National Educational Goals Panel, for which she also led an advisory council.

8. See *Detecting Growth in Language* and the chapter "Evaluation" in *Student-Centered Language Arts, K-12*.

9. *The New Standards Project: An Overview*, Learning Research and Development Center of the University of Pittsburgh (directed by Lauren Resnick and Daniel Resnick) and the National Center on Education and the Economy (directed by Marc Tucker), p. 1.

10. Quoted from page 22 of a transcript of a presentation by Daniel Resnick to the Alliance for Curriculum Reform at a meeting I attended in Aspen, Colorado, on August 26, 1991.

11. Douglas D. Noble, "Who Are These Guys: Corporate Involvement in the 'New American Schools'," *Rethinking Schools*, March/April 1992, p. 20.

12. These quotations are from "Sound Bites," *ASCD Update*, May 1991, p. 5.

13. Ibid., p. 5.

14. Tim Brookes, "A Lesson to Us All," *Harper's*, May 1991, p. 27.

15. Ibid., no page number.

16. Mary Lou McClosky and D. Scott Enright, "America 2000—Two TESOL Members Respond," *TESOL Matters*, 1 (August/September 1991):1.

17. Ibid., p. 8.

18. "Shorts," *Rethinking Schools*, March/April 1992, p. 7.

19. Stan Karp, "Massachusetts 'Choice' Plan Undercuts Poor Districts," *Rethinking Schools*, March/April 1992, p. 4.

20. John E. Chubb and Terry M. Moe, *Politics, Markets, and America's Schools* (Washington, D.C.: The Brookings Institute, 1990).

21. Robert Lowe, "The Illusion of 'Choice'," *Rethinking Schools,* March/April 1992, p. 22.

22. See Geraldine Joncich Clifford, "A Sisyphean Task: Historical Perspectives on Writing and Reading Instruction," *Collaboration through Writing and Reading: Exploring Possibilities*, ed. Anne Haas Dyson (Urbana, Ill.: National Council of Teachers of English, 1989).

23. Patrick Shannon, *The Struggle to Continue: Progressive Reading Instruction in the United States* (Portsmouth, N.H.: Heinemann Educational Books, 1990).

24. Alfred North Whitehead, "The Mathematical Curriculum," presidential address to the London branch of the Mathematical Association, in *The Aims of Education* (New York: Dutton, 1949), p. 85. Originally published in 1929.

25. Ibid., pp. 18 and 19.

26. Ron Miller, *What Are Schools For?: Holistic Education in American Culture* (Brandon, Vt.: Holistic Education Press, 1990).

27. "Creating Educational Futures: A Historical Perspective," an insert to *Changing Schools*, February 1992; also obtainable from Don Glines at P.O. Box 2977, Sacramento, Calif. 95812; telephone (916)393-8701.

Chapter Seven

1. For more on this, see pp. 124–130 of *Harmonic Learning*.

2. See, for example, *Changing Schools* (Colorado Options in Education, 98 N. Wadsworth Blvd. No. 127, Box 191, Lakewood, CO 80226), *Rethinking Schools* (1001 E. Keefe Ave., Milwaukee, WI 53212), and the *Holistic Education Review* (39 Pearl St., Brandon, VT 05733-1007). These refer to and sometimes list experimental schools and other organizations useful for alternative networking.

3. I was inspired to conceive these particular games by the research experiments with conjunctive and disjunctive logic discussed in *A Study of Thinking*, by Jerome S. Bruner, Jacqueline J. Goodnow, and George A. Austin (New York: Wiley, 1965).

4. Burton White, *The First Three Years of Life* (Englewood Cliffs, N.J.: Prentice-Hall, 1975).

5. In an essay titled "Writing, Inner Speech, and Meditation" in *Coming on Center*.

6. James Haughton Woods, ed., *The Yoga-System of Patanjali* in the Harvard Oriental Series (Delhi, India: Motilal Barnarsidass, 1966).

7. Holt Associates can be contacted at 2269 Massachusetts Ave., Cambridge, MA 02140; telephone (617)864-3100. Susanah Scheffler is director.

8. An ex-teacher put together a collection of essays written by home-schooling children to give others an idea of what the experience and the problems are like. These are testimonials by adolescents who like it but who also convey through the particularities of their cases the realities of what it entails. See Grace Llewellyn, ed., *Real Lives:*

Eleven Teenagers Who Don't Go to School (Eugene, Oreg.: Lowry House, 1993).

9. Maurice Gibbons and others, "Toward a Theory of Self-directed Learning: A Study of Experts without Formal Training," *Journal of Humanistic Psychology*, Spring 1980, pp. 41–56.

10. Ibid., quotations excerpted from p. 54.

Chapter Eight

1. Part Three of *Harmonic Learning.*

2. Mathematics Sciences Education Board, *Reshaping School Mathematics: A Philosophy and Framework for Curriculum* (Washington, D.C.: National Academy Press, 1990); *Curriculum and Evaluation Standards for School Mathematics* (Reston, Va.: National Council of Teachers of Mathematics, 1989); *Project 2061: Science for All Americans* (Washington, D.C.: American Association for the Advancement of Science, 1989); and *The Content Core: A Guide for Curriculum Designers* (The National Science Teachers Association, 1991).

Chapter Nine

1. The genesis and ramifications of the Alliance for Curriculum Reform (ACR) are treated in more detail in Part Three of *Harmonic Learning.* For further information write to ACR, 2000 Clarendon Boulevard, Arlington, Va. 22201.

2. Warren McCulloch, *Embodiments of Mind* (Cambridge, Mass.: M.I.T. Press, 1965). This question is the title of a chapter in this book.

3. In Part Three of *Harmonic Learning*.

4. Suzanne Langer, *Mind: An Essay on Human Feeling*, 2 vols. (Baltimore, Md.: Johns Hopkins University Press, 1967).

5. James Watson, *The Double Helix* (New York: Atheneum, 1968).

6. See *Student-Centered Language Arts* for the full exposition of what is said in this section, especially the chapter titled "Becoming Literate."

7. David Lancy, *Children's Emergent Literacy from Research to Practice* (New York: Praeger, 1994).

8. Frank Smith, *Understanding Reading* (Hillsdale, N.J.: Lawrence Erlbauer Associates, 1988).

Chapter Ten

1. The following description and quotations are drawn from Draft 7/91 of *Project 2061: Educating for a Changing Future: McFarland Model*, put out by the American Association for the Advancement of Science (AAAS). For further or updated information write to Project 2061 at the AAAS, 133 H St. NW, Washington, DC 20005. All quotations are from pp. 11–14.

2. Progressive Education Association, ed., *Adventure in American Education*, vol. 5: *Thirty Schools Tell Their Story* (New York: HarperCollins, 1943), p. xvii.

3. Ibid., p. xxiii.

4. Ibid.

5. For some notion of the failure of a liberal arts education to have a significant positive effect on students' lives, based on research done well before the financial and curricular dilemmas of the 1980s and 1990s, see Nevit Sanford, *Where Colleges Fail* (San Francisco: Jossey-Bass, 1967).

6. *National Observer*, July 28, 1969, p. 4.

7. Interested parties can contact Don Glines, Educational Futures Projects, P.O. Box 2977, Sacramento, CA 95812; telephone (916)393-8701. His relating of this experience to current reform, *Educational Futures and Mankato Wilson,* may be obtained there.

   The fifty-minute videotape *Mankato Wilson Campus School: Remembered, 1992* may be obtained for $18 from the College of Education, Mankato State University, Mankato, MN 56001.

   A dissertation drawing on the Mankato experiment, Kathleen Long's *Individual Teacher Perspectives on School Restructuring* (University of Oregon, 1992) may be obtained from the library of the University of Oregon or from Kathleen Long, Division of Education, Indiana University, South Bend, IN 46615. After 1994 it will be available as a book.

8. All quotations describing these NASDC projects are taken from NASDC's unpaginated announcement in 1992 of its awards, titled "NASDC Facts." Information about the progress of these projects can be obtained from NASDC at 1000 Wilson Blvd., Suite 2710, Arlington, VA 22209; telephone (703) 908-9500; FAX (703) 908-0622.

9. Ivan Illich, *Deschooling Society* (New York: HarperCollins, 1971).

10. Ronald Barnes, "New Age Education," *J C Penney Forum,* May 1984, p. 15. See also Jim Atkinson, "MXC: A City with a Taste of Tomorrow," *Northwestern Bell Magazine,* special edition, 1972.

Chapter Eleven

1. Erik H. Erikson, *Childhood and Society* (New York: Norton, 1950, 1963).

2. Jerome S. Bruner, *Toward a Theory of Instruction* (Cambridge, Mass.: Harvard University Press, 1966).

3. Lev Semenovich Vygotsky, *Thought and Language* (Cambridge, Mass.: MIT Press, 1962).

4. George Herbert Mead, "Self," in *On Social Psychology: Selected Papers*, ed. Anselm Strauss (Chicago: University of Chicago Press, 1954).

5. Handily summarized from Piaget's many books in Henry W. Maier, *Three Theories of Child Development* (New York: HarperCollins, 1965).

6. Heinz Werner, *Comparative Psychology of Mental Development* (New York: Science Editions, 1948).

7. Ibid., p. x of foreword by Gordon Allport.

8. Claude Levi-Strauss, *The Savage Mind* (Chicago: University of Chicago Press, 1962).

9. Maria Montessori, *The Absorbent Mind* (New York: Holt, Rinehart & Winston, 1967).

10. Burton White, *The First Three Years of Life* (Englewood Cliffs, N.J.: Prentice-Hall, 1975).

11. Rudolf Steiner, *The Essentials of Education* (London: Rudolf Steiner Press, 1982), p. 39. First published in 1926.

12. Bronson Alcott, *Conversations with Children on the Gospels*, 2 vols. (New York: Arno Press). First published in 1837.

13. Robert Coles, *The Spiritual Lives of Children* (Cambridge, Mass.: Harvard University Press, 1990).

14. Joseph Chilton Pearce, *The Magical Child* (New York: Dutton, 1977), and Thomas Armstrong, *The Radiant Child* (Wheaton, Ill.: Theosophical Publishing House, 1985).

15. James Peterson, "Extrasensory Abilities of Children: An Ignored Reality?" *Learning*, December 1975, pp. 11–14.

16. *The Boy Who Saw True*, introduction, afterword, and notes by Cyril Scott (London: Neville Spearman, 1953).
17. Steiner, *The Essentials of Education*, p. 81.
18. Joseph Head and S. L. Cranston, eds., *Reincarnation: An East West Anthology* (Wheaton, Ill.: Theosophical Publishing House, 1961). It quotes from this poem among hundreds of texts by famous Western thinkers and literary figures—and even practical creators like Thomas Edison, Henry Ford, and Luther Burbank—showing that they all believed in or took seriously the idea of reincarnation.
19. Caleb Gattegno, *For the Teaching of Elementary Mathematics* (Mt. Vernon, N.Y.: Cuisenaire Company of America, 1963).
20. *Teaching the Universe of Discourse.*
21. Charles Tart, *Altered States of Consciousness* (Novato, Calif.: Psychological Processes, 1992).

Chapter Fourteen

1. In Part Two of *Harmonic Learning* I explored this thesis.
2. See Ken Wilbur, ed., *The Holographic Paradigm and Other Paradoxes* (Cambridge, Mass.: Shambhala, 1982).
3. George Leonard had the right idea twenty-five years ago in his *Education and Ecstasy* (New York: Delacorte Press, 1968), in which he was already drawing on spiritual disciplines and proposing counterculture practices for public education.

▲

BIBLIOGRAPHY

▲

Author's Works Cited

Ed. with Kenneth R. McElheny, *Points of View: An Anthology of Short Stories* (New York: Dutton, 1966, 2nd edition 1994).

Teaching the Universe of Discourse (Portsmouth, N.H.: Boynton/Cook Heinemann, 1968).

With Betty J. Wagner, *Student-Centered Language Arts, K-12* (Portsmouth, N.H.: Boynton/Cook Heinemann, 1968, 4th edition 1992).

Senior editor, *Interaction: A K-12 Language Arts and Reading Program* (Boston: Houghton Mifflin, 1973, out of print).

Coming on Center: Essays in English Education (Portsmouth, N.H.: Boynton/Cook Heinemann, 1981, 2nd edition 1988).

Storm in the Mountains: A Case Study of Censorship, Conflict, and Consciousness (Carbondale: Southern Illinois University Press, 1988).

Harmonic Learning: Keynoting School Reform (Portsmouth, N.H.: Boynton/Cook Heinemann, 1992).

Detecting Growth in Language (Portsmouth, N.H.: Boynton/ Cook Heinemann, 1992).

Bibliography for Universal Spiritual Traditions

This list of suggested reading is roughly sequenced from most comprehensive to most specialized.

BOOKS

Manley P. Hall, *The Secret Teachings of All Ages: An Encyclopedic Outline of Masonic, Hermetic, Cabalistic, and Rosicrucian Symbolical Philosophy* (Los Angeles: Philosophical Research Society, 1978). Such a fascinating book to begin with that one may never come out of it. Though it includes only the West and its sources, it is richly multicultural and extracts multitudinous quotations and graphics from early texts.

Max Heindel, *The Rosicrucian Cosmoconception* (Oceanside, Calif.: The Rosicrucian Fellowship, 1909). As complete and helpful an exposition of esoteric understanding as one volume might contain.

Itzhak Bentov, *Stalking the Wild Pendulum: On the Mechanics of Consciousness* (New York: Dutton, 1977). A brilliant, original, colloquial rendering of esoteric cosmology and physiology in terms of recent physics. This is an excellent way for the postmodern layman to come upon and entertain concepts of spiritual evolution, reincarnation, and transformation of consciousness keyed to a cyclic universe.

Aldous Huxley, *The Perennial Philosophy* (New York: World, 1944). Emphasizes universal ideas among the world's religions and philosophers corresponding in more exoteric form to the esoteric tradition.

Éliphas Lévi, *The History of Magic* (New York: Samuel Weiser, 1969). Originally published in French around 1860; translated into English in 1913 by A. E. Waite. The book that pioneered rediscovery in the nineteenth century of occult traditions, which is essentially what "magic" means here.

H. P. Blavatsky, *The Secret Doctrine: The Synthesis of Science, Religion, and Philosophy*, 3 vols. (Wheaton, Ill.: Theosophical Society, 1893). The cornerstone of modern Theosophy and hence a major source of understanding of esoteric traditions.

Swami Vyas Dev Ji, *Science of Soul (Atma Vijnana): A Practical Exposition of Ancient Method of Visualization of Soul* (Bharat, India: Yoga Niketan Trust, 1964). A pure, clear contemporary presentation of the Vedantic anatomy of the human being as sheaths or vehicles corresponding to clairvoyant realities.

E. A. Wallis Budge, *The Egyptian Book of the Dead* (New York: Dover, 1967). Originally published in 1895. This pioneering translation of the Papyrus of Ani, containing copious notes and commentary, makes clear that the ancient Egyptians also believed in a scale of such bodies or vehicles.

Walter Scott, *Hermetica: The Ancient Greek and Latin Writings Which Contain Religious or Philosophical Teachings Ascribed to Hermes Trismegistus*, vols. 1–4 (London: Dawsons of Pall Mall, 1924). Transmission of Egyptian thought as mediated through Neoplatonists.

Kenneth Sylvan Guthrie, comp. and trans., and David Fideler, ed., *The Pythagorean Sourcebook and Library* (Grand Rapids, Mich.: Phanes Press, 1978). Definitive compilation on Pythagoreanism, which was pivotal between Eastern and Western esoteric traditions.

Plato, *Timaeus*, vol. 7 of Plato's works in the Loeb Classical Library (Cambridge, Mass.: Harvard University Press, 1929). His most esoteric work, closest to Pythagoras, constructs a cosmology based on numerical ratios that are fundamental musical intervals.

Marie-Louise von Franz, *Number and Time: Reflections Leading Toward a Unification of Depth Psychology and Physics* (Evanston, Ill.: Northwestern University Press, 1974). A remarkable fusion of esoteric doctrine with recent scientific thought.

Charles Williams Heckethorn, *The Secret Societies of All Ages and Countries* (New Hyde Park, N.Y.: University Press, 1965). Originally published in 1875, updated in 1895. Aside from Jesuitical conspiracy theories following the French Revolution, this is the first, still authoritative, work of scholarship on strands of underground spiritual and political organizations throughout history.

Mircea Eliade, *Yoga: Immortality and Freedom*, Bollingen Series 56 (Princeton, N.J.: Princeton University Press, 1958). A fine, comprehensive treatment of yoga by a student of it who is also a renowned scholar of comparative religions.

Swami Hariharananda Aranya, ed., *Yoga Philosophy of Patanjali* (Calcutta, India: Calcutta University Press, 1963). Contains Vyas's famous commentaries on this key distillation of yoga. For a brief and simple version for Westerners, see Swami Prabhavananda and Christopher Isherwood, eds., *How to Know God: The Yoga Aphorisms of Patanjali* (Hollywood, Calif.: Vedanta Press, 1953).

Mircea Eliade, *Shamanism: Archaic Techniques of Ecstasy*, Bollingen Series 56 (Princeton, N.J.: Princeton University Press, 1958). This magnificently cross-cultural work relates Native American to worldwide shamanic traditions and, in comparing shamanism with yoga, connects scattered indigenous teachings with Vedanta.

Idris Shah, *The Sufis* (New York: Doubleday, 1964). His most general book about this Islamic variation on illuministic or esoteric spirituality.

Farid al-din Attar, *The Conference of the Birds* (New York: Samuel Weiser, 1954). A thirteenth-century Sufi allegory of individuals rejoining the All through a pilgrimage together. Unacknowledged as a precursor of Chaucer's secularized rendition, *The Parliament of Fowls*.

Edwin A. Burtt, ed., *The Teachings of the Compassionate Buddha* (New York: Dutton, 1955). A compilation of basic Buddhist texts, which often focus on issues of incarnation and reincarnation.

D. T. Suzuki, *Zen Buddhism* (New York: Doubleday, 1956). A classic introduction to the equivalent of yoga and Sufism, all three being esoteric quintessences of their respective cultures' religions.

Gershom Scholem, *On the Kabbalah and Its Symbolism* (New York: Schocken Books, 1965). Translated by Ralph Manheim. The seminal work of scholarship on this Jewish mystical teaching. With this in hand, one might look at the basic texts themselves, the *Zohar,* or *Book of Radiance*, which includes the successive emanations, and the *Sepher Yetzira* or *Book of Formation*, which interprets the book of Genesis esoterically as a cosmology. Both are currently being made available—not to say, declassified—in various editions for modern readers.

Dion Fortune, *Mystical Qaballah* (New York; Ibis Books, 1979). Originally published in 1935. Some other approaches to Cabalism by someone versed in the various movements and organizations of the twentieth-century revival of esoteric traditions.

Rudolph Steiner, *Christianity as a Mystical Fact and Occult Mysteries of Antiquity* (Blauvelt, N.Y.: Steinerbooks, 1969). Originally published in 1902. Describes, as Annie Besant, Édouard Schuré (see Note 4, Chapter One, in Notes section), and others have, the truer, esoteric Christianity, kept alive by heretical groups like the Bogomils and Albigensians.

Rudolf Steiner, *Eleven European Mystics* (Blauvelt, N.Y.: Steinerbooks, 1971). Originally given as lectures in 1900. The deeper, inner Christianity as seen in the lives and works of some medieval and Renaissance mystics.

Origen, *On First Principles* (New York: HarperCollins, 1966). Edited by G. W. Butterfield. This leading second-century Christian theologian's doctrine on the existence of the soul before and after its incarnation in the body was orthodox until Pope Julian anathematized it in 553 A.D.

Origen, *Commentary on The Gospel According to John,* (Washington, D.C.: Catholic University of America Press, 1989). Translated by Ronald Heim. Contains evidence of Origen's and hence the early Christians' assumption of reincarnation. Many of Christ's utterances seem clearly to assume it also, as Sybil Leek brings out in *Reincarnation: The Second Chance* (New York: Random House, 1974).

Alvin Kuhn Boyd, *Shadow of the Third Century: A Reevaluation of Christianity* (Wheaton, Ill.: Theosophical Society, 1949). A well-argued thesis that Christianity was quite different—less spiritual—after this period, when earlier teachings like Origen's were suppressed.

Hans Jonas, *The Gnostic Religion* (Boston: Beacon Press, 1958). The seminal work on Gnosticism, which at first blended with and then was purged from ecclesiastical Christianity.

Elaine Pagels, *The Gnostic Gospels* (New York: Random

House, 1979). One of the translators of these recently discovered texts, unknown to Jonas when he wrote the first edition of the book above, documents Gnostic differences with Christianity, which define some of the distinctions between exoteric and esoteric.

Joseph Campbell, ed., *Spiritual Disciplines* and *The Mysteries*, Bollingen Series 30, vols. 4 and 2 (Princeton, N.J.: Princeton University Press, 1960 and 1955). These collections of papers, given at two of the Eranos conferences by eminent international scholars, give infinite opportunities to cross-reference spiritual traditions around the world, but readers will mostly have to draw similarities themselves.

Jill Purce, *The Mystic Spiral: Journey of the Soul* (New York: Thames & Hudson, 1980). Captures cross-cultural manifestations of the common spiritual traditions through pictures of universal glyphs like oculi and mazes explained by text.

Frances A. Yates, *The Occult Philosophy in the Elizabethan Age* (London: Ark, 1979). A highly regarded British historian, Dame Yates relates the Christian Cabalist/Rosicrucian transmission of esoteric traditions with which Shakespeare, Marlowe, and Spenser seem to have been acquainted.

JOURNALS

Gnosis, Lumen Foundation, P.O. Box 14217, San Francisco, CA 94110–0217. A quarterly featuring different topics each issue about Western spiritual traditions and their sources.

The Upper Triad, P.O. Box 1370, Manassas, VA 22110–1370. Follows the main Vedantic and Theosophical traditions.

Alexandria, Phanes Press, P.O. Box 6114, Grand Rapids, MI 49516. An annual with fascinating, high-quality articles on all aspects of esoteric traditions.